The Other Tiger

Recent Poetry from Latin America

The Other Tiger

Recent Poetry from Latin America

Selected and translated by
Richard Gwyn

Seren is the book imprint of
Poetry Wales Press Ltd
Nolton Street, Bridgend, Wales

www.serenbooks.com
facebook.com/SerenBooks
Twitter: @SerenBooks

The right of Richard Gwyn to be identified
as the Author of this Work has been asserted
in accordance with the Copyright, Designs
and Patents Act, 1988.

Original poems in Spanish © the individual authors.

ISBN 978-1-78172-334-0

Cover painting: Franz Marc, The Tiger, 1912.

A CIP record for this title is available from
the British Library.

All rights reserved. No part of this publication
may be reproduced, stored in a retrieval system,
or transmitted at any time or by any means
electronic, mechanical, photocopying, recording
or otherwise without the prior permission
of the copyright holders.

The publisher works with the financial assistance
of the Welsh Books Council.

Printed by Bell & Bain Ltd, Glasgow.

de 'El otro tigre'

Un tercer tigre buscaremos. Éste
Será como los otros una forma
De mi sueño, un sistema de palabras
Humanas y no el tigre vertebrado
Que, más allá de las mitologías,
Posa la tierra. Bien lo sé, pero algo
Me impone esa aventura indefinida,
Insensata y antigua, y persevero
En buscar por el tiempo de la tarde
El otro tigre, el que no está en el verso.

Jorge Luis Borges (1899-1986)

from 'The Other Tiger'

Let us look for a third tiger. This one
will be a form in my dream like all the others,
a system, an arrangement of human language,
and not the flesh-and-bone tiger
that, out of reach of all mythologies,
paces the earth. I know all this; yet something
drives me to this ancient, perverse adventure,
foolish and vague, yet still I keep on looking
throughout the evening for the other tiger,
the other tiger, the one not in this poem.

Translated by Alastair Reid (1926-2014)

Índice

1. 'Dónde vivimos

Daniel Samoilovich: La Casa del Tigre	44
Rómulo Bustos Aguirre: Balada de la casa	44
Siomara España: La casa vacía	46
Fabio Morábito: Época de crisis	48
Jaime Luis Huenún: En la casa de Zulema Hualquipán	52
Damsi Figueroa: Execración de la luz	52
Ricardo Herrera Alarcón: Un hombre solo en una casa sola	54
Gustavo Barrera: El espacio vacío	56
Laura Wittner: Luna de plástico	60
Verónica Zondek: Progreso	62
Jorge Aulicino: La ciudad y los bárbaros	66
Gabriel Chávez Casazola: He nacido en los confines	66
Julián Herbert: Los Mezquites	68
Alicia García Bergua: Metafísca zoológica	70
Rafael Courtoisie: Los que no están	70
D.G. Helder: No clarea y ya se oyen cacareos...	72
Pedro Serrano: Berwick	74
Laura Wittner: Otra ciudad	74
Jorge Fondebrider: Regent's canal (a la altura de Danbury Street)	76
Carolina Dávila: Postal de Buenos Aires	78
Andrés Neuman: Buenos Aires al vuelo	80
Humberto Ak'Abal: Chonimutix	84
Jaime Pinos: Vista general	86
Otoniel Guevara: Nunca tuve una casa	88

Contents

1. 'Where we live'

Daniel Samoilovich: The House in Tigre	45
Rómulo Bustos Aguirre: Ballad of the House	45
Siomara España: The Empty House	47
Fabio Morábito: Time of Crisis	49
Jaime Luis Huenún: In the House of Zulema Hualquipán	53
Damsi Figueroa: Execration of the Light	53
Ricardo Herrera Alarcón: A lonely man in a lonely house	55
Gustavo Barrera: The Empty Space	57
Laura Wittner: Plastic moon	61
Verónica Zondek: Progress	63
Jorge Aulicino: The City and the Barbarians	67
Gabriel Chávez Casazola: I was born within the confines	67
Julián Herbert: Los Mezquites	69
Alicia García Bergua: Zoological Metaphysics	71
Rafael Courtoisie: Those who are not here	71
D.G. Helder: It is not yet light and the cock crows...	73
Pedro Serrano: Berwick	75
Laura Wittner: Another City	75
Jorge Fondebrider: Regent's Canal (by Danbury Street)	77
Carolina Dávila: Postcard from Buenos Aires	79
Andrés Neuman: Buenos Aires on the Fly	81
Humberto Ak'Abal: Chonimutux	85
Jaime Pinos: Panorama	87
Otoniel Guevara: I never had a house	89

2. 'De dónde venimos'

Jessica Freudenthal Ovando: Fragmento del libro *Árbol*	94
Gioconda Belli: Dios dijo	96
Nadia Prado: Siempre escribía	98
Piedad Bonnett: Biografía de un hombre con miedo	100
Wendy Guerra: Un rostro en la muchedumbre (Graffitis)	100
Darío Jaramillo Agudelo: Testimonio acerca del hermano	102
Irene Gruss: El té	106
Clemente Riedemann: El hombre de Leipzig	106
Micaela Chirif: Un amigo	108
Mirta Rosenberg: Una carta convertida en cosa	110
Gabriel Chávez Casazola: La canción de la sopa	112
Enrique Winter: Polaca	118
Diana Bellessi: de 'Detrás de los fragmentos'	120
Edgar Dobry: Mandado	120
Fabián Casas: Tratando de sepultar	122
Alejandro Cortés González: Jurar en vano	124
Jessica Freudenthal Ovando: La casa del loco	124
Alessandra Molina: Ronda infantil	128
Beatriz Vignoli: Escrito en la mesa de luz de un Hotel ****	130
Damaris Calderón: Instantánea	130
Osvaldo Hernández: Canción para Manuel	132
Carlos Decap: American Bar	132
Beatriz Vignoli: Función de la lírica	134
Carlos López Beltrán: Desabrigo	134
Héctor Abad Faciolince: Memento	136

2. 'Where we come from'

Jessica Freudenthal Ovando: Fragment from *Tree*	95
Gioconda Belli: God said	97
Nadia Prado: I would always write	99
Piedad Bonnett: Biography of a Fearful Man	101
Wendy Guerra: A Face in the Crowd (Graffiti)	101
Darío Jaramillo Agudelo: Testimony Concerning my Brother	103
Irene Gruss: Tea	107
Clemente Riedemann: The Man from Leipzig	107
Micaela Chirif: A Friend	109
Mirta Rosenberg: A Letter Transformed into a Thing	111
Gabriel Chávez Casazola: The Song of Soup	113
Enrique Winter: Polish Woman	119
Diana Bellessi: from 'Behind the Fragments'	121
Edgar Dobry: Errand	121
Fabián Casas: Trying to Bury	123
Alejandro Cortés González: To Swear in Vain	125
Jessica Freudenthal Ovando: The Madman's House	125
Alessandra Molina: A Children's Round	129
Beatriz Vignoli: Written on the Bedside Table of a Hotel ★★★★	131
Damaris Calderón: Snapshot	131
Osvaldo Hernández: Song for Manuel	133
Carlos Decap: American Bar	133
Beatriz Vignoli: Function of lyric poetry	135
Carlos López Beltrán: Exposed	135
Héctor Abad Faciolince: Memento	137

3. 'El mundo que compartimos'

Pedro Serrano: Dark Ages	146
Alejandro Crotto: En el Haras Vadarkablar	148
Fabio Morábito: Ajusco	150
Darío Jaramillo Agudelo: Gatos	152
Daniel Samoilovich: Libélulas	154
Mirta Rosenberg: Si alguien querría ser una tortuga	156
Eduardo Chirinos: Un perro mojado de rocío	158
Rómulo Bustos Aguirre: Del cangrejo ermitaño	160
Igor Barreto: Ladrón de gallos	160
Pura López Colomé: Y el anturio, impávido	162
Rómulo Bustos Aguirre: Escena de Marbella	164
Alejandro Crotto: Las Palomas	166
Antonio Deltoro: Primavera	168
Pedro Serrano: El conejo y la chistera	170
Jorge Aulicino: de *Cierta dureza en la sintaxis*	172
Coral Bracho: Cabras	174
Sergio Raimondi: Qué es el mar	174
Camilo Brodsky: Las naturalezas muertas: mirlos, tordos y otras aves	176
Eduardo Milán: decir ahí	178
Piedad Bonnett: Lección de supervivencia	182
Mauricio Molina: El Viejo licántropo	184
Javier Bello: de *El fulgor del vacío*	186
Rómulo Bustos Aguirre: Cuento	186
D.G. Helder: Intrascedencia	188
Eduardo Milán: El salto del tigre	190

3. 'The world we share'

Pedro Serrano: Dark Ages	147
Alejandro Crotto: At the Vadarkablar Stud Farm	149
Fabio Morábito: Ajusco	151
Darío Jaramillo Agudelo: Cats	153
Daniel Samoilovich: Dragonflies	155
Mirta Rosenberg: If anyone wanted to be a tortoise	157
Eduardo Chirinos: A dog wet with dew	159
Rómulo Bustos Aguirre: Of the Hermit Crab	161
Igor Barreto: Rooster Thief	161
Pura López Colomé: And the Anthurium, Undaunted	163
Rómulo Bustos Aguirre: Marbella Scene	165
Alejandro Crotto: Pigeons	167
Antonio Deltoro: Spring	169
Pedro Serrano: The Rabbit and the Top Hat	171
Jorge Aulicino: from *A somewhat difficult syntax*	173
Coral Bracho: Goats	175
Sergio Raimondi: What the Sea Is	175
Camilo Brodsky: Still lives: Blackbirds, Thrushes and Other Birds	177
Eduardo Milán: to say	179
Piedad Bonnett: Lesson in Survival	183
Mauricio Molina: The Old Lycanthrope	185
Javier Bello: From *The Glow of Emptiness*	187
Rómulo Bustos Aguirre: Story	187
D.G. Helder: Insignificance	189
Eduardo Milán: The Tiger's Leap	191

4. 'Lo que hacemos y dónde vamos'

Darío Jaramillo Agudelo: Razones del ausente	196
Juan Manuel Roca: Lo que ocurre en el poema	198
Frank Báez: Maullido	200
Ariel Williams: de *Discurso del contador de gusanos*	200
Tomás Harris: Argel	204
Teresa Arijón: de 'La vida nueva'	206
Tedi López Mills: Fiestas	210
Jorge Fernández Granados: Las cosas	212
Sergio Raimondi: El verbo inglés ante la acción del fuego	214
Miguel Petrecca: Novelista	216
Marina Serrano: Nunca decías sí	218
Marina Serrano: ¿Qué fuimos a ver, Simón...?	218
Paula Piedra: Sí hay sueño americano	220
Frank Báez: Los Beach Poets	222
Damaris Calderón: Esta será la única mentira en la que siempre creeremos	224
Julio Trujillo: Diez tequilas	226
Juan Manuel Roca: Paisaje con mendigos	226
Beatríz Vignoli: La caída	230
Marcelo Guajardo Thomas: Cochrane	232
Juan Manuel Roca: Mester de servidumbre	232
Roberto Appratto: Es la voz de tu conciencia la que te habla	234
Fabricio Estrada: El espejo	240
Humberto Ak'Abal: Camino al revés	240
Wendy Guerra: El viaje inverso	240
Jorge Aulicino: La ley de la calle	242
Carlos Decap: Batalla del Ebro	244
Verónica Zondek: Profundo en el mapa	244
Catalina González Restrepo: Viaje	246
Enrique Winter: El piso sucio y la luz prendida	248
Roberto Appratto: Todos los poetas esconden algo	248
Juan Ramón Saravia: De cómo algunas curaciones resultan peor que la enfermedad misma	250
Tedi López Mills: La Guerra sutil	250
Javier Bello: La jaula de la sentencia	254

4. 'What we do and and where we go'

Darío Jaramillo Agudelo: Reasons for his Absence	197
Juan Manuel Roca: What Happens in the Poem	199
Frank Báez: Miaow	201
Ariel Williams: from *Discourse of the Teller of Worms*	201
Tomás Harris: Algiers	205
Teresa Arijón: from 'The New Life'	207
Tedi López Mills: Fiestas	211
Jorge Fernández Granados: Things	213
Sergio Raimondi: English words regarding the effect of the fire	215
Miguel Petrecca: Novelist	217
Marina Serrano: You never said yes	219
Marina Serrano: What did we go to see, Simón...?	219
Paula Piedra: Sure, there's an American Dream	221
Frank Báez: The Beach Poets	223
Damaris Calderón: This will be the only lie in which we'll always believe	225
Julio Trujillo: Ten Tequilas	227
Juan Manuel Roca: Landscape with Beggars	227
Beatríz Vignoli: The Fall	231
Marcelo Guajardo Thomas: Cochrane	233
Juan Manuel Roca: Craft of Servitude	233
Roberto Appratto: It's the voice of your conscience speaking to you	235
Fabricio Estrada: The Mirror	241
Humberto Ak'Abal: Walking Backwards	241
Wendy Guerra: Reverse journey	241
Jorge Aulicino: The Law of the Street	243
Carlos Decap: Battle of The Ebro	245
Verónica Zondek: Deep in the map	245
Catalina González Restrepo: Journey	247
Enrique Winter: The floor dirty and the lights on	249
Roberto Appratto: All poets hide something	249
Juan Ramón Saravia: How some cures end up being worse than the illness itself	251
Tedi López Mills: The Subtle War	251
Javier Bello: Cage of Verdicts	255

5. 'Lo que somos y cómo amamos'

John Galán Casanova: Poema de la primera vez	262
Wendy Guerra: Palabra de esquimal	264
Siomara España: El regreso de lolita	264
Malú Urriola: de *Hija de perra*	268
Diego Maquiera: la Tirana	268
Edwin Madrid: de 'Delicias de la noche'	270
Carlos Henrickson: Pequeña canción realista	272
Osvaldo Bossi: Fragmentos de *Tres*	274
Luis Felipe Fabre: Imagen de la desconocida	276
Carmen Ollé: Bares	278
Fabián Casas: Despertarte	280
Jorge Fondebrider: All the Thing You Are	280
Jorge Fondebrider: De cómo el armor se vuelve recuerdo del armor	282
Diana Bellessi: Crucero ecuatorial	282
Tania Montenergro: El ñatazo	284
Eduardo Chirinos: La herida	286
Aleyda Quevedo Rojas: Por fortuna la luna	286
Osvaldo Sauma: Mirándola dormir	288
Miguel Ildefonso: Odiseo	290
Ana Franco: Peligro de extinción	290
Alicia Torres: Como Perceval	292
Catalina González Restrepo: Alimento	294
Edwin Madrid: Muchacho de corazón amarillo	296
Daniel Samoilovich: Porto dos Ossos	298
Alejandro Schmidt: Mi corazón era un hotel	300
Eduardo Espina: Razón de todas la cosas	302
John Galán Casanova: Poema de la última vez	304

5. 'What we are and how we love'

John Galán Casanova: Poem of the First Time	263
Wendy Guerra: Eskimo's Word	265
Siomara España: The Return of lolita	265
Malú Urriola: from *Bitch's Daughter*	269
Diego Maquiera: The Tyrantess	269
Edwin Madrid: from 'Pleasures of the Night'	271
Carlos Henrickson: Little Realist Song	273
Osvaldo Bossi: Fragments from *Three*	275
Luis Felipe Fabre: Image of the Unknown Woman	277
Carmen Ollé: Bars	279
Fabián Casas: To Awaken	281
Jorge Fondebrider: All the things you are	281
Jorge Fondebrider: How love becomes a memory of love	283
Diana Bellessi: Equatorial Cruise	283
Tania Montenergro: Snort	285
Eduardo Chirinos: The Wound	287
Aleyda Quevedo Rojas: Luckily the Moon	287
Osvaldo Sauma: Watching her sleep	289
Miguel Ildefonso: Odysseus	291
Ana Franco: Danger of Extinction	291
Alicia Torres: Like Percival	293
Catalina González Restrepo: Nourishment	295
Edwin Madrid: Boy with the Yellow Heart	297
Daniel Samoilovich: Porto dos Ossos	299
Alejandro Schmidt: My heart was a hotel	301
Eduardo Espina: Reason for All Things	303
John Galán Casanova: Poem of the Last Time	305

6. 'Lo que será de nosotros'

Mario Rivera: Los Muertos	310
Beatriz Vignoli: La Guerra de los tontos	320
Luis Felipe Fabre: Xochicuicatl	320
Osvaldo Hernandez: Vinieron los muretos	323
Mónica Velásquez Guzmán: Siete maneras de decir el dolor	324
Juan Manuel Roca: Palimpsesto desde Rimbaud	326
Verónica Zondek: Ausencia	328
Ramón Cote Baraibar: Premonición en San Librario	328
Julián Herbert: Oscura	330
Jacqueline Goldberg: El moribundo nos convoca	334
Luis Chaves: Traducción libre de un tema inédito de Chan Marshall	334
D.G. Helder: Cuerpos de todos los tamaños por donde corre la misma sangre	340
Leonardo Sanhueza: Puño	342
Irene Gruss: Mientras tanto	344
Luis Felipe Fabre: Infomercial	344
Beatriz Vignoli: Plaza St.Exupéry	348
Jorge Fondebrider: Desmantelar la casa	348
Irene Gruss: La muerte está en casa	350
Raúl Zurita: de 'El desierto'	350
Claudia Hernández de Valle-Arizpe: Mato por rabia	354
Fabio Morábito: Sollozos	358

6. 'What becomes of us'

Mario Rivera: The Dead	311
Beatriz Vignoli: The War of the Idiots	321
Luis Felipe Fabre: Xochicuicatl	321
Osvaldo Hernandez: The Dead Arrived	323
Mónica Velásquez Guzmán: Seven Ways of Talking about Pain	325
Juan Manuel Roca: Palimpsest from Rimbaud	327
Verónica Zondek: Absence	329
Ramón Cote Baraibar: Premonition in San Librario	329
Julián Herbert: Dark	331
Jacqueline Goldberg: The dying man	335
Luis Chaves: Free translation of an unpublished piece by Chan Marshall	335
D.G. Helder: Bodies of all sizes where the same blood runs	341
Leonardo Sanhueza: Fist	343
Irene Gruss: And in the meantime	345
Luis Felipe Fabre: Infomercial	345
Beatriz Vignoli: Plaza St.Exupéry	349
Jorge Fondebrider: Closing up the House	349
Irene Gruss: Death is At Home	351
Raúl Zurita: from 'The Desert'	351
Claudia Hernández de Valle-Arizpe: I kill out of Rage	355
Fabio Morábito: Sobbing	359

Preface

It is 14th July, 2014: Bastille Day. I am in a house in Galloway, south west Scotland, having the only conversation I shall ever have with the poet and translator Alastair Reid. He tells me that barely a day goes by without him reading something by Borges. During our conversation he frequently speaks of Borges in the present tense, despite the Argentinian writer having died in 1986.

The first story I read by Borges, at the age of eighteen, was *Tlön, Uqbar, Tertius Orbis*. The first poem I remember reading by Neruda, a year or so later, was 'To Don Asterio Alarcón, Clocksmith of Valparaíso'. Although the name would have meant nothing to me at the time, both translations were by Alastair Reid. Forty years on, when I finally get to meet the man, Alastair is a little frayed around the edges, but alert and bright-eyed as a moorland bird. He lives in New York City but spends part of every summer in the region of Scotland where he was born and spent his earliest years. I have been advised that he will prove an invaluable repository of experience and anecdote for my research into Latin American literature, since, apart from translating both Borges and Neruda, he knew them personally, and was on first name terms with most of the writers of the *El boom*: Gabriel García Márquez, Mario Vargas Llosa, Álvaro Mutis – but Borges was a special case, and Alastair speaks of him as of a respected friend.

Two things stand out in our conversation. The first is that, even as we talk of poetry, Alastair insists that for Borges everything was a fiction (though throughout our conversation he uses the Spanish word *ficción*). I know this already, because it appears in one of the essays in *Outside In*, a selection of Alastair's prose writings: 'Borges referred to all his writings as fictions... A fiction is any construct of language – a story, an explanation, a plan, a theory, a dogma – that gives a certain shape to reality.'[1] Including, Borges insisted, a poem.

And here we get to the tiger. It was a leap in the conversation that did it, the leap of a figurative tiger perhaps, and the next thing I know Alastair is reciting a section of the poem. 'That's such an amazing poem,' he says, 'the very last stanza is extraordinary... *I know all this; yet something / drives me to this ancient, perverse adventure, / foolish and vague, yet still I keep on looking / throughout the evening for the other tiger, / the other tiger, the one not in this poem.*[2] He pauses, and adds: 'That's forever and ever and ever and ever. It's a great corrective to poets, that one.'

Forever and ever and ever and ever. How strange that Alastair should choose these words to complete his memory of the poem. In Edwin Williamson's biography of Borges we find this: 'And yet something imposed on him "the senseless and ancient" adventure of searching for "this other tiger, the one that is not in the verse," even though, as he would later observe to Antonio Carrizo, he knew that the quest was "infinite and vain" because "reality is unreachable through art."'[3]

Alastair starts telling me about one occasion in Buenos Aires when he and Borges were wandering around the Recoleta cemetery, and Borges wanted to show him something, but being blind, he couldn't see the thing that he wanted Alastair to see; he wasn't even sure that they were standing in the right place: 'he was showing me something that he couldn't *see*, and immediately there was something very bizarre about this and in all the encounters with Borges I began to realise that this notion of a fiction...'

He drifts into silence. Perhaps he is getting tired. We've been talking for three hours: he is eighty-eight years old, and is not well, as I later discover. What was he going to say? That Borges' failure to see the thing that he was showing was, in its way, an invention, or re-invention of the thing being shown, a seeping through of memory into reality, and therefore a 'fiction' also? He could not see it, but he could at least remember, and so re-imagine it. And weeks later, reflecting on this ellipsis in the conversation, I find the following passage in Williamson's biography, in which Borges is speaking of his blindness: 'and there was I, in some way the centre of 900,000 volumes in various languages. I discovered I could hardly make out the title pages or the spines.'[4]

And all I can think when I read that is Alastair's description of

Borges: 'he was showing me something in Buenos Aires that he couldn't see.'

I wasn't sure where to start looking for the third tiger, the one that was not in Borges' poem: and even though the quest might be 'infinite and vain' I decided to try and track it down. I thought perhaps I might glimpse its shadow in the poems gathered here.

*

Before discussing the origins and evolution of this anthology, a few words on translation – and on the translator's role in the process of compiling a work of this kind – seem in order.

I have a distinct memory of the first time I gave translation serious critical thought. It was during a visit to Florence, when I was in my early twenties. I was staying at the house of the poet Michele Ranchetti (the uncle of my partner at the time), and he was showing me an Italian translation of the poem 'Missing Dates', in a bilingual collection of English language poetry. In it, the Italian translation of Empson's villanelle, rather than conveying, in tones of doomed grandeur, the perennial poetic concerns of time and loss, addressed instead the dried fruit of the date palm, *Phoenix dactylifera*. How, I wondered, during the course of the translation process, could no one – not the translator, nor the copy editor, nor even the proof reader – have spotted such a rudimentary error?

It was in part my shock at how bewilderingly incompetent or bizarre some translated poetry was – and the number of mistakes and mistranslations contained in works published in major anthologies – that led me, through an immodest desire to see if I could do any better, to attempt translations of my own. It made sense to begin with something that I liked, and my first attempts were of poems by Antonio Machado (much too difficult for a beginner) and, more successfully, Jaime Gil de Biedma, a couple of which were published. The addiction grew, but I was aware of my technical limitations, so enrolled on a formal course of study in Spanish to English translation. At the same time, I read more poetry and novels in the original language, and began to understand something of the complexity of the translator's craft, as well as to appreciate –

something I had long suspected – the intrinsic 'creativity' of the pursuit. Most writing involves thinking stuff up and putting it down in words; hopefully the right words, in the right order. The only significant difference was that, with translation, someone else had given you a template for the first part, the 'thinking stuff up' phase.

As a writer, I was excited to discover that the frontiers between my 'own' writing and translation began slowly to erode, and I came to develop an appreciation of the process whereby reading, writing and translating became part of a single continuum. More concretely, I reached the same conclusion as the one noted by William Carlos Williams, who, in a letter from 1940, wrote: 'If I do original work all well and good. But if I say it... by translating the work of others that also is valuable. What difference does it make?'[5]

The impulse to translate is a curious one. As Lydia Davis has put it: 'I still don't understand the urge ... [It] is a kind of hunger; maybe the polite word would be appetite – I want to consume the text, and reproduce it in English ... I don't have a completely satisfactory answer. The desire to translate may be something of an inexplicable addiction.'[6] And sometimes that compulsion or addiction can lead us to turn a thing loved in another language into English – as my early attempts at Machado and Gil de Biedma proved – and are done simply for the hell of it, a kind of obsessive curiosity to see *how it works*. And one learns that there are times when some almost indefinable element in the original text, something that I have heard one translator refer to as the 'temperature' of the words, and another as the 'mood' of a piece, needs to be translated, if at all possible, just as much as the meaning of the words themselves. And, of course, it is the words that constitute that effect, but only by the alchemy of their contiguity is that temperature or mood or tone achieved. Only those particular words in that particular order have produced this effect in the original, so how to set about doing something equivalent with a different set of words, in a different language?

'If I am to be faithful to anything in the opening passage of a novel, or a short story, or a memoir, it will be to its mood. It will be to the trance it sets up ... the magic trick that takes the reader though the page and into the secret realm beyond,' writes

Maureen Freely in her autobiographical essay, *Angry in Piraeus*.[7] How true this is of the translation of poetry. It is, after all, the mood of the poem that first makes you take notice, or, in extreme cases, causes a shiver of recognition. This is the initial buzz, the urge that makes you want to see how it might be done in English. Reading a lot of poems, sometimes up to 30 or 40 a day, you begin to spot quite quickly if something is a little different, offers an unknown quality, or simply appeals because it does, without any apparent reason. On such occasions my first thought would always be: 'I must translate that in order to find out what it is about it that appeals to me'. This connects, no doubt, to an innate need in the translator's psychological make-up to examine and assimilate difference, but whatever the rationale, the drive is compulsive and more than a little obsessive.

It is no secret that the translation of poetry is a special case. You come to expect an almost universally quizzical reaction when you tell people that you translate poetry. It is regarded as a strange and perverse activity. As Edith Grossman observes:

> '[P]oetry can seem completely localized, thoroughly contextualised, and absolutely inseparable from the language in which it is written in ways that prose is not. The textures of a language, its musicality, its own specific tradition of forms and meters and imagery, the intrinsic modalities and characteristic linguistic structures that make it possible to express certain concepts, emotions and responses in a specific manner but not in another – all of these inhere so profoundly in a poem that its translation into another language appears to be an act of rash bravado verging on the foolhardy.' [8]

However, Grossman is merely putting up the case for the opposition, the dreaded and, to my mind, misguided *traduttore/traditore* school of thought, embellished by Robert Frost's peevish old saw about poetry being what is lost in translation. What Grossman really thinks, as she goes on to say, is that a 'particular rendering' of a poem is always possible, as long as one stays loyal to the original, not in a servile or literalistic fashion, but by braving up to the fact that, as Walter Benjamin once wrote: "No translation would be possible if in its ultimate essence it strove for likeness to the original'"⁹ – and to pose the question, instead, as Grossman does: 'How would I write the poem if I were composing it in English within the formal constraints set by the poet?'¹⁰

That problem – how would I write the poem If I were composing it in English? – lies at the heart of the matter, and no amount of theory will help you at this point. Nor, indeed, does a familiarity with the literary traditions of the country out of which the poem emerged. You might become interested afterwards, and wish to find out more about that poem's creator and his or her literary affiliations, but knowing beforehand that they belonged to such and such a faction, or were enemies of so-and-so, are of no great interest or concern at the moment of translation: ignorance is, on occasion, an advantage, or privilege, of one's outsider's position.

Quite apart from any other influences, I have learned a good deal about the process of translation from taking part in workshops of the 'Poet to Poet' method, as described by W.N. Herbert in his introduction to *The Third Shore*, his second anthology of Chinese Poetry, and have applied that knowledge to my dealings with some of the poets whose work is here represented. As with the Poet to Poet method – in which translator and poet communicate, either directly or through intermediaries fluent on the source and target languages – my objective in consulting with the poets in the anthology was to realize 'a high level of discussion about formal issues ... achieving more of an agreed equivalence in metrical, imagistic and, where suitable, idiomatic finish. Effectively, the Poet to Poet method allows for a strong engagement with the issue of cultural translation on the level of craft.'¹¹ This last point is crucial, and where I was fortunate enough to converse in detail with those poets who could read and understand my translations – at least a dozen of the poets represented in this book come to mind – I was able to employ a 'pared/paired down' version of Herbert's methodology to complement and assist the more traditional single translator method. Both have their hazards: the Poet to Poet method frequently ends in compromise, especially when clear consensus cannot be reached and the more 'risky' translation is dismissed; while the single translator, as Herbert points out, is more susceptible to 'personal habit.'

Sometimes a poet, despite knowing English well, would rather leave it to the translator. As Jeremy Munday has observed: 'The input to the translation from the ST [Source Text] author can vary enormously, depending on the author's level of competence in English and interest in the process.'[12]

Anthologies of this size, representing a country or a region – let alone a region that spreads over two continents – tend to include work by a selection of different translators. One of the potential hazards of *The Other Tiger* – for the reader – is the intrusion of the single translator's own voice. While one might take steps to prevent this 'personal habit' becoming intrusive, it is bound to be there, as Ezra Pound famously proved. It is for this reason that I put my translation through the filter of other readers' responses, where possible the poets themselves, as well as through trusted and patient translator friends. But no doubt this did not prevent the intrusion, on occasion, of 'personal habit.'

★

The Other Tiger was conceived following a commission by the magazine *Poetry Wales*, back in 2010, to provide a two part 'introduction' to recent Latin American poetry. It was only once I'd embarked on the first few translations that I realised the hubris I had committed; how utterly unrealistic the task I had set myself, and how selective, or arbitrary, I was going to have to be. But the short essays were duly published over two issues, accompanied by my own translations of a fairly random assortment of poets.[13] By dipping my toe into an ocean of possibilities, I became aware of how daunting the selection of an anthology from this vast territory would be. Nevertheless, I did not take much persuading when, the following year, it was suggested I embark on an anthology of Latin American Poetry for *Poetry Wales*' publishers, Seren.

I should clarify, firstly, that the poets represented in this anthology write in the Spanish language, as I have not tackled the poetry of other languages of the Americas (notably Brazilian Portuguese, French, and the innumerable indigenous languages). I might have used the term 'Spanish American' but for the fact that many poets would feel that this tied them too closely to their colonial pasts, and besides, the term would also apply to North Americans for whom Spanish is a first language, whose writers (apart from those in Mexico) are not represented in this book either.

Secondly – and this was crucial to the design – I wanted an anthology of *poems*, rather than of *poets*, and did not want it laid out chronologically by author, or by country. What I wanted, first and foremost, was the freedom to select individual poems by a wide range of poets, and therefore decided that the book was going to be themed by topic rather than by nationality or date of birth.

Thirdly, since my intention was to focus on poetry of the late 20th and early 21st centuries, I decided to limit my selection to poets born after 1945; and the poets needed to be alive, as I was keen to discuss my translations with them wherever possible. Consequently, I wrote to all of the poets represented here, or else, in many cases, met them in person, and they have all received my translations and been invited to comment on or question them. Many of them have taken up this opportunity, raising interesting and sometimes perplexing choices for the translator – or else pointing out small but often crucial details of vocabulary or presentation.

The decision to confine the anthology to living poets meant the exclusion of some notable names, for example the Chileans Gonzalo Millán and Roberto Bolaño, and the Peruvian Jose Watanabe; but also the 1945 stipulation discounts poets from an earlier generation, some of whose poems I have translated previously – such as Nicanor Parra (born 1914), Claribel Alegría (1924), and Ernesto Cardenal (1925), to name only three – who also published poetry during the latter years of the 20th Century (and into the 21st) and are alive at the time of writing. This is unfortunate, but any anthology has to abide by certain criteria for consideration, and these, after much deliberation, were mine. As it stands, the oldest poet in the anthology was born in 1946, and the youngest in 1982.

The desire to make this collection as contemporary as possible was, to a significant degree, a reaction against the tendency of the available bilingual anthologies of Latin American poetry to take an historical perspective. The three major collections, published over the past 20 years by the University of Texas (1996)[14], Oxford University Press (2009)[15], and Farrar, Strauss & Giroux (2011)[16] – are heavily historical in content, with only the last of these offering anything more than a thin smattering of poets born after 1945. Charles Simic and Mark Strand's excellent anthology, *Another Republic*[17], provided a precedent of sorts, but that was published in 1976 and dealt with an earlier generation of poets.

I wanted to make available poetry that spoke to contemporary readers – those whose lives coincided or overlapped in time with those of the poets selected. This has not been done before in the UK nor, to the best of my knowledge, in the USA or anywhere else in the English-speaking world. A 2014 publication, *Pinholes in the Night*, selected and edited, respectively, by Raúl Zurita and Forrest Gander, sought to provide a representative collection of 'essential' poems from Latin America, but this too was historical in design, with only two of the selected poets still living at the time of publication.[18]

I believe that the current anthology is representative of Latin American poems written in Spanish today, although only time will tell which of them is 'essential.' They are the poems that stuck – for whatever reason – among the thousands I have read since embarking on the process of selection in 2011.

★

My first encounter with many of these poems was through listening to them, while attending readings at poetry festivals and book fairs across Latin America. If I liked a particular poem, I tracked down the poet responsible – either then, in person, or else later, by email. This is perhaps the smallest, but by no means insignificant group represented in the anthology, and accounts for the inclusion, to name names, of: Jaramillo, Fondebrider, Galán, Báez, Roca, Cote, Fabre, Freudenthal, Chirif, González Restrepo, López Mills and Samoilovich.

Next, I was steered towards other names through conversations with the many Latin American poets I spoke with over the course of five years, names I then sought out in bookshops and libraries and online.

Finally – the most extensive and time-consuming method by far – I searched independently, both on the internet and using whatever print anthologies were available, country by country, often acquiring a far greater quantity of poets and poems than I needed, and even making draft translations of poems I was never going to include, but which I felt obliged to sample and try out, in order to 'get the feel' of an unknown poet's writing.

Having made a selection, I would then edit and revise the poems into a further draft, and where I detected problems with my translations I consulted either with the poets themselves or, where the poet's knowledge of English was insufficient, with one or other intermediary, preferably from the same country (or province of a country) as the poet, in case of any local or specialist language variations.

By whichever method I came into contact with a poem, I needed to be attracted to some special characteristic or energy, a particular use of language or imagery or rhythmic power, provoking the same kind of response that I might have towards a poem in my own language, with the proviso that at the same time I needed to be alert as to whether or not it was likely to work well in English, and what the possible pitfalls of translation might be – those problematic words or phrases that can cause the poem to fail in its new garb. It only takes one of these for the whole poetic edifice to fall apart.

Occasionally, and perversely, it is those very problems of translation that will sometimes appeal: the lines on which you feel certain to come unstuck. Conversely, the most transparently 'translatable' poems are not always the best choices. As Susan Bassnett has commented: 'Translating poems that seem to be very straightforward and easily understandable in the source language all too often end up as banal in English. Translating the apparently simple is, in a different way, as tough as translating a very complex text, for the effect of simplicity is only achievable with considerable skill, and a translator needs comparable skills.'[19] Those particular skills, as I discovered, are perhaps the most underestimated in the translator's repertoire.

Nor did I necessarily select – in cases where the poet was particularly well-known in his or her own country – the most 'famous' or well-circulated poem or poems by that individual. I chose poems because they interested me, and because they helped provide a broader overview of what is being written across the Hispanic American world.

*

If there is a bias towards poems from Argentina, Chile, Mexico and Colombia, it is because these are the countries to which my travels have taken me; travels which coincided with my reading of those countries' poetries, and with incipient thoughts of translation, so that travel, my own writing, and translation have became thoroughly linked in my memory of those journeys.[20] Over the period 2011-2015 I made four trips to Argentina, three to Chile, and two each to Mexico and Colombia. I also made two visits to Nicaragua. Sometimes these trips were only a matter of a week or ten days, to attend a poetry festival at which I had been invited to read my own work; other trips were more substantial, including a tour of Patagonia with three other poets from Wales during August-September 2013, and month-long stays in Mexico, Colombia and Chile during 2014 and 2015, while carrying out research for another project. It is, however, precisely these countries that have – with the possible inclusion of Peru – the strongest literary tradition of the region and the infrastructure to support it. I confess to having read more individual collections from these countries, and to having learned more of their literary culture. So, while my selection leans heavily in the direction of certain territories – both geographic and poetic – there is a reason for it, even a method.

But the preponderance of poems from certain national states did not prevent me from reading anthologies and individual collections from the other countries of Spanish-speaking America. Apart from the fine national anthologies of poetry published by the Chilean publishers LOM – and many others besides – there were several general collections that were especially useful. I might single out two: Sergio Ramírez' *Puertas Abiertas* (2011),[21] which provided a much-needed and extensive summary of Central American poetry over the period, and

Gustavo Guerreo's *Cuerpo Plural* (2010),[22] whose title not only invokes a sense of Latin American poetry as parts of the same pluralistic entity – the Bolivarian ideal, or Pan-Americanism, if you will – but also insinuates a variously gendered body: a body that resists definition within the traditional binary of male/female, offering a more fluidly gendered body (and world).

As I began to read more deeply within these poetries, certain themes began to emerge, certain overriding preoccupations. These varied, depending on the generation of the poets, and the countries they come from, but the recurrent patterns or themes became more apparent the more I read. Of course, it might be argued that I started looking for certain kinds of poems, seeking them out in order to fit in with a pre-ordained set of categories, but that was not the case, at least not in any conscious sense. I began the process of sorting the poems much later because, just as with my 'own' writing, I did not know what I was putting together until I had started.

The sections into which I divided the anthology followed an interior logic that only became apparent after around one third of the poems had been completed in draft form. I noticed that the pieces I had chosen seemed to fall into broad categories that coincided, unsurprisingly, with human universals; or rather of the relationships that humans maintain with distinct realms of experience, wherever they are in the world. These were:

> (i) The home and the immediate environment; buildings; a spirit of place, which I abbreviated to 'Where we live.'
>
> (ii) Childhood, family, friendship and the ways in which memory configures the past: 'Where we come from.'
>
> (iii) Animals and the natural world, both in reality and as metaphor: 'The world we share.'
>
> (iv) The social and political world, journey, exile and writing: 'What we do and where we go.'
>
> (v) Love, sex and the body: 'What we are and how we love.'

(vi) Conflict, sickness, violence and death: 'What becomes of us.'

Poems do not fall conveniently into ready-made categories, so these sections are, at best, provisional. It was not my intention to confine the constituent poems to a set of interpretations limited to the category into which I have placed them. But the sections do provide a structure for the reader, and the arrangement avoids the – to my mind – rather more arbitrary arrangement by birth date or nationality. The layout is also intended to provide a narrative, for anyone who might wish to consume the entire collection at a sitting – from birth to death, as it were – as though reading a complex, multi-voiced novel.

*

Despite the subtitle of this book, there is no such animal as 'Latin American Poetry': there is, rather, a collection of discrete poetries associated with particular countries, which occasionally indicate points of overlap and interaction with the poetries of other countries in the hemisphere, and with Spain – and within those poetries are different movements, groupings and subgroupings, some linked to parallel movements in other Latin American countries, others more or less indigenous. There has, historically, been a good deal of travel and interaction between the different nations of Hispanic America and across the Atlantic, especially as a consequence of the serial civil wars and dictatorships that have been visited upon most of these countries over the past two centuries, and this has brought with it new influences, especially from the direction of France, and latterly, of the United States.

Towards the end of the 19th century, Spanish (Castilian) prosody underwent a revolution of sorts in Latin America, initiated to a large extent by the Nicaraguan poet Rubén Darío, and the movement associated with him, *modernismo*. This movement, not to be confused with the later, European modernism, swept through Latin America, though I would hasten to add that some countries were affected more than others. Poets such as the Chilean Vicente Huidobro, the Peruvian César Vallejo, and the

Argentinian Oliverio Girondo brought about changes in poetic language that had no equivalent in Spain. If we then consider that each region of Spanish America has its own particularities, uniformity was never likely to occur. In Mexico, a heavy rhetorical leaning and preference for metaphysical speculation (exemplified in the 20th century by Octavio Paz) linked that country's poetry more closely to its Spanish roots. Colombian poets, like their Mexican peers, prided themselves on a close allegiance to classical Spanish prosody. Cuba – and through its influence, other parts of the Caribbean – was (and is) more inclined to the baroque (consider, for example, Lezama Lima, Carpentier, Cabrera Infante) and syncretism. Chile, by contrast, displayed in some of its leading poets – Pablo de Rokha, Pablo Neruda, Enrique Lihn, and in our own time, Raúl Zurita – the stamp of the epic. The River Plate region, in turn, partly due to its Atlantic-facing geography, was more receptive to influences from Europe, and – from the 1950s onward – the United States; a feature which had always been evident in the poetry of Central America, but which was accentuated by the translations of José Coronel Urtecho and Ernesto Cardenal, who collaborated in making Ezra Pound's work available in Spanish. [23]

When considering poetry in Latin American countries, we should always bear in mind a preference for poets to consider themselves a part of a group or movement; of belonging to a literary collective specific to a geography and a point in time. Thus in Argentina, to take a representative example, the last four decades have seen movements – generally centred around particular magazines – falling into two main groups: the *neo-baroque* (a tendency apparent across several Latin American countries but, as I have mentioned above, especially prevalent in Cuba and in Mexico) and *objectivism*. Practitioners of the neo-baroque tend towards extensive wordplay, indulge in 'alliteration ... anagram puzzles, hipograms and other *calembours* (puns)', prefer opacity to clarity of communication, even, according to the same critic 'dissipating all referential illusion and hindering the search for semantic depth.' [24]

Objectivism, meanwhile, according to one of its leading theorists, takes on a more directly communicative pathway, avoiding 'verbal and sentimental excesses', engaging with the visible (as opposed to the metaphysical) universe, and 'comes to a clean narrative or a more or less elegant technique for description.'[25] Similar, if not parallel distinctions are discernible in the 'poetry wars' of the UK in the 1970s, but what I am suggesting is that group identity, the sense of belonging to a certain poetic tendency, and one's 'generation' (the 'generation of the 80s', for example, referring to poets whose work began to be published during that decade) held more importance for a Latin American poet than it did for a British, Irish, or (North) American – at least until quite recently.

Gustavo Guerrero, the Venezuelan editor of the anthology *Cuerpo Plural*, writes that the tendency to categorise poets according to their generation is no longer useful, and has effectively been replaced by individualistic agendas, as poets' lives begin to be run as concerns about the promotion and publicity of their work – which can be shared far more rapidly and extensively since the rise of the internet, and the self-promotion which that allows. In his anthology, Guerrero selects poets who, he claims, 'prioritise a critique of the modern sacralisation of poetry.' Nowadays, writes Guerrero, poetry's role is more democratic, more diverse and lodged in the vernacular rather than the 'sublime' language associated with a literary elite.[26] This would seem to support the decision to lead an anthology such as this by *poems* rather than by *poets*, since the contemporary (or its *zeitgeist*) has moved away from the sweeping polarisations of earlier generations, and is suspicious of absolutist definitions by movements, factions, or gurus.

In this descent from the poetic heights, it is impossible not to make mention of the Chilean Nicanor Parra, aged 101 at the time of writing, and perhaps the single most influential Spanish language poet of the past hundred years. By the 1930s – eighty years ago – Parra was already asserting that what was needed was a vernacular poetry that related to everyday life and which was accessible to the general public. These ideas, as manifested in *Poesia y antipoesia* (1954) had a huge impact on poets of a younger generation, especially those who were caught up in the politics of resistance. Parra's 'antipoetry' advocated ordinariness of voice and the avoidance of elitist language in poetic expression, using a declarative tone, simple, though not simplistic vocabulary, and more prose-like rhythms.[27] Parra's later work is often a mesh of word association games, intentional cliché and spectacularly straightforward rants about the environment, inequality and corporate corruption. He is, if one can be both, a ludic poet, while remaining a poet of intense seriousness. Parra's influence – whether one approves of it or not – is already more lasting than that of either Pablo Neruda or his fellow Nobel laureate, the Mexican Octavio Paz, because his ideas on the significance of poetry in the lives of ordinary people are seen by many to be more informed and more resonant with contemporary attitudes.

Partly as a result of Parra's influence, along with a greater appreciation of the kind of poetry being written in the USA, from William Carlos Williams to the Beats, many poets have tended towards the colloquial, the fragmentary and the inconclusive. At the same time, there is also a tendency – especially in Central America – towards a kind of populism, a reminder that in countries such as Nicaragua, poetry was once (and for some remains) a song sheet for the revolution, a sadly moving and ironic reminder of how one particular revolution went astray.[28]

As was occurring with other art forms, poetry in the second half of the twentieth century was exposed to a post-colonial modernity – and, as Jill Kuhnheim notes,[29] far from being an arcane diversion for literati (a zone into which 'serious' or 'academic' poetry is often perceived to have slipped in European cultures) much of the poetry from the region remains politically engaged and willingly participates in the social issues of its time. A good example of this would be the role taken by the International Poetry Festival of Medellín, in Colombia, which, since 1991, and under the curatorship of Fernando Rendón, has consistently stood up for the rights of ordinary Colombians in the struggle against fear and violence and the almost continuous war between the armed forces of the state, narco-terrorists, and FARC militants, that kept the country in a state of near breakdown for half a century. The International Poetry Festival at Granada, Nicaragua, also seemed to attract displays of 'agenda' poetry on occasion. It goes without saying, perhaps, that a poet's political and social engagement should never be confused with the quality of their work; nevertheless, the temptations for a poet to crowd-please are manifest in an audience hungry for social justice, who might easily confound rousing words with good poetry, or else not care to differentiate between the two.

Occasionally – and Chile is a case in point – there is a tendency to hold the figure of the poet in high esteem, almost as a guru, which can be a little bewildering for a northern European poet, accustomed to reciting poems in the back room of a pub to a scant gathering of sceptics. The poet in many Latin American societies is still addressed as 'maestro'. There is also the more extreme phenomenon of the *vate*, which refers to the kind of poet, who is regarded (especially by himself, and he is usually, though not invariably, male) as a kind of seer or prophet. It could be that the elevated status of poets in Chile harkens back to the sixteenth century national epic *La Aracauna*, written by the soldier-poet Alonso de Ercilla y Zúñiga.[30] As I have already indicated, Chilean poets have tended towards the epic form ever since.

With the concept of the *vate*, one can almost be overcome by the fumes of bardic hocus-pocus. It can at times resemble nostalgia for the figure of the shaman-storyteller in indigenous cultures, with a thick overlay of European Romanticism. However, the *vate* is saved from caricature by a tendency towards political activism and resistance, a role pertinent to those Chilean poets who actively opposed the Pinochet regime.

Resistance has long been a theme in Latin American poetry, stretching back to the wars of independence from Spanish rule, continuing into the twentieth century with a repudiation of the neo-colonialism posed by a United States that all too frequently has regarded Central and South America as its back yard. The rise of revolutionary movements and the indigenism that often accompanied them, found early expression in the radical poetry of the Peruvian César Vallejo, whose brand of active resistance to any form of neo-colonialist hegemony has inspired many Latin American poets. Rebecca Seiferle, in her preface to *The Black Heralds*, suggests that Vallejo 'disarticulates the Spanish language in order to disarticulate many of the dominant assumptions of Western culture.'[31] Vallejo's abiding influence is undeniable in

Latin American poetry, his concerns about the mythic inheritance of a neglected indigenous population being taken up in the poetry of Ernesto Cardenal, for example, notably in *Los ovnis de oro* (*Golden UFOs*).[32] In the current collection it is possible to detect strains of his influence in poems by Jaime Huenún, Javier Bello and Otoniel Guevara, to give but three examples, and although the notion of indigenousness can be seen very much as a class as well as an ethno-cultural divide in much of Latin America, it is clearly more of an issue in some countries than it is in others.

The political upheaval, and crackdown on all forms of resistance, that manifested itself most evidently in Pinochet's coup of 1973, had an abiding effect on many Latin American writers, and were summarised by Roberto Bolaño, in his acceptance speech for the Rómulo Gallegos Prize in 1999:

> '[M]y own generation, those of us who were born in the 1950s ... gave what little we had—the great deal that we had, which was our youth—to a cause that we thought was the most generous cause in the world and in a certain way it was, but in reality it wasn't... [W]e fought our hardest, but we had corrupt leaders, cowardly leaders... and now those young people are gone, because those who didn't die in Bolivia died in Argentina or Peru, and those who survived went on to die in Chile or Mexico, and those who weren't killed there were killed later in Nicaragua, Colombia, or El Salvador. All of Latin America is sown with the bones of these forgotten youths...'[33]

But the revolutionary struggle of many of the writers who lived through the various dictatorships throughout Latin America in the seventies and early eighties seems no longer to be of direct relevance to many of the poets who are emerging now. It may be unfair to generalise in these terms, but it would appear, to an onlooker, as if Bolaño's generation has been followed by one more concerned with a literature of intimacy, and less interested in a political agenda, veering even towards the narcissistic playground of self-empowerment exemplified in social media, just as similarly globalised younger people have across Europe and Asia. Or is it, rather, that the political has become personalised in the lives of younger poets to the extent that discriminating between the two domains is no longer useful? In any case, it should be borne in mind that many of the poets in this volume were not born when Pinochet took power in Chile, were small children at the time of the Sandinista revolution in Nicaragua or the Falklands/Malvinas conflict in Argentina, and have not lived out their adult lives against a backdrop of dictatorships and disappearances. There is a new interiority in the work of many of them – which pitches the individual against the same cacophony of unending but meaningless choice, the serial crises of consumer identity, and the distinct but nonetheless destructive dictatorship of the saturated psyche which we all, as citizens of the new millennium, must either share in or endure.

*

Translations, like poems themselves, are never really finished. Conversations about translation even less so.

Towards the end of our meeting in July 2014, Alastair Reid invited me to catch up with him in New York the following April – when I was due to travel to the United States – and take up our chat where we left off. Sadly, in September, only a few weeks after our meeting, he died. I am sorry not to have had the chance to meet him again, but I hope, in some small way, to have helped keep his legacy intact: had he not, through his translations, introduced me to the work of Borges and other Latin American writers, it is unlikely I would ever have become a translator. Which is why this book is dedicated to his memory.

*

The reading of a poem is itself a kind of translation, an act of decipherment.[34] In this sense we are all translators, because a translator is – as Borges himself pointed out – 'a very close reader; there is not much difference between translating and reading.'[35]

Nor, for that matter, is there much difference between reading and writing. Nor even between reading and travelling. Or writing and travelling, whose synergetic relationship I have remarked upon above. As Lydia Davis has it: 'to translate is also to read, and to translate is to write, as to write is to translate and to read is to translate. So that we may say: To translate is to travel and to travel is to translate.'[36]

This selection of poems from Latin America came about through just such a confluence of travel, reading, and writing. The translations that ensue are a part of the continuum.

Rabós D'Empordà, May 2016

1. Alastair Reid, 'Fictions', in *Outside In: Selected Prose*. Edinburgh: Polygon, 2008 (p. 311).
2. J.L. Borges. *Selected Poems* (ed. Alexander Coleman). London: Penguin, 1999 (pp, 116-9).
3. Edwin Williamson, *Borges: A Life*. New York: Viking, 2004. (p. 341).
4. ibid.
5. William Carlos Williams, cited in Edith Grossman, *Why Translation Matters*. New Haven: Yale University Press, 2010 (p. 8).
6. Lydia Davis, 'Freelance.' *Times Literary Supplement*. 26 February 2014 (p.16).
7. Maureen Freely, *Angry in Piraeus*. London: Sylph Editions, 2014 (p.14).
8. Edith Grossman, *Why Translation Matters*, pp. 93-4.
9. Walter Benjamin, 'The Task of the translator,' translated by Harry Zohn, in Rainer Schulte and John Biguenet: *Theories of Translation*, 71-82. Chicago: Chicago University Press, 1992.
10. Edith Grossman, *Why Translation Matters*, p. 96.
11. W.N. Herbert, *The Third Shore: Chinese & English-Language Poets in Mutual Translation*. Bristol: Shearsman, 2013 (pp 25-6).
12. Jeremy Munday, *Style and Ideology in Translation: Latin American Writing in English*. New York: Routledge, 2008 (p.198).
13. 'The Green Whale of Summer: Reflections on Latin American Poetry, Part One' appeared in *Poetry Wales* Vol 46. No, 3 (2010) with translations of poems by Nicanor Parra, Claribel Alegría, Ernesto Cardenal and Alejandra Pizarnik. 'Enigmas of the night: Reflections on Latin American Poetry, Part Two' appeared in *Poetry Wales* Vol 47 No 1 (2011), along with translations from Jorge Fondebrider, Wendy Guerra, Siomara España and Andrés Neuman.
14. Stephen Tapscott (ed.) *Twentieth Century Latin American Poetry: A Bilingual Anthology*. Austin: University of Texas, 1996.
15. Cecilia Vicuña and Ernesto Livon-Grosman (eds.) *The Oxford Book of Latin American Poetry: A Bilingual Anthology*. New York: Oxford University Press, 2009.
16. Ilan Stavans (ed.) *The FSG Book of Twentieth Century Latin American Poetry*. New York: Farrar, Strauss & Giroux, 2011.
17. Charles Simic and Mark Strand (eds.) *Another Republic: 17 European and South American Writers*. New York: Ecco Press, 1976.
18. Forrest Gander (ed.) & Raúl Zurita, *Pinholes in the Night: Essential Poems from Latin America*. Port Townsend, Washington: Copper Canyon Press, 2014.

19. Susan Bassnett, cited on the Stephen Spender Trust website: 'Advice from the judges.' http://www.stephenspender.org/poetry_translation_advice_from_judges.html
20. *Ricardo Blanco's Blog*, written by the author's eponymous alter ego: https://richardgwyn.me/
21. Sergio Ramírez, ed, *Puertas Abiertas: Antología de poesía centroamericana*. México DF: Fondo de cultura económica, 2011. I am grateful to Sr. Ramírez for his kind cooperation in providing access to most of the Central American poets in this anthology.
22. Gustavo Guerrero, *Cuerpo plural: Antología de la poesía hispanoamericana contemporánea*. Valencia: Pre-Textos, 2010.
23. Much of this paragraph derives from the author's correspondence with Jorge Fondebrider, personal communication, May 2016.
24. Both quotations are from Daniel García Helder, 'El neobarroco en la Argentina', in *Diario de Poesía*, Buenos Aires 1, no. 4, 1987. For further discussion of the neo-baroque, in English, see Chapter 4 of Jill S. Kuhnheim's *Textual Disruptions: Spanish American Poetry at the End of the Twentieth Century*. Austin: University of Texas Press, 2004.
25. Daniel Freidemberg, 'El modo en las cosas' in *Diario de Poesía*, Buenos Aires 5, no. 21, 1991.
26. Gustavo Guerrero, *Cuerpo plural*, p.23 et seq.
27. For an in-depth analysis of Parra's poetry over this period, see Edith Grossman, *The Antipoetry of Nicanor Parra*. New York: New York University Press, 1975.
28. The Sandinista Revolution of 1979, and the progressive regime that ensued with the likes of Sergio Ramírez as Vice-President, and Ernesto Cardenal as Minister of Culture, inspired hope, however briefly, that radical change to social conditions and the education policy in Nicaragua might be effected. Sadly, the war with the US-sponsored 'contras', incessant internal wrangling and the cynical capitulation to greed and corruption undergone by Daniel Ortega since his return to power in 2007 have rendered redundant any optimism about the future of this unhappy country.
29. Jill S. Kuhnheim, see note 24.
30. Alonso de Ercilla y Zúñiga, *La Aracauna*. Madrid: Ediciones Catedra, S.A., (updated version, 2001).
31. Rebecca Seiferle, 'César Vallejo: The Thread of Indigenous Blood'. Introduction to César Vallejo, *The Black Heralds* trans. Rebecca Seiferle). Port Townsend, Washington: Copper Canyon Press, 2003.
32. Ernesto Cardenal, *Los ovnis de Oro/Golden UFOs*. Bloomington: Indiana University Press, 1992.
33. Roberto Bolaño, from *Between Parentheses*, trans. Natasha Wimmer. New York: New Directions, 2011 (p 35).
34. Andrés Neuman, cited by W.N. Herbert, in his introduction to *The Third Shore* (p 21).
35. Norman di Giovanni, *The Lesson of the Master: On Borges and his work*. London: Continuum, 2003 (p. 181).
36. Lydia Davis, 'To Reiterate' (trans. Rebecca Seiferle), from *Almost no Memory*, 1997, in *The Collected Stories of Lydia Davis*. London: Picador, 2014 (p. 215).

Introduction to Part 1: 'Where we live.'

This first section addresses poetic responses to *habitat* in the broadest sense, notably through a poem's engagement with the idea of home, buildings, place or environment. 'Home' is very often the place from which we set out on a journey, and to which we will, eventually, return. The home is therefore the embodiment of familiarity, but 'houses' can be unfamiliar places, and the geographies that serve as a locus for other people's homes can exhibit qualities that, on returning to our own homes, imbue the familiar with strangeness.

From the first line of Samoilovich's 'Tigre' – 'We have a house in South America' – it was clear that this poem must open the anthology. Tigre (meaning 'tiger', appropriately) is a town and complex of islands and rivers to the north of Buenos Aires. Weeping willows grow abundantly along the riverbanks, and the islanders are reputed to suffer from a kind of wistful lethargy, a condition known locally as *mal del sauce*[1] or 'weeping willow sickness', that afflicts a person who spends too many hours gazing at the slow passage of water. Samoilovich's gently sardonic poem encapsulates this labyrinthine backwater of faded dreams, and a community of people brought together by 'an oversight of death'.

In 'Ballad of the House' (p45), Rómulo Bustos Aguirre invites the reader inside a house 'with a strange name', and even though 'you' will 'not drink the red plum wine / that expands memories', you have already become a participant in the fiction, so that the story the child is reading – from 'a half-open book' – and the poem itself bleed into each other. In Siomara España's 'The Empty house' (p47), visitors are not welcome: they will discover things that the speaker would rather were not known: they will 'whisper mischievously' and 'discover our absurdities'. But the real threat posed by these unwanted guests is revealed only at the end of the poem.

The theme of houses and the home under threat is sustained over several poems, peaking in Fabio Morábito's 'Time of Crisis', (p49) which warns of the fragility of architecture itself: the houses we live in are not safe, and even our kisses can go missing. For the occupants of this building, existence is precarious, and the children leave as soon as they can, to travel the world and find a place where walls are walls and a roof is a roof. Although he has lived in Mexico since the age of fifteen, Morábito was born in Alexandria to Italian parents, and his poems often – as here – invoke an outsider's insight into the infrastructure of a society under threat from within.

Jaime Luis Huenún's poem 'In the house of Zulema Hualquipán' (p53) reflects, through the metaphor of the house, on the status of the indigenous Mapuche community in Chile, induced (or 'reduced' as the poet would have it) to living in government reservations.[2] Huenún himself writes: 'My poems are a silent gesture, a territory for dreamers who want to rid our heads of who we are when we are at our worst: an irreparable error, a much-despised species.'[3] But the tragedy of the Mapuche past evoked by the words 'so many sons ago for the red dust of the road' does not prevent those building Zulema Hualquipán's house from driving their names into the sand 'like stakes' to hold up the roof.

In Veronica Zondek's 'Progress' (p63), the paradox of any such concept is weighed against a return to the poet's childhood home, after a long absence, where everything has changed for the worse, and yet the past reconfigures itself through a tentative process of remembering. Zondek's unique displacement of language, her use of neologism and sudden shifts in tone, while causing a nest of problems for the translator, manages to revisit the emotional geography of childhood with disturbing effect, slipping in an allusion to the 'snatching' away of innocence (by the military coup) that signals the end of childhood.

A shift occurs in the second half of the section, as less poems concern the home itself and locations diversify. In Pedro Serrano's poem 'Berwick' (p75), the town and surrounding landscape is almost animate, but the pathetic fallacy lodges trees and animals within an historical setting, the swans oblivious to the tides of invasion to which the town has been subject, just as the birds, at the opening of the poem 'orbit a charmed present'. The speaker in Laura Wittner's 'Another City' (p75) reflects on places where she is not, keeps suitcases 'packed for ever / and ready on the sofa.' But is this another way of being absent while remaining present; the 'black pit of packed bags / the reverse of disembarking'? Is the 'human desire for the incomplete' complemented by the fragmentation of the self that comes from leaving, rather than staying? It is a question in part answered by Jorge Fondebrider's crow, in 'Regent's Canal (by Danbury Street)' (p77), a bird that knows the speaker is not 'from around here', and therefore doesn't 'have time to waste on a stranger'. The foreigner to London could hardly be more at a loss 'in this city of brick houses and slow ceremonies' and so, as foreigners do, feels his outsider status reinforced as much by the inanimate objects around him as by the bird and 'the sound of ghostly footsteps crossing Noel Road.'

The speaker in Carolina Dávila's 'Postcard from Buenos Aires' (p79), by contrast, identifies (and identifies with) the city as a woman, and 'notices at once' her sisterhood in the qualities of 'its loose cobblestones . . . its dilapidated balconies', and in its 'rain, / more impassioned than any weeping'. Following on, a native of the same city, Andrés Neuman, who left Argentina at the age of 14 to settle with his family in Granada, Spain, revisits his childhood in 'Buenos Aires on the Fly' (p81), a poem that begins on 'the third floor of the past' and gallops through a kaleidoscopic array of sights and sounds and memories, some sensuous, some terrifying (the 'sinister helicopter flights' bringing to mind the Junta's custom of throwing political prisoners into the freezing waters of the south Atlantic), and comes full circle, helter-skelter, unable to reconcile a 'yesterday / with the memory of tomorrow.'

The spare, allusive poems of the Guatemalan Humberto Ak'Abal, who is of the Maya k'iche people, and writes in both that language and Spanish, often resemble puzzles or *koans*. The imagery in 'Chonimutux' (p85) replaces the expectations of a European mind with the internal logic of a dream: the substantiality of night, the inversion of earth and sky. In 'I never had a house' (p89), Otoniel Guevara, from El Salvador, offers a poem that reflects on a simple wish – to own a house, a place in which the speaker and his partner can make love without the neighbours hearing. The ideal – a garden, a patio where children play – is suddenly interrupted by the memory of the speaker at age twelve 'and the endless dead bodies', reminding us that lodged within the poem's (or the poet's) memory is an implacable image of the violence wreaked on El Salvador not very long ago, with massacres such as that of El Mozote,[4] when more than 800 civilians were murdered by the Salvadoran armed forces. The poem ends ambiguously with the entry of Death, feeling 'as though / he's in his own home'.

1. For a fictional evocation of *mal de sauce* or 'weeping willow sickness', see Inés Garland's novel *Piedra, papel o tijera (Stone, paper, scissors)*, Buenos Aires: Alfaguara, 2009.
2. On Jaime Huenún see, for example, 'Las reducciones en *Reducciones de Jaime Huenún*' by Sonia Betancour Sánchez y Orietta Geeregat Vera, in *Estudios filológicos* no. 55, Valdivia, June 2015. http://www.scielo.cl/scielo.php?pid=S0071-17132015000100002&script=sci_arttext
3. 'My poems are a silent gesture . . .' 'Mi poesía es un gesto de silencio, un territorio para ilusos que quisieran sacar de sus cabezas aquello que somos cuando somos lo peor: un error irreparable, una especie muchas veces deleznable'. Cited in *Foja de poesía* no. 094, 09 Nov 2009: http://circulodepoesia.com/2009/11/foja-de-poesia-no-jaime-huenun/
4. El Mozote: Like other writers from Central America, Osvaldo Hernández Alas' poetry is set against a background of armed conflict. During the Salvadoran civil war (1980-82), several episodes of indiscriminate mass murder took place, the most notorious of which was *El Mozote*, on 11 December 1981, in which the Salvadoran army killed more than 800 civilians. See, for example, *The Massacre at El Mozote*, by Mark Danner, Granta Books, 2005.

La Casa del Tigre

Tenemos una casa en Sudamérica.
Aquí están los perros sin dueño,
el río, las palmeras, el verano,
el arbolito enmarañado
de las rosas silvestres,
las luces diagonales en otoño.
Acá vino a parar la ropa vieja, el silencio
los vasos desparejos,
los miembros más longevos
de razas diferentes, hermanados
por el azar, por un descuido de la muerte.

Daniel Samoilovich (Argentina)

Balada de la casa

Hallarás una casa con un nombre extraño
            que intentarás descifrar en vano
Y muros del color de los buenos sueños
Pero tú no verás ese color
Tampoco beberás el vino rojo de los ciruelos
            que ensancha los recuerdos
En la verja
un niño con un libro entreabierto
Pregúntale por el camino de los grandes árboles
cuyos frutos guarda un animal
que adormece a los andantes con sólo mirarlos
Y él contestará mientras conversa
            con un ángel de alas verdes
(como si fuera otro niño que juega al ángel
y se hubiera colocado anchas hojas de plátano a la espalda)
moviendo apenas los labios en un leve conjuro
"el canto del gallo no es azul sino de un rosa dormido
como el primer claro del día"

The House in Tigre

We have a house in South America.
Here are the dogs with no owner,
the river, palm trees, summer,
the little tangled bush
of wild roses,
slanting light in autumn.
Here's where old clothes end up, silence,
non-matching glasses,
the most long-lived members
of different races, made siblings
by chance, by an oversight of death.

Daniel Samoilovich (Argentina)

Ballad of the House

You will find a house with a strange name
                        that you will attempt in vain to decipher
And walls the colour of good dreams
But you will not see that colour
Nor will you drink the red plum wine
                        that expands memories
On the fence
a child with a half-open book
Ask him the way to the big trees
whose fruits are guarded by an animal
that sends passers-by to sleep just by looking at them
And he will answer while conversing
                        with a green-winged angel
(as if it were another child playing at being an angel
with wide banana leaves stuck to his back)
barely moving his lips in a gentle spell
"the cockerel's song isn't blue but a sleepy pink
like the first light of day"

Y tú no entenderás. Y sin embargo
hallarás un zaguán que yo recorrí inmenso
donde cuelga el retrato de un señor que resplandece
              levemente, con el corazón en la mano
Y al fondo, muy al fondo
el alma de la casa sentada en una mecedora, cantando
Pero tú no la escucharás

Pues, en ese instante
un sonido lejano ajará el horizonte
Y el niño habrá pasado la última de las páginas

Rómulo Bustos Aguirre *(Colombia)*

La casa vacía

No invites a nadie
a nuestra casa,
pues repararán en
puertas, paredes, escaleras
y ventanas,
mirarán la polilla en
los rincones,
los cerrojos oxidados,
las lámparas ciegas, arruinadas.
No traigas a nadie a nuestra casa
pues no tendrán más
que angustia de tu mesa,
de tu cama, del mantel,
del mobiliario se reirán
de pena por las tazas, fingirán
nostalgia de mi nombre,
y reirán también de nuestra hamaca.
No traigas más gente a nuestra casa
pues te escribirán canciones,
te entusiasmarán el alma,

And you will not understand. And nevertheless
you will find an immense hallway that I crossed
where the portrait of a lord hangs, shimmering
                      slightly, his heart in his hand
And at the back, right at the back,
the soul of the house seated in a rocking chair, singing
But you will not heed her

Because in that instant
a distant sound shall crumple the horizon
And the child will have finished the last page

Rómulo Bustos Aguirre (Colombia)

The Empty House

Invite no one
into our house,
for they will notice
the doors, walls, staircase
and windows,
they will see the moths
in the corners,
the rusty locks,
the blind, ruined lamps.
Don't bring anyone to our house
for they will only be distressed
by your table,
your bed, the tablecloth,
the furniture, laugh pityingly
at the cups, pretend to
be nostalgic for my name,
make fun, what is more, of our hammock.
Don't bring people to our house any more
for they will write you songs,
excite your soul,

te susurrarán traviesos,
sembrarán una flor en tu ventana.

Por eso no debes, te lo ruego,
traer más gente a nuestra casa
pues se pondrán rosados,
verdosos, rojizos o azulados,
al descubrir paredes rotas
las plantas marchitadas.
Querrán barrer en los rincones
querrán abrir nuestras persianas
y encontrarán seguro entre mis libros
las excusas perversas que buscaban.

No traigas más nadie a nuestra casa,
así descubrirán nuestros absurdos
te llevarán lejos a otras playas
te contarán historias de naufragios
te sacarán a rastras de esta casa.

Siomara España (Ecuador)

Época de crisis

Este edificio tiene
los ladrillos huecos,
se llega a saber todo
de los otros,
se aprende a distinguir
las voces y los coitos.
Unos aprenden a fingir
que son felices,
otros que son profundos.
A veces algún beso
de los pisos altos
se pierde en los departamentos

whisper mischievously,
plant a flower at your window.

That's why – I beg you – you must
not bring people to our house,
for they will turn pink,
greenish, reddish, bluish,
on discovering broken walls
and withered plants.
They will want to sweep out the corners
they will want to open our blinds
and find, tucked away among my books
the depraved excuses they were searching for.

Don't bring anyone to our house any more,
for they will discover our absurdities,
will carry you off to faraway beaches
tell you tales of shipwrecks,
drag you from our house.

Siomara España (Ecuador)

Time of Crisis

This building
has hollow bricks,
you get to know everything
about the others,
learn to distinguish
the voices and the couplings.
Some learn to pretend
that they are happy,
others that they are deep.
At times a kiss
from the upper floors
gets lost in the lower

inferiores,
hay que bajar a recogerlo:
"Mi beso, por favor,
si es tan amable."
"Se lo guardé en papel periódico."
Un edificio tiene
su época de oro,
los años y el desgaste
lo adelgazan,
le dan un parecido
con la vida que transcurre.
La arquitectura pierde peso
y gana la costumbre,
gana el decoro.
La jerarquía de las paredes
se disuelve,
el techo, el piso, todo
se hace cóncavo,
es cuando huyen los jóvenes,
le dan vuelta al mundo.
Quieren vivir en edificios
vírgenes,
quieren por techo el techo
y por paredes las paredes,
no quieren otra índole
de espacio.
Este edificio no contenta
a nadie,
está en su época de crisis,
de derrumbarlo habría
que derrumbarlo ahora,
después va a ser difícil.

Fabio Morábito (México)

apartments,
you have to go down and fetch it:
"My kiss please,
if you would be so kind."
"I kept it wrapped in a newspaper."
A building has
its golden age,
the years and fatigue
wear it thin,
so that it resembles
the life that passes by.
The architecture loses weight
and habit gains ground,
propriety gains ground.
The hierarchy of the walls
dissolves,
the roof, the floor, everything
turns concave,
this is when the young people flee,
travel the world.
They want to live
in virgin buildings,
they want a roof for a roof
and walls for walls,
they don't want
another kind of space.
This building doesn't satisfy
anyone,
it is in its time of crisis,
to knock it down you'd have
to knock it down right now,
later it's going to be difficult.

Fabio Morábito (Mexico)

En la casa de Zulema Hualquipán

Junto al río de estos cielos
verdinegro hacia la costa
levantamos la casa de Zulema Hualquipán.
Hace ya tantas muertes los cimientos,
hace ya tantos hijos para el polvo
colorado del camino.
Frente al llano el lomaje del oeste,
levantamos la mirada de mañío
de Zulema Hualquipán.
Embrujados en sus ojos ya sin luz
construimos las paredes de su sueño.
Cada tabla de pellín huele a la niebla
que levantan los campos de la noche.
Cada umbral que mira al río y los lancheros
guarda el vuelo de peces y de pájaros.
Bajo el ojo de agua en el declive
donde duermen animales de otro mundo
terminamos las ventanas.
Y en la arena hemos hincado nuestros nombres
como estacas que sostienen la techumbre
de la casa de Zulema Hualquipán.

Jaime Luis Huenún (Chile)

Execración de la luz

Desde hoy viviré bajo la tierra
Oír los pasos que arando con espinas, invocan el miedo
ahuyentan el miedo para invocarlo nuevamente
tan vano es como sostener el Misterio

Me despido de la lluvia, crin del viento
de la sal que se revuelca en los océanos
Mas, extrañaré las rocas retrocediendo hacia la playa

In the House of Zulema Hualquipán

Next to the river of these skies
dark green towards the coast
we raise the house of Zulema Hualquipán.
The foundations so many deaths ago,
so many sons ago
for the red dust of the road.
Opposite the plain and the low ridge to the east,
we raise the mañío tree gaze
of Zulema Hualquipán.
Spellbound in her already lightless eyes
we build the walls of her dream.
Every plank of oak smells of the fog
that rises from the fields at night.
Every threshold that looks to the river and the boatmen
preserves the flight of fish and birds.
Under the spring on the slope
where animals from another world are sleeping
we finish the windows.
And into the sand we have driven our names
like stakes that hold up the roof
of the house of Zulema Hualquipán.

Jaime Luis Huenún (Chile)

Execration of the Light

As of today I will live beneath the earth
To listen to footsteps that plough with thorns, that invoke fear
and banish fear so as to invoke it anew
is as vain as sustaining the Mystery

I take my leave of rain, horsehair of the wind
of salt that is sent churning through the ocean
even though I will miss the rocks retreating towards the beach

eterna huida de espuma y sangre
la sal sobre la llaga, su caricia

Desde hoy viviré bajo la tierra
donde la salamandra teje su llama de coral
y una serpiente roja late en el corazón de un magma extraordinario

Invocando el nombre de las aguas remotas
vadearé los ríos que se abrazan
los diminutos ríos que se abrazan y se quedan abrazados
los diminutos ríos que conservan el pensamiento sin voz.

Damsi Figueroa (Chile)

Un hombre solo en una casa sola

Qué hace un hombre solo en una casa sola?
Lee un poema de Teillier?
Enciende el fuego?
Y si no tiene deseos de encender el fuego?
Llama por teléfono a su esposa?
Llama por teléfono a una amiga?
Llama por teléfono a sus hijos?
Se embriaga y trata de escribir?
Se embriaga y lee?
Se embriaga y piensa en el futuro?
Y si no quiere oír más la palabra futuro?
Se mete a la tina con agua tibia y cuchillo?
O se pone a ver una película?
Escribe cartas?
Y si quiere dormir y no puede?
Y si debe estar despierto y no quiere?
Coloca entonces una a una en su lengua el Seconal, el Veronal?
Imagina que su casa es un barco ebrio?
Imagina que su casa es un bar pintado por van Gogh como dice un poema de Decap?

eternal flight of sea-spray and blood
salt on the wound, its caress

As from today I will live beneath the earth
where the salamander weaves his coral flame
and a red snake beats in the heart of an astonishing magma

Invoking the name of remote waters
I will wade across rivers that embrace
the small rivers that embrace and remain embraced
the small rivers that hold onto unspoken thoughts.

Damsi Figueroa (Chile)

A lonely man in a lonely house

What does a lonely man do in a lonely house?
Read a poem by Teillier?
Light a fire?
What if he has no wish to light the fire?
Call his wife on the telephone?
Call a woman friend on the telephone?
Call his children on the telephone?
Get drunk and try to write?
Get drunk and read?
Get drunk and think about the future?
What if he no longer wishes to hear the word future?
Climb in the bathtub with lukewarm water and a knife?
Or settle down to watch a film?
Write letters?
And what if he wants to sleep and can't?
And what if he must stay awake and doesn't want to?
Place on his tongue, one by one, a Seconal, a Veronal?
Imagine that his house is a drunken boat?
Imagine that his house is a bar painted by van Gogh, as a poem by Decap has it?

Se pone a conversar con Decap?
Conversa con Kerouac?
Llama por teléfono a un cuchillo?
Enciende el fuego con un magnolio?
Con la escarcha que ha empañado las ventanas?
Lava la sangre de las sábanas en una tina?
Ve una película donde un tipo escribe cartas en una casa enferma?
Un tipo que se encama con una enferma en una casa sola?
Un tipo enfermo que escucha el teléfono ocupado de su esposa?
La voz de una mujer enferma en el teléfono apagado de una amiga?
Qué hace la casa con este tipo enfermo?
Y si la casa quiere estar sola?
Y si los muebles quieren que nadie los mire?
Y el aire reniega de todo respiro?
Y la tina de toda sangre?
Y la chimenea de todo fuego?
Y el papel en blanco de toda letra?
Y la muerte de todo señorío?

Un hombre solo en una casa sola?

Un hombre solo en una casa enferma?

Ricardo Herrera Alarcón (Chile)

El espacio vacío

Todos los ingredientes se mezclarán esta noche

(la casa proyecta sus pasillos hacia los cuatro puntos cardinales)

los invitados visten adecuadamente

Todo indica que en ese lugar ocurrirá algo

algunos rastros indican que ya han sucedido cosas

Have a conversation with Decap?
Have a conversation with Kerouac?
Call a knife on the telephone?
Light a fire with a magnolia tree?
With the frost that has misted over the windows?
Wash the blood from the sheets in the bathtub?
Watch a film in which some guy writes letters in a sick house?
A guy who has sex with a sick woman in a lonely house?
A sick guy who listens to the occupied tone on his wife's phone?
The voice of a sick woman on the switched-off phone of a woman friend?
What does the house do with this sick guy?
And if the house wants to be alone?
And if the furniture wants no one to look at it?
And if the air refuses all breath?
And the bathtub all blood?
And the chimney all fire?
And the paper blank of all words?
And death all dominion?

A lonely man in a lonely house?

A lonely man in a sick house?

Ricardo Herrera Alarcón (Chile)

The Empty Space

All the ingredients will be mixed together tonight

(the house extends its corridors to the four cardinal points)

the guests dress suitably

Everything suggests that something is going to happen in this place

a few clues suggest that things have already happened

en ese lugar

Los invitados comienzan a inquietarse esperando la función

buscan en su horizonte algo en qué ocupar las manos
pero descubren que la casa está completamente vacía

no existe un lugar donde sentarse

no existe algo que beber o que comer

Alguien anuncia la presentación de una película

los invitados se dirigen hacia algún recinto distinto
del cual ocupan en ese momento

(es posible que ahí estén pasando una película)

los invitados comienzan a inquietarse esperando la función

algunos rastros indican que ya ha sucedido algo

algunos rostros indican que ya ha sucedido algo

Alguien anuncia la presentación de los músicos

lo cierto es que nadie habla
lo cierto es que a los invitados les gustaría encontrar

un lugar donde sentarse
o un vaso para ocupar las manos

no existe un lugar donde sentarse

no existe algo que beber o que comer

Los invitados comienzan a inquietarse esperando la función

in this place

The guests start to become anxious waiting for the performance

they search the horizon for something with which to occupy their hands
but discover that the house is completely empty

there is no place to sit down

there is nothing to drink or eat

Someone announces the screening of a film

the guests make their way towards a different area
from the one they are in just now

(it's possible a film is being shown there)

the guests start to become anxious waiting for the performance

a few clues suggest that something has already happened

a few faces suggest that something has already happened

Someone announces the presentation of the musicians

what is certain is that nobody talks
what is certain is that the guests would like to find

a place where they could sit down
or a glass to occupy their hands

there is no place to sit down

there is nothing to drink or eat

The guests start to become anxious waiting for the performance

siguen llegando invitados
pero descubren que la casa está completamente vacía

algunos rastros indican que ya ha sucedido algo

algunos rostros indican que ya ha sucedido algo

Cuando observan un sector específico dentro de la casa
descubren que está completamente vacío

pero el espacio inmediatamente contiguo
está repleto de invitados que siguen llegando

Cuando observan un sector específico dentro de la casa

descubren que está completamente vacío

Gustavo Barrera *(Chile)*

Luna de plástico

Estamos en un living oscuro
donde quiero todo menos lo que tengo.
Sin zapatos, en el piso, tomando vino
en vasos de cristal, ponen música fuerte
y me pregunto: ¿por qué nosotros nunca
ponemos esta música?
La posibilidad del placer me está haciendo levitar
y la imposibilidad del placer me marea.
Voy a asomarme a la ventana a tomar aire,
pero no hay más, aquí, que la estrecha confluencia
de patios traseros y escaleras para incendio,
la ausencia de sonido mordazmente agitada
por la música mágica, una oscuridad de afueras de la ciudad
apenas conocida. Así que necesito ir a la calle.
Me pongo los zapatos, salgo,

guests keep arriving
but they discover that the house is completely empty

a few clues suggest that something has already happened

a few faces suggest that something has already happened

When they look at a particular section inside the house
they discover that it's completely empty

but the space immediately adjacent
is full of guests who keep arriving

When they notice a particular section inside the house

they discover that it's completely empty

Gustavo Barrera (Chile)

Plastic moon

We are in a dark living room
where I want everything except what I have.
Without shoes, on the floor, drinking wine
from crystal glasses, they put on loud music
and I ask myself: why do we
never play this music?
The possibility of pleasure is lifting me off the ground
and the impossibility of pleasure is making me dizzy.
I lean out of the window to take in some air,
but there's no more here, only the tight alignment
of back patios and fire escapes,
the absence of sound sarcastically shaken
by the magical music, a darkness of the city's suburbs
barely known. That's why I need to go out on the street.
I put on my shoes, leave,

bajo la luz marrón que el piso a cuadros se chupa como esponja,
y mientras tanto pienso, pienso.
¿Por qué nosotros nunca ponemos esta música?
Me paro en la vereda congelada. No hay olores.
No puedo distinguir la ventana
de donde vengo. Un grupo de hombres en la sombra
me vuelven al temor. Ay, pero, gracias.

Laura Wittner *(Argentina)*

Progreso

Lo sé sin traición ni documento.
Esta es mi casa y ya no es.
Hierven y suben los recuerdos de escalón en escalón
y altísimos hasta el piso 15 se pierden en la nada del cielo
gris ahora y no azul del no, ya recuerdo.
Tres peldaños con pisadas y barro en la entrada
una herradura quejumbrosa en un clavo de la puerta
y un aura que defiende el hálito familiar.
Sí, un piso cuadriculado en la cocina
Un pulcro tablero y una Clorinda para el buen aseo
Un pan que presto se amasa en la memoria
Un horno que cuece la torta del barro infantil.
Sí, recuerdo la sombra alternada de los postigos
y el eterno recuento de líneas en desvelo
y las voces celestiales
y también las otras
esas
las que amonestan
las que invaden mi cabeza en reposo pretendido
y obligan la lectura a la luz de una linterna
para que Dios mediante no cunda el pánico.
Sí, una quejumbrosa escalera recibe mis zapatos colegiales
y destapa y ondea esa independencia de pelo en pecho.
Sí, una entonces bravucona y vociferante

under the muddy light that the chequered floor sucks in like a sponge,
and in the meantime I think, I think.
Why do we never play this music?
I stop on the frozen pavement. There are no smells.
I can't make out the window
from which I have come. A group of men in the shadows
makes me afraid again. Oh, but thanks.

Laura Wittner (Argentina)

Progress

I know it without betrayal or evidence.
This is my house and yet it's not.
Memories boil and bubble from step to step
and towering up to the 15th floor, get lost in the nothingness of sky
grey now and not the blue of No, I remember.
Three stairs with footprints and mud in the entrance
a cranky horseshoe on a nail in the door
and an aura that protects the family's breath.
Yes, a chequered floor in the kitchen
a spruce chess board and *Clorinda* for thorough hygiene
bread that is promptly kneaded in memory
an oven that bakes the cake of childhood's clay.
Yes, I remember the shifting shade of the shutters
and the eternal counting of lines in sleeplessness
and the voices from heaven
and also the others
those
those that reprimand
those that invade my head in supposed sleep
and make me read by the light of a torch
so that God willing panic doesn't spread.
Yes, a squeaky staircase absorbs my school shoes
and reveals and flaunts that strident independence.
Yes, once loud and swaggering,

una hinchada en llanto y risa y nervios de principiante
una colgada como todos en el ojo del tiempo propio.
Tantos y tantos días errantes en el desierto del hogar
concentrada en el decir aparte de los mayores
llenando el vacío que a ratos hincha
para luego hilvanar una historia en demasía propia
inteligible, por supuesto, en un otrora tan cuerdo
y ese armario con sorpresas en el pasillo
no otra cosa que un mar antañoso con su completo oleaje
encerrado bajo una y siete llaves de cancerbero
silencio y secreto pocas veces entreabierto
baúl de piratas y cueva de duende maldito
deseando la dolencia para violarle el sello
y las albas paredes de adobe
desnudas y sin cáscara en medio de las tembladeras
y los libros que derrumban sobre la cabeza
y la invasión de maestros componedores
y el polvo y el desorden y el silencio arrinconado
y la tremenda molestia del ajetreo.

Vanidad.
Vanidad de la materia que acoge el recuerdo
cual cofre silente entregado a la retroexcavadora.

Progreso
frío y bello como el hielo azul de los glaciares
que pudiendo apenas y con la venia de dónde la carretera
tampoco sabe ni pregunta
y toma la sartén por la mango y entierra bajo el trueno del hacer
el bellísimo pensar y encadenado al fuego
que una vez ya nos fue arrebatado.

Verónica Zondek (Chile)

swelling with laughter and tears and the nerves of a beginner,
hooked, like everyone, in the eye of their own time.
So many days wandering in the desert of the home
concentrating on the alien talk of adults
filling the emptiness that occasionally swells
to later stitch together a too personal story,
only intelligible, of course, in one formerly so sane,
and that wardrobe of surprises in the corridor
nothing less than an ancient sea in full surge
buried beneath one and seven keys of Cerberus
silence and secret seldom ajar
pirates' chest and cave of cursed elf
wishing for illness so as to break the seal
and the shining white walls of adobe
naked and without a shell when the earth shakes
and the books that collapse on your head
and the invasion of master bonesetters
and the dust and the mess and the cornered silence
and the tremendous bother of hustle and bustle.

Vanity.
Vanity of the matter that shelters memory
like a silent treasure box surrendered to the digger.

Progress
cold and beautiful like the blue ice of glaciers
that barely able and with the road's consent
neither knows nor asks
and takes control and buries beneath the thunder of doing
the loveliest thought and chained to the fire
that already once was snatched from us.

Verónica Zondek (Chile)

La ciudad y los bárbaros

Bajaban a la ciudad desde montañas explosivas, rojas
con barrenos y fósforo y mataban con cuchillos
y tenían olor a bosta, pero reivindicaban sus ojos azules.
Y después de matar robaban a los muertos,
los que a su vez habían bajado de la montaña roja
con barrenos y habían matado a todos con
fósforo y cuchillos y habían robado a los muertos.
Quienes habían bajado de la montaña en medio de explosiones
rojas y habían matado con barrenos y bosta
y habían robado a los muertos.
Todos, en general, reivindicaban sus ojos azules
pero ninguno se enamoró de ninguna mujer ni tuvo descendencia.
El origen de la ciudad se perdía en los tiempos,
pero los desconocidos llegaban siempre
cuando la población estaba a punto de extinguirse.

Jorge Aulicino (Argentina)

He nacido en los confines

He nacido en los confines de un imperio inasible
rodeado por líneas imaginarias y huidizas.

Desde niño quise conocer el corazón de la comarca,
acudir a su norte que era también su centro.

Después de muchos años de soñar con caminos
me resigno a saber que no he partido.

Esta mañana un hombre enfrente mío conversa con los pájaros.
Les instruye la forma de llegar al palacio de jade.

Yo lo escucho pensando en el norte,
en el centro,

The City and the Barbarians

They came down on the city from the explosive mountains, red
with blasthole and phosphorous and they killed with knives
and smelled of dung, but flaunted their blue eyes.
And after killing they robbed the dead,
who in their time had come down from the red mountain
with blastholes and had killed everyone
with phosphorous and knives and had robbed the dead.
Who had come down from the mountain amid red explosions
and had killed with blastholes and dung
and had robbed the dead.
All of them, by and large, flaunted their blue eyes
but none of them fell in love with a woman nor had descendants.
The origin of the city was lost in time,
but strangers always arrived
when the population was at the point of extinction.

Jorge Aulicino (Argentina)

I was born within the confines

I was born within the confines of an elusive empire
bordered by imaginary and evasive lines.

Since childhood I wanted to know the heart of the region,
to visit the north, which was also the centre.

After many years of dreaming about roads
I resign myself to the knowledge that I have not left.

This morning a man across from me is talking to the birds.
He tells them how to arrive at the jade palace.

I listen to this, thinking of the north,
of the centre,

en mi viejo deseo.

Pero ya estoy cansado y los días me pesan.

He de conformarme con aprender ese idioma de aves
y, ya solo, en mi cuarto, planear sobre las sábanas.

Gabriel Chávez Casazola (Bolivia)

Los Mezquites

Para Hernán Bravo Varela

Es más cómodo flotar sobre honduras tranquilas
que estar de pie en el lodo, con el agua hasta el cuello.
Quédate quieto un rato y vendrán las tortugas
a comerte los dedos entre helechos y hierba,
sin siquiera mirarte. (Tres millones de años
sitiadas en un charco en medio del desierto;
¿qué piedad o qué rencor puede causarles
el manso enjambre de tu futuro?)

Cavan salud los brazos en la calma.
Apenas emerges, un alfiler de sol
te llama desde el fondo: un anillo
que gira entre el deseo y la generosidad.
Nada tras él, cabeza abajo, con los ojos abiertos,
hundiendo puños en el fango de la ciénaga.
Pero el anillo es sólo un rumor.

*Dicen que Los Mezquites forman parte de los restos
de un mar que en la prehistoria cubría esta región.
Su flora y fauna incluyen estromatolitos,
endémicas tortugas de bisagra y ciegos peces
que nadan en cavernas a donde no cae luz.*

of my old desire.

But now I am tired and the days weigh on me.

I have to be content with learning that language of birds
and, alone now, in my room, to soar above the sheets.

Gabriel Chávez Casazola *(Bolivia)*

Los Mezquites

For Hernán Bravo Varela

It is more comfortable to float on calm, deep waters
than to stand in mud, up to your neck in water.
Stay quiet a moment and the tortoises will come
to nibble at your toes between the grass and ferns,
without even looking at you. (Three million years
holed up in a pond in the middle of the desert;
what piety or rancour might the steady swarm
of your future cause in them?)

Your arms dig for health in the calm.
As soon as you emerge, a pinprick of sun
calls you from the depths: a ring
that spins between desire and generosity.
Swim towards it, head down, eyes open,
sinking fists into the silt of the swamp.
But the ring is only a rumour.

They say that Los Mezquites are part of the remains
of a sea that, in prehistory, covered this region.
Its flora and fauna includes stromatolites,
native terrapins and blind fish
which swim in caves where no light enters.

Nunca llega, el viento: viene hacia acá
como un rumor, haciendo rizos
cada vez más pequeños en el agua.
Así suenan al ras de superficie las palabras, el anillo:
es más cómodo flotar que estar de pie.

Preferible bucear debajo de los nenúfares negros:
arden los ojos abiertos, hojas de agua
tapian el sol sobre la sien.
Ciego como los peces de una gruta líquida.
No hay más joya nupcial que un rumor en la boca.
Con el agua hasta el cuello.

Julián Herbert (México)

Metafísica zoológica

Como la oveja que regresó a parir
a la granja donde había nacido,
algunas noches sueño que aún estoy en la casa
donde vivió la persona que salió un día
a ser quien soy ahora.

Alicia García Bergua (México)

Los que no están

      Para las almas los cuerpos valen oro. Pero es un oro carnal, de ruido tibio, un oro en trazos y fibras, oscuro, más oscuro que la muerte que lleva y devuelve las almas a su origen, la muerte como un mar que las devora.
      Los cuerpos flotan.
      Sin la muerte, un cuerpo es más grave que su sombra. La muerte los levanta, los madura, hace de los cuerpos un sueño

It never arrives, the wind: it comes towards this place
like a rumour, making smaller and smaller
ripples on the water.
This is the way words sound at the rim of the surface, the ring:
it is more comfortable to float than to stand.

Preferable to dive beneath the black water lilies:
your open eyes sting, floating leaves
block the sun from your temples.
Blind like the fish in a liquid grotto.
There is no better nuptial gem than a rumour in the mouth.
Up to your neck in water.

Julián Herbert (Mexico)

Zoological metaphysics

Like the sheep who returns to the farm
where she was born to give birth,
some nights I dream that I'm still in the house
where the person lived who went out one day
to be who I am now.

Alicia García Bergua (Mexico)

Those who are not here

      For souls, bodies are worth their weight in gold. But it is a carnal gold, that makes a lukewarm noise, a gold in traces and fibres, dark, darker than the death that carries and returns souls to their place of origin, death as a sea that devours them.
      Bodies float.
      Without death, a body is graver than its shadow. Death raises them up, matures them, makes of the bodies an unrepeat-

irrepetible en el que el deseo encuentra materias claras para hacer la casa.

    La casa se levanta y se derrumba, pero los trozos esparcidos son duras gotas del agua del deseo, humedecen la vida que les falta.

Rafael Courtoisie (Uruguay)

No clarea y ya se oyen cacareos . . .

No clarea y ya se oyen cacareos.
De nuevo lo mismo, lo que ayer era mañana
ahora es hoy, mañana lo que es hoy
va a ser ayer y así siempre.
El que está descalzo, en la cocina,
y arranca una hoja del almanaque
recién pensaba en sueños que estaba muerto,
eso dicen las viejas alarga la vida.
Espinas, hojas, flores blancas picadas
de púrpura entre las ramas del limonero
donde tiene su parada Rufo el zorzal
– ahora no, pero vamos a hablar
de cuando en una vida suya anterior
pretendió valerse de la rivalidad
entre César y Pompeyo. Muy bien,
digamos que una brisa sacude todo eso,
incluso los limones que por descuido
faltó apuntar más arriba
entre espinas y hojas.

D.G. Helder (Argentina)

able dream in which desire finds clear materials with which to make the house.

The house is raised and falls down, but the scattered bits are hard drops of the water of desire, they moisten the life that they lack.

Rafael Courtoisie (Uruguay)

It is not yet light and the cock crows . . .

It is not yet light and the cock crows.
The same thing again, what yesterday was tomorrow
now is today; tomorrow, what is today
will be yesterday and so on for ever.
He who is barefoot, in the kitchen,
and tears a page from the calendar
just now thought in a dream that he was dead,
the old women say that means a longer life.
Thorns, leaves, white flowers dotted
with purple between the branches of the lemon tree
where Rufo the thrush perches
– not now, but let's talk soon
of when, in an earlier life,
he tried to benefit from the rivalry
between Caesar and Pompey. Okay,
let's say a breeze shakes all that away,
even the lemons which, carelessly,
someone failed to point out above
between thorns and leaves.

D.G. Helder (Argentina)

Berwick

Se levanta una polvareda de pájaros
en el campo apenas resembrado.
Rastrean el alimento, orbitan en un presente
subyugado. Firman parábolas y planos curvos,
picotean. En el codo de la colina
se asienta el pueblo. Planea
sobre el brazo de mar que lo acuna.
Da de comer a las gaviotas y a los perros.
Mira hacia el otro lado como si esperara
años de invasión. Una fila de árboles bajos,
como corderos, otean el horizonte.
Las ovejas en cambio echan raíces
y brotan algodonales
en apretadas frondas blancas.
Las vacas son cuajos pardos en los pastizales.
Aquí atracaron las olas de la latinidad y la germanía.
Abajo pasa el Tweed, nadan los cisnes
como si cualquier cosa desde siempre.

Pedro Serrano (México)

Otra ciudad

Cuando levanto la vista veo nieve,
nieve refulgiendo desde el televisor.
Como siempre, titilan sobre el mapa
los lugares donde una no está.
Seguro extrañaría el mercado de flores
y despertar en este piso octavo
que se abre desafiando al viento.
La verdad es que hubo un solo día de nieve
y que hay una posible segunda versión
para las cosas conocidas.

Berwick

A dust cloud of birds stirs
in the newly planted field.
They follow the trail of food, orbit a charmed
present. They execute parabolas and level curves,
they peck about. In the lee of the hill
sits the town. It hovers over
the arm of sea that rocks it to sleep.
It feeds the seagulls and the dogs.
It looks towards the other shore, as
if it awaited years of invasion. A line of low trees,
like sheep, scan the horizon.
The real sheep, by contrast, cast down roots
and cotton fields spring up
in cramped white fronds.
The cows are a dull brown, curdling in the pastures.
Here waves of Romans and German tribes docked.
Below flows the Tweed, and swans swim
as if nothing had happened, ever.

Pedro Serrano (Mexico)

Another City

When I raise my eyes I see snow,
snow gleaming from the television.
As always, places where one is not
shimmer on the map.
Certainly, I'd miss the flower market
and waking in this eighth-floor flat
which opens out in defiance of the wind.
The truth is there was just one day of snow
and there is a second possible version
of things known to us.

Las valijas están hechas desde siempre
y además están sobre el sofá
en posición de espera.
Ese momento dura, se sostiene,
es una manera de estar:
estar a punto de ser abandonado.
El pozo negro de las valijas hechas,
reverso del desembarco:
el deseo humano por lo incompleto
que se refleja, dicen,
en la predilección por lo pequeño,
lo breve, el fragmento.

Laura Wittner (Argentina)

Regent's Canal (a la altura de Danbury Street)

De la tierra helada del invierno, apenas los contrastes:
las aguas verdes del canal a la deriva,
la lluvia inglesa y ese cuervo trepándose a la rama.
como quien dice estoy,
yo soy de aquí
y tengo poco tiempo que perder con un extraño.

De esta ciudad de casas de ladrillo y lentas ceremonias,
el cuervo es otro dato de la tarde,
una constancia más que el hombre acepta
y suma a la barcaza, a la botella,
al tipo con su caña y sobretodo
pescando desde el borde
con gusanos que guarda en una caja de zapatos.

El extranjero entonces se aferra a ese canal
y busca detrás de las esclusas,
de los barcos dormidos hasta la primavera,
de pasos fantasmales que cruzan Noel Road

Suitcases have been packed for ever
and ready on the sofa
waiting to be off.
That moment lasts, is sustained,
it's a way of being:
to be at the point of being abandoned.
The black pit of packed bags
the reverse of disembarking.
The human desire for the incomplete
reflected, it is said,
in a preference for small things,
brevity, fragments.

Laura Wittner *(Argentina)*

Regent's Canal (by Danbury Street)

From the frozen winter earth, only the contrasts:
the drift of the canal's green waters,
the English rain and that crow shuffling along the branch,
as if to say
I'm from around here
and I don't have time to waste on a stranger.

The crow joins the afternoon's information
in this city of brick houses and slow ceremonies,
one more constant that the man takes as given
along with the barge, the bottle,
the character with his rod and raincoat
fishing from the bank,
with worms that he keeps in a shoebox.

So the foreigner sticks to that canal,
searching behind the locks,
behind the hibernating boats
behind the sound of ghostly footsteps crossing Noel Road

una costumbre que no tiene,
un modo de las cosas que no entiende.

Jorge Fondebrider (Argentina)

Postal de Buenos Aires

Esta ciudad está viva
y es como la gorda mujer que canta mientras todo tiembla

Como esa mujer a la que no le importa que el mundo
vaya a pique
porque se levantó hermosa
o se maquilló demasiado
o usó zapatos altos, unos zapatos rojos, altísimos
que le alargaban las piernas

Y es también como esa mujer que soñó algo obsceno
muy sucio
y sonríe toda la jornada,
            frente a la pantalla
                        en su oficina.

Sí, esta ciudad está viva
y es una mujer

O tal vez es un film italiano largo, muy largo
que en el minuto noventa y cinco se harta de si mismo
y entonces canta, vibra
y decide ser un homenaje
algo menos real y más histriónico

Yo
(que sé de ciudades que también son mujeres)
lo noté de inmediato
en sus adoquines flojos

for a custom he is lacking
a way of things he cannot understand.

Jorge Fondebrider (Argentina)

Postcard from Buenos Aires

This city is alive
and is like the fat lady who sings while everything trembles

Like that woman who doesn't care if the world
is going to hell
because she started the day beautiful
or she put on too much make up
or used high heels, red shoes, the highest heels
to make her legs longer

And is also like the woman who dreamed something obscene
truly filthy
and smiles all day long,
       in front of the computer screen
              in her office.

Yes, this city is alive
and is a woman.

Or perhaps it's a long Italian film, very long
that in the ninety-fifth minute becomes tired of itself
and so sings, vibrates
and decides to be an homage
somewhat less real and more histrionic

I
(who know about cities that are also women)
noticed it at once
in its loose cobblestones

en sus balcones desvencijados
en su lluvia,
      más pasional que cualquier llanto,
que viene fuerte y se detiene
como una mujer que cede y luego se arrepiente
para al final ceder de nuevo.

Carolina Dávila (Colombia)

Buenos Aires al vuelo

Todo comienza en la tercera planta del pasado,
la quinta puerta al fondo del olvido.
Ábrela, ciérrala: hay viento suficiente
para escapar, y tiempo para entender al fin.

Las calles coloniales y todavía sucias de San Telmo
que alguien en mi nombre recorre alucinado,
con su viejo almacén (la esquina de los gritos)
donde guardan los víveres de alguna semifusa
o la Plaza Dorrego, balones y raíces como músculos,
los domingos en venta su sol artesanal,
aquel otro mercado (hangar de contraluces)
cuando el precio del pan subía cada tarde,
quedarme con el cambio, tan sólo dos monedas
y dos también, y solos, los amores:
la rara pelirroja de la calle Juncal,
la bailarina-yegua del galopar en leves zapatillas,
más allá las mañanas borrosas y de escarcha
camino al puerto, dársenas y grúas
(soñolienta gimnasia de sus amaneceres), la marrón
pestilencia del río, avergonzado de la historia
y del vuelo siniestro de helicópteros,
el terror, ciertos golpes, piruetas para entrar en los potreros,
un reloj alemán que se llevó consigo algunas horas,
abre, ciérrate,

in its dilapidated balconies
in its rain,
> more impassioned than any weeping,
that comes on strong and then holds back
like a woman who yields and later regrets it
only to yield again.

Carolina Dávila (Colombia)

Buenos Aires on the Fly

It all begins on the third floor of the past,
the fifth door at the end of forgetting.
Open it, close it: there's enough wind
to escape, and time to finally understand.

Someone with my name wanders dazed
the colonial and forever filthy streets of San Telmo,
with its old store (the corner of shouts)
where they keep a supply of semiquavers
on the Plaza Dorrego – balls, and roots like muscles,
its artisan sun on sale every Sunday,
that other market (a back-lit hangar)
when the price of bread rose every evening
and I would pocket the change, only two coins
and two loves, also:
the strange redhead on Juncal Street,
the dancer-mare galloping in flimsy shoes,
and then fuzzy mornings and the frosty
road to the port, docks and cranes
(drowsy gymnasium of its dawns), the brown
pestilence of the river, ashamed of its history
and of sinister helicopters flights,
the terror, blows – so hard, pirouettes to get on those scrappy playgrounds,
a German wristwatch that took a few hours from me,
open, shut it,

el grito de ese niño que me aturde
despertando algún miedo en otro idioma,
nombres que aún traduzco, el ajedrez color
pomelo en la avenida Independencia, mi amigo el heladero,
su desaparecer, las bicicletas en el Parque Lezama
(la azul velocidad con que se alejan),
las risas maquilladas, los zapatos, los columpios
de los domingos húmedos en Plaza Francia
(entre parques y plazas huye el tiempo),
la libertad, el Once, el bus 86,
el sueño de haber sido futbolista u hombre muerto,
aquel temible patio de los puñetazos
(jugar al escondite era un alivio),
pero qué libertad, ciérrate, ciérrate,
un club donde nadar era aprender a ahogarse,
un abuelo con gorra lúcido hasta el suicidio,
otro que vive en hábitos y gestos que aprendí
mucho más tarde, desandando la escala,
una pequeña casa en las afueras, un jardín con enanos
y aquel raro almanaque y las canicas grises
y un cuadro con un circo, la pianista de manos
que se rompen, un balón de colores ascendiendo,
el templo azul y oro, su garganta de césped,
el transistor oculto debajo de un manual, el laberinto
en Alsina y Moreno, la muerte junto al álgebra,
esas únicas fiestas en las cuales bailaste (¿recuerdas que bailaste?),
el Teatro Colón o la caverna donde secuestraban
el violín de mi madre cada día, el corredor
desierto y enemigo, las intrusas con vaqueros rosados,
un balón de colores descendiendo,
aquel mirar vacío de cierto amigo muerto en delantal
(su cara detenida como en un papel pálido),
los varios ataúdes que me hicieron adulto,
la madera del ébano, un arco y un caballo,
un Dodge naranja incendio
(el viento suficiente para que se propague),
un limonero roto, un sauce en pie, ladrones
sin sombra y una puerta perforada,

the cry of that boy dumbfounds me
waking some kind of fear in another language,
names which I still translate, the grapefruit coloured chess set
in Independencia Avenue, my friend the ice-cream vendor,
his disappearance, bicycles in Lezama Park
(the blue speed with which they move away),
the made-up laughter, the shoes, the swings
on humid Sundays in Plaza Francia
(between parks and plazas time flees),
freedom, the *Once* neighbourhood, the 86 bus,
the dream of having been a footballer or a dead man,
that fearful patio of the fistfight
(playing hide-and-seek was a relief),
but what freedom, shut it, shut it,
a club where to swim was to learn to drown,
a behatted grandfather lucid to the point of suicide,
another who lives on in habits and gestures that I learned
much later, coming back down the ladder,
a little house in the suburbs, a garden with gnomes
and that rare almanac and the grey marbles
and a painting of a circus, the pianist with broken
hands, a bright ball ascending,
the blue and gold temple, its neck of lawn,
transistor radio hidden beneath a manual, the labyrinth
of Alsina and Moreno Streets, death next to algebra,
the only fiestas on which you danced (remember that you danced?),
the Colón theatre or the cave where they confiscated
my mother's violin every day, the deserted and hostile
corridor, the gatecrasher girls in pink jeans,
a bright ball descending,
the empty look of a friend, dead in his apron,
(his face paused in time as if a blank sheet)
the various coffins that made an adult of me,
ebony wood, a bow and a horse,
a flame-red Dodge
(wind enough for the fire to spread),
a broken lemon tree, a willow standing, thieves
without shadow and a door with holes,

un ladrón diferente en el espejo: esos balcones
al otro lado, asómate, del tiempo
y del aire y del plano que se acerca
a dos ojos cerrados, las luces y los pozos,
el pronto aterrizaje, su riesgo necesario,
(las calles de allá abajo y aquí dentro),
el bobo señalar de un obelisco,
la bóveda nublada, la veloz
repetición de la caída,
su materia inasible,
su resplandor...

Igual que en el mercado yo quisiera
quedarme con el cambio, ser ayer
teniendo la memoria de mañana.
A mí se me hace cuento que existiera un lugar
al que pertenecer, un árbol sin raíces, una línea
que ya no tiene suelo, palpita de invisible,
traza su propio mapa en mi reverso, habla,
duele y remonta el vuelo.

Andrés Neuman (Argentina)

Chonimutux

Las noches en Chonimutux
son espesamente negras.

Puede llevarse
un poco entre las manos
y tapar con ella
hoyitos en las paredes.

Son como barrancos boca abajo.

Si te quedás viendo su hondura

a different thief in the mirror: those balconies
on the other side, check it out, from time
and from the air and the map that approaches
two closed eyes, lights and wells,
the prompt landing, its necessary risk,
(the streets of down there and inside here),
the stupid pointing of an obelisk,
the cloudy vault, the speedy
repetition of the fall,
its ungraspable material,
its radiance ...

Just as in the market, I would like
to pocket the change, and to be yesterday
with the memory of tomorrow.
Hard to believe there might exist a place
to belong, a tree without roots, a line
that has no ground, that flutters invisibly,
traces its own map on my back, talks,
hurts, and takes flight again.

Andrés Neuman (Argentina)

Chonimutux

The nights in Chonimutux
are thick and black.

You can pick up a little
between your hands
to seal off
small holes in the walls.

They are like inverted ravines.

If you keep looking at their depths

sentís irte de cabeza

como si la tierra estuviera arriba
y uno parado en el cielo.

Humberto Ak'Abal *(Guatemala)*

Vista general

En el espacio,
la ciudad se extiende
sin control,
como una hoguera,
piedra por piedra,
calle por calle,
consumiendo el paisaje,
llenándolo de gente, ratas y pájaros sucios.
Aquí,
la cultura es salvaje
y se construye lo mismo de savia que de sangre.
El hábitat,
un pequeño gran vertedero de la modernidad periférica
al pie de Los Andes,
bajo el inmenso cielo de América.

En el tiempo,
la ciudad se desvanece
bajo el rigor de los cíclicos terremotos
o a manos de la afición nacional por las demoliciones.
Aquí,
nada se conserva,
todo se destruye.
Los lugares y las cosas
apenas ofrecen resistencia
a la continua disolución de este pueblo fantasma,
ahogado en el río del olvido

you will feel yourself falling headfirst

as if the earth were above you
and you were standing on the sky.

Humberto Ak'Abal *(Guatemala)*

Panorama

The city expands
in space
without restraint,
like wildfire,
stone by stone,
street by street,
consuming the countryside,
filling it with people, rats and grimy birds.
Here,
culture is savage
and is built with equal parts of sap and blood.
The habitat
a big little rubbish tip of peripheral modernity
at the foot of the Andes
beneath the immense sky of America.

With time,
the city fades away
under the harshness of cyclical earthquakes
or due to the national fondness for demolitions.
Here,
nothing is preserved,
everything is destroyed.
Places and things
barely offer any resistance
to the continual dissolution of this phantom town,
lodged in the river of oblivion

donde todo cambia sin permanecer.

Jaime Pinos (Chile)

Nunca tuve una casa

Quiero una casa

donde no escuchen tus gritos los vecinos
tus gritos de placer
        inocultables

donde siempre caiga el agua
del cielo
        y de la regadera

Quiero un hogar con patio
donde juegue la infancia
su más torrente abecedario

donde el sol no me recuerde
los cadáveres incesantes de mis doce años

donde no haya que colocar semáforos
        bajo las puertas
donde quepa el amor que nos lazamos
        y los hijos

donde La Muerte finalmente llegue
y se sienta
        como en su propia casa

Otoniel Guevara *(El Salvador)*

where everything changes without remaining.

Jaime Pinos (Chile)

I never had a house

I want a house

where the neighbours cannot hear your cries
your irrepressible
        cries of pleasure

where there is always water falling
from the sky
        and from the watering can

I want a garden and a patio
where childhood plays out
its most torrential alphabet

where the sun does not remind me
of being twelve and the endless dead bodies

where I don't have to put red signals
        under doors
where there's room for the bond of love
        and the children

where Death arrives finally
and feels as though
        he's in his own home.

Otoniel Guevara (El Salvador)

Introduction to Part 2:
'Where we come from.'

Roots, family and friendship form the unifying thread for the poems in this section.

Jessica Freudenthal Ovando's opening poem uses an incantatory style to explore the sometimes horrifying complexities of family history among the Bolivian ruling class, in which, for example, 'my father's father was imprisoned by my mother's father' – a line followed by the deadpan: 'I am the daughter of my mother and my father'. The list technique might run the risk of becoming overstretched were it not for the variation in content (and manners of meeting with death) and the pathos of its delivery. Freudenthal's other poem in Part 2, 'The Madman's House' (p125) offers a further glimpse into personal territory, where 'Indian and Spanish blood / flow' within a 'bastard fatherland' (the title of an online collection of Freudenthal's poems).[1]

A biblical quotation opens her brief reflection on neighbourly violence in Gioconda Belli's five-liner (p97), 'God said'. Belli's memoir, *The Country under My Skin*[2], is a celebrated account of how a young woman from Nicaraguan high society became a Kalashnikov-wielding *Sandinista* before and during the 'contra' war. Meanwhile, and by contrast, the Chilean Nadia Prado – a specialist in the prose poem – likes to find correspondences and connections with the everyday, hence her likening of writing to her mother's sewing (p99).

In reading for this section I encountered numerous poems that addressed difficult or conflictual relations with fathers, and a few are included here. Piedad Bonnett's 'Biography of a Fearful Man' (p101) seems almost to equate the father's 'goodness' ('he was a good man' . . . 'a decent man') with that of fearfulness ('like a whining dog, muzzled / and tied to its stake'). Paradox lies at the core of other paternal portraits: Beatriz Vignoli's hospitalised father is rescued from a fall by his daughter's embrace just as 'Rigoletto hugs the corpse / of his daughter' on the ward's TV; Alejandra Cortés González (p125) extends an image of his bloodied father, razor in hand, 'with that satyr's smile hidden between the cracks of a broken mirror' – where the speaker now sees only himself, shaving his own face. The Cuban poet Damaris Calderón (p131) offers a minimum of goodwill in her 'Snapshot' (of my father): 'On wretched nights he would mount my mother / like someone who catches a train by mistake'; and yet the father too falls prey, 'eaten by vultures / (his children)' in this short, startling poem. The only father to emerge as wholly admirable is Héctor Abad's, in 'Memento' (p137), and he is brutally murdered, a political assassination at the height of Colombia's Dirty War, documented more extensively in the author's devastating account, *Oblivion*[3], the title (like the last few lines of the poem) deriving from an unpublished piece by Borges, discovered in his father's pocket after his murder: 'already we are the oblivion we shall be.'

Relationships with siblings offer no source of comfort here, only further distress. Darío Jaramillo, in his 'Testimony concerning my Brother' (p103), delivers an hypnotic, weaving account of a life of excess and debauch, but the poem is also haunted by a sense of immanence, and of loss, and always compromised by paradox – including the suspicion as to whether, indeed, this 'brother' actually exists, or is an aspect of the speaker: 'he has told me he would never die, that one day he will leave, / perhaps disappear, / but that we will always be together, in some way, / as always.' Irene Gruss' speaker takes tea with her sister in the aptly titled 'Tea' (p107), but the beverage spills, and as it seeps across the table towards the her, she realizes that the liquid 'scares me, and at the same time / I know that what it's asking for / is pity, help'.

Friendship seems to bear greater potential for a rewarding relationship than family, even when – as in the case of Micaela Chirif's poem (p109) – the friend with whom her speaker holds telephone conversations that 'sometimes last the whole evening' is dead. The writer in Mirta Rosenberg's 'Letter transformed into a thing' (p111) complains that 'memories are foolish things', but the letter's quiddity or 'thing-ness' somehow transmutes the epistle itself into a 'matter of metaphor': solid matter somehow being 'more ungraspable or more gaseous' that 'what has been lost' over the years.

The recounting of family origins is a topic of interest, even anxiety, for many Americans, North and South: two Chileans from different generations, Clemente Riedemann (born 1953) and Enrique Winter (1982), reflect on their respective German and Polish ancestors' journeys to a Chile, where, in Riedemann's case (p107), fake land rights[4] were handed out, while Winter's grandmother worked as a domestic servant for her German husband's family (p119). The collective memory of Diana Bellessi's Italian ancestors (p121), however, died 'with the death / and memory of my grandparents', although she retains, as her inheritance, 'a gleaming of the Adriatic / and an enormous hoe'.

Two Argentinians born in the 1960s, Edgardo Dobry (p121) and Fabián Casas (p123), offer poems of a very different tenor: in Dobry's poem, the nine-year old narrator follows his mother's instruction to 'bring her / a kilo of those pears that Augustine / stole in Thagaste in 370 AD', the temporal disjunction not merely adding a surrealist spin, but providing a sense of the essentially unchanging nature of experience, as the boy – just like Neuman's younger persona in Part 1 – is able 'keep the change'. Casas' powerful meditation on mortality (p123) suggests that after 'trying to bury / our parents' story' in adolescence, we may be obliged to have the same story told back to us (by a psychotherapist, perhaps) in order to become 'better people'. The poem's descent into darkness, literally, encompasses, en route, the disarming image of the wife who cooks while 'the husband masturbates in the bathroom'.

Finally, special mention should be made of Gabriel Chávez Casazola's 'Song of Soup' (p113). In this poem, the traditional big Latin family of 'grandfather's day' is nostalgically evoked – a time when everything was big, and soup was 'dished out with big ladles / from enormous tureens.' But even here 'Father' embodies authority, and fantasizes about a younger replacement for 'Mother', and 'riding in a big car or on a big horse or /walking with big style, not yet aged with time.' Fathers, in these poems, have a lot to answer for.

1 *Patria bastarda* can be found at: http://www.puntoenlinea.unam.mx/images/stories/pdf/cartografias-54-jessica-freuedentahl.pdf
2 *The Country under my Skin*, Anchor, 2003. First published in Spanish as *El país bajo mi piel* (Vintage Español, 2001).
3 *Oblivion: A Memoir*, Farrar, Straus and Giroux, 2012. First published in Spanish as *El olvido que seremos* (Seix Barral, 2006).
4 These land rights in southern Chile were known as *rewes*, a term borrowed from Mapudungun, the Mapuche language, and which might be paraphrased as 'engraved totemic logs that mark a place of spiritual purity.'

Fragmento del libro *Árbol*

I

mi padre tiene una novia de mi edad
mi padre dice engañó a mi madre con seis mujeres
de las que se enamoró
mi padre siempre engañó a mi madre
-siempre- puede reducirse a quince o veinte años
mi padre y mi madre se hicieron novios a los quince años
y se casaron al borde de la mayoría de edad
mi madre es hija de un militar
mi madre es hija de un militar que dicen estuvo involucrado
en la muerte del che guevara y la nacionalización de la gulf oil
company
mi padre es hijo del hombre de confianza del presidente que hizo
la revolución de 1952
el padre de mi padre fue confinado por el padre de mi madre
yo soy hija de mi madre y de mi padre
tengo una hermana y dos hermanos
mi hermano mayor lleva el nombre de mi padre y el nombre del
    hermano mayor de mi madre
el hermano mayor de mi madre murió en un accidente de
aviación
-dicen que no fue un accidente-
dicen que sabotearon el avión para que cayera el gobierno de mi
abuelo militar que nacionalizó la gulf y el estaño
mi hermano menor lleva el nombre del sid campeador y el del
hermano menor de mi madre que es también el de su padre
yo llevo mi nombre y el nombre de la hermana mayor de mi
padre muerta por un ataque de epilepsia en el oriente boliviano
la madre de mi padre dice que nació en un lugar donde el
cementerio es más grande que el pueblo, y que no conoció la
palabra amor
mi hermana lleva su nombre y los dos nombres de mi madre
el hermano menor de mi madre lleva el nombre de su padre
-pero no lo usa nunca-
la hermana menor de mi madre es adoptada

Fragment from *Tree*

I

my father has a girlfriend of my age
my father says he cheated on my mother with six women
with whom he fell in love
my father always cheated on my mother
"always" could be reduced to fifteen or twenty years
my father and my mother became engaged at fifteen years of age
and were married as soon as they were legal adults
my mother is the daughter of a military man
my mother is the daughter of a military man they say was involved
in the death of che guevara and the nationalization of the gulf oil
company
my father is the son of the right hand man of the president who led
the revolution of 1952
my father's father was imprisoned by my mother's father
I am the daughter of my mother and my father
I have a sister and two brothers
my older brother has the same name as my father and the older
    brother of my mother
the older brother of my mother died in an airplane
accident
– they say that it wasn't an accident –
they say that the plane was sabotaged to bring about the fall of my
military grandfather's government that nationalized oil and tin
my younger brother has the name of sid campeador and of the
younger brother of my mother which is also the name of her father
I have my name and the name of the older sister of my father who
died during an epileptic attack in eastern bolivia
my father's mother says that she was born in a place where the
cemetery is bigger than the village, and she never knew the word
love
my sister has her name and the two names of my mother
my mother's younger brother has his father's name
– but never uses it –
my mother's younger sister is adopted

—pero ese es un secreto a voces—
yo soy esposa de mi esposo
yo no uso el apellido de mi esposo
mi esposo era el novio de la hija segunda del hermano menor de mi madre
mi madre y el padre de mi esposo tuvieron un romance
mi padre se puso algo celoso
madre y padre
madre patria
pacha mama
el árbol familiar no conoce sus raíces
no puede verlas
en la oscuridad y profundidad de la tierra
allí debajo escondidas
lejanas a la copa
al aire
y a las ramas
en las ramas de este árbol
cuelgan los muertos
los suicidios
el hermano de la madre de mi padre
se pegó un tiro la noche de navidad
el tercer hermano de mi padre aspiró cocaína hasta detener su corazón
el primo hermano de mi madre se lanzó por las cataratas del niágara
muertes poéticas
muertes
el padre de mi madre murió de cáncer de páncreas
el padre de mi padre murió de enfisema
el hermano segundo de mi padre murió de un paro cardiopulmonar
a este árbol le cuesta respirar
no conoce sus raíces
los apellidos recorren toda la estructura
se desvanecen
se hacen transparentes

Jessica Freudenthal Ovando (Bolivia)

– but this is an open secret –
I am the spouse of my spouse
I do not use the surname of my spouse
my spouse was the boyfriend of the second daughter of my
mother's younger brother
my mother and my spouse's father had a fling
my father became somewhat jealous
mother and father
mother fatherland
pacha mama
the family tree doesn't know its roots
it can't see them
in the darkness and depth of the earth
there hidden underground
far from the crown
from the air
and from the branches
from the branches of this tree
hang the dead
the suicides
my father's mother's brother
shot himself on christmas night
my father's third brother snorted cocaine until his heart stopped
my mother's first cousin threw himself off the niagara falls
poetic deaths
deaths
my mother's father died of cancer of the pancreas
my father's father died from emphysema
my father's second brother died of cardiopulmonary arrest
it costs this tree to breathe
it doesn't know its roots
the surnames run all along its structure
they vanish
they become transparent

Jessica Freudenthal Ovando (Bolivia)

Dios dijo

Dios dijo:
Ama a tu prójimo como a ti mismo.
En mi país
el que ama a su prójimo
se juega la vida.

Gioconda Belli *(Nicaragua)*

Siempre escribía

Siempre escribía mirando a mi madre trabajar. La vigilaba por el agujero de la puerta. Si la vigilaba podía escribir segura de que ella no me viera. Su rostro era el papel blanco donde esparcía el alfabeto. La lluvia mojaba mi espalda, el trazo era su mano paseándose en la mía. Mi madre encerrada y transformada en máquina de coser salía a escribir por mí del otro lado de la puerta.

Nadia Prado *(Chile)*

God said

God said:
Love your neighbour as yourself.
In my country
he who loves his neighbour
is dicing with death.

Gioconda Belli (*Nicaragua*)

I would always write

I would always write while watching my mother work. I kept an eye on her through the gap in the door. If I kept an eye on her I could write safe in the knowledge that she could not see me. Her face was white paper on which I scattered the alphabet. The rain wet my back, the stroke of my pen was her hand ambling along mine. My mother, shut inside and transformed into a sewing machine, ventured out to write through me from the other side of the door.

Nadia Prado (*Chile*)

Biografía de un hombre con miedo

Mi padre tuvo pronto miedo de haber nacido.
Pero pronto también
le recordaron los deberes de un hombre
y le enseñaron
a rezar, a ahorrar, a trabajar.
Así que pronto fue mi padre un hombre bueno.
("Un hombre de verdad", diría mi abuelo).
No obstante – como un perro que gime, embozalado
y amarrado a su estaca –, el miedo persistía
en el lugar más hondo de mi padre.
De mi padre,
que de niño tuvo los ojos tristes y de viejo
unas manos tan graves y tan limpias
como el silencio de las madrugadas.
Y siempre, siempre, un aire de hombre solo.
De tal modo que cuando yo nací me dio mi padre
todo lo que su corazón desorientado
sabía dar. Y entre ello se contaba
el regalo amoroso de su miedo.
Como un hombre de bien mi padre trabajó cada mañana,
sorteó cada noche y cuando pudo
se compró a cuotas la pequeña muerte
que siempre deseó.
La fue pagando rigurosamente,
sin sobresalto alguno, año tras año,
como un hombre de bien, el bueno de mi padre.

Piedad Bonnett (Colombia)

Un rostro en la muchedumbre (Graffitis)

Mis padres una vez tuvieron la razón
Se conocieron en una plaza abarrotada cantando a coro
Se amaron en un mar de diez literas acalladas por la voz

Biography of a Fearful Man

As soon as he was born my father was fearful of life.
But just as soon
he was reminded of the duties of a man
and he was taught
to pray, to save, to work.
So that soon my father was a good man.
("A real man," my grandfather would have said).
Nevertheless – like a whining dog, muzzled
and tied to its stake – the fear persisted
in the deepest part of my father.
Of my father,
who as a child had sad eyes, and as an old man
hands as clean and earnest
as the silence of early mornings.
And always, always, the air of a lonely man.
So that when I was born my father gave me
all that his confused heart
knew to give. And amid that was included
the loving gift of his fear.
Like a decent man my father worked every morning,
navigated every night and when he could
he bought, by instalments, the little death
that he always desired.
He paid for it rigorously,
without alarm, year after year,
like a decent man, my dear old father.

Piedad Bonnett (Colombia)

A Face in the Crowd (Graffiti)

My parents were in their right minds once
They met in a packed square singing in a choir
They loved each other in a sea of ten bunks silenced by

       de «silencio»
Me trajeron al mundo en un salón de camas ordenadas
       en emociones compartidas
Nadamos en playas atestadas de bañistas confundidos
       por trajes idénticos y camiones colectivos
Los sábados en la noche vimos las mismas películas
llorando a la par de un país subtitulado en blanco y negro
Los domingos nos dijimos adiós
confusos en el azul   uniformado que nos separó
Mis padres   cuando por fin se quedaron solos
Perdieron la razón.

Wendy Guerra (Cuba)

Testimonio acerca del hermano

Mi hermano tiene la línea de la vida corta y marcada intensamente,
una señal profunda, como si una estrella de fuego le hubiera horadado la
mano y el rumbo.
Mi hermano sabe decir que no con la dureza y la suavidad de los
       hombres vigorosos.
Mi hermano le ha enseñado a su cuerpo la alucinación y el éxtasis,
ha cantado y reído, mi hermano ha vivido siempre como un sabio,
pisando el límite exacto de la demencia, tocando su borde alucinado,
en la fiebre del hongo o el alcohol, en el delirio del amor o de la orgía.
Pero siempre mi hermano ha sido fuerte y sabio,
con la sabiduría de quien sabe el límite de su destrucción
y con la sabiduría de quien se conserva intacto,
mi hermano juega con el tiempo, yuxtapone colores,
mi hermoso quinto hermano me enseña con su historia el fondo
       transparente de su calma
y me extiende la misma mano que quemó todas sus naves
jugándose el todo por el todo, siempre,
y siempre incólume
como quien sabe el final y no le duele.
Mi hermano, el sabio transgresor, regresándome a la ebriedad y al

         the command to "be silent"
They brought me into the world in a room of beds tidied
         into shared emotions
We swam at beaches packed with bathers confused
         by their identical swimsuits and communal trucks
Saturday nights we watched the same films
crying in the same way a subtitled country cries in black and white
Sundays we said our goodbyes
hazy in the uniform   blue that separated us
My parents   when at last they were left alone
Lost their minds.

Wendy Guerra (Cuba)

Testimony Concerning my Brother

My brother has a short and deeply furrowed life-line,
a profound sign, as if a shooting star had pierced his hand
         and his path.
My brother knows how to say no firmly and smoothly
         like all strong men.
My brother has taught his body hallucination and ecstasy,
has sung and laughed; my brother has always lived like a sage,
pacing the exact limits of insanity, touching its deluded edge,
in mushroom or alcohol fever, in the delirium of love or orgy.
But my brother has always been strong and wise,
with the wisdom of one who knows the limits of his self-destruction
and with the wisdom of one who keeps himself intact,
my brother plays with time, juxtaposes colours,
my beautiful fifth brother teaches me with his story the transparent
         depths of his calm
and offers me the same hand that burned all his boats
always playing for all and everything,
and always unharmed
like one who knows the end but it does not hurt him.
My brother, the wise transgressor, furiously free, unchained from all

        incesto,
el furiosamente libre, el desatado de toda obligación que no sea su
        instinto.
Mi quinto hermano es duro y seco con la gente, intolerante como yo,
pero mucho más recio, como quien está acostumbrado a guardar su
        territorio de invasiones.
Mi hermano regala una cálida ternura a quienes ama,
y entonces es locuaz y regocijante y más hermoso.
Mi hermano habla poco
y en ciertos momentos de lucidez alcohólica me dijo que él nunca
        moriría, que algún día se irá,
que a lo mejor desaparezca,
pero que siempre estaremos juntos, de algún modo,
como siempre.
Debimos conocernos cuatro años antes, también me dijo mi hermano
        en esa noche,
pero yo creo que todo tiene su día, su destiempo,
su oscura constelación de alborozado abrazo.
Desde muy joven, sabiendo lo que hacía,
mi quinto hermano quemó todas sus naves,
y abrió los ojos y descubrió su hermoso cuerpo
y supo también que la belleza es la sabiduría del cuerpo
y siempre estuvo atento, creciendo hacia dentro en afiebrada vigilia.
Mi hermano fabrica conmigo fantasías de diecisiete pisos, con risas y
        palabras,
mi hermano hace música y dice disparates y le gusta echar mentiras que
        no le hacen daño a nadie,
y le fascinan los perfumes y hacer ejercicio y quemarse bajo el sol
y le gusta estar solo, organizando los oficios diarios.
Mi quinto hermano es fuerte y sabio
y ambos sabemos que nunca nosotros, solitarios, dejaremos de estar
        juntos.
Falta también aquí el sabor amargo que vela tras la sombra de mi quinto
        hermano,
la pesadilla y el descenso a los infiernos:
él siempre se jugó el todo por el todo
y desaparecerá en la plenitud,
cuando el agrio fantasma que lo sigue sin tocarlo, decida por él,

         obligation
except to his instinct,
returning me to drunkenness and incest.
My fifth brother is hard and dry with people, intolerant like me,
but much tougher, like one who is used to securing his territory
         from invaders.
My brother bestows a warm affection on those he loves,
and then he is talkative and lovely and full of joy and more beautiful.
My brother talks little
and at given moments of alcoholic lucidity has told me he would never
         die, that one day he will leave,
perhaps disappear,
but that we will always be together, in some way,
as always.
We should have met four years earlier, my brother told me
         that night too,
but I think that everything has its day, its bad timing,
its dark constellation of jubilant embrace.
From a young age, knowing what he was about,
my fifth brother burned all his boats,
and opened his eyes and discovered his beautiful body
and knew also that beauty is the wisdom of the body,
and he was ever alert, growing inward in a feverish wakefulness.
My brother and I invent fantasies of seventeen storeys, with laughter
         and words,
my brother makes music and talks nonsense and likes to tell lies
         that don't harm anyone,
and is captivated by perfumes and working out and burning in the sun
and he likes to be alone, going about his daily tasks.
My fifth brother is strong and wise
and we both know that the two of us, loners, will never be apart.
The sour taste that keeps vigil over my fifth brother's shadow
         is also missing from this poem,
the nightmare and the descent to hell:
he always played for all or nothing
and will disappear when at his peak,
when the bitter ghost that follows without touching him,
         decides for him,

y caiga,
y con él caiga lo que quede de mí,
si entonces algo queda.

Darío Jaramillo Agudelo (Colombia)

El té

Está sentada frente a mí
y hace ruidos con la taza, la golpea sin querer.
Está loca pero la que desea
matarla soy yo.
Si le comento cualquier asunto, ella pregunta
con tono de loca más que dubitativa: ¿ah, sí?
Ahora está
diciéndome que hay vidrios rotos
en su barriga, la cortan, duele.
Miro la taza que golpeaba, intacta,
y el té que viene hacia mí, de a poco,
rogando algo que no entiendo. El líquido
toma una forma que me asusta, y al mismo tiempo
sé que lo que pide
es piedad, ayuda; es té tibio
sobre la mesa y
es mi hermana.

Irene Gruss (Argentina)

El hombre de Leipzig

El padre del padre de mi padre traía todo el mar en sus mejillas. Trajo un cormorán en la mirada y una flauta dulce en los bolsillos.
No trajo papeles ni osamentas. Le quitaron su historia en las aduanas y venía de lejos.

and he falls,
and with him falls what is left of me,
if, by then, anything is left.

Darío Jaramillo Agudelo (Colombia)

Tea

She is sitting across from me
and she makes noises with her cup, knocking it heedlessly.
She's crazy but I'm the one
who wants to kill her.
Anything I comment upon, she asks
with a tone more crazy than doubtful: *is that so?*
Now she is
telling me there is broken glass
in her stomach, it's cutting her, it hurts.
I look at the cup she was knocking, it's undamaged,
and at the tea that's gradually making its way towards me,
asking me something I don't understand. The liquid
takes a shape that scares me, and at the same time
I know that what it's asking for
is pity, help; the tea is lukewarm
on the table and
it is my sister.

Irene Gruss *(Argentina)*

The Man from Leipzig

My father's father's father carried the whole sea in his cheeks. He brought a cormorant in his gaze and a melodious flute in his pockets. He didn't carry papers or skeletons. They took away his story at customs, and he was coming from far away.

Al llegar, sólo la niebla, pañal de maíz para envolver los viejos barcos de
madera: la "Steinward", el "Hermann", el bergantín "Susanne" y el
"Alfred". Todos buscando el paraíso. Para todos, desengaño y selva.
(El daguerrotipo muestra a unas familias apiñadas y sin saber a qué
atenerse. Allí dormitan en el suelo el hacedor de calamorros y la mujer
del peluquero. También, un niño con paperas).
¡Oh viejos barcos de madera! ¡Oh germánicos famélicos! Les
prometieron la tierra pero la tierra tenía dueños falsos. Falsas estacas de
papel y no auténticos rewes milenarios. El padre del padre de mi padre
hubo de hablar en otra lengua, gotear, de nuevo, el semen de la aurora.
A fundar cosas es que vino el hombre de tan lejos.
Corral, después de un siglo pronuncio tu nombre en la mañana. Estoy
de pie sobre una lancha arrojando trozos de carne podrida a las gaviotas.
Por aquí entró en América el perseguido, uno que no fue rico ni famoso
sino bello. Porque bello es todo cuanto sigue siendo, a pesar de la
muerte, el deterioro y el olvido.
El hombre de Leipzig, el carpintero, me trajo a tierra en el lápiz de su
oreja, de donde he bajado para organizar el mundo con palabras.

Clemente Riedemann (Chile)

Un amigo

a veces me llama por teléfono
un amigo muerto desde hace años
contrariamente a lo que podría pensarse
la conversación es bastante normal:
yo le cuento los chismes de acá
y él me cuenta los de allá
yo miro el día oscurecerse en la ventana
él se corta las uñas con pereza
y así
compartiendo historias
pasamos a veces la tarde entera

cuando llega el momento de colgar

On arrival, only fog, a maize napkin to wrap up the old wooden ships: the *Steinward*, the *Hermann*, the brigantine *Susanne* and the *Alfred*. All in search of paradise. For all of them: disappointment and forest.
(The daguerreotype shows a few families squeezed in and not knowing what to adjust to. There, snoozing on the floor, the boot-maker and the barber's wife. Also, a child with mumps.)
Oh, old wooden boats! Oh, famished German types! They promised them land but the land had false owners. False paper stakes instead of authentic thousand year *rewes*. My father's father's father had to speak in another language, to squeeze out, once more, the semen of daybreak. To found things is what brought the man from so far away.
Corral, after a century I utter your name in the morning. I am standing on a launch tossing pieces of rotten meat to the gulls. Through here, the persecuted man entered America, one who wasn't rich or famous, but handsome. Because handsome is everything he still is, whatever else happens, despite death, decline and oblivion.
The man of Leipzig, the carpenter, brought me to earth in the pencil behind his ear, from which I have come down to organise the world with words.

Clemente Riedemann *(Chile)*

A Friend

a friend dead for some years now
sometimes calls me on the phone
contrary to what might be expected
the conversation is normal enough:
I give him the gossip from hereabouts
he gives me the gossip there
I watch the day darkening in the window
he lazily cuts his nails
and in this way
sharing stories
we sometimes spend the entire evening

when the time comes to hang up

y siempre llega
nos da entonces muchísima tristeza
y nos ponemos a llorar
pero eso sí
    por delicadeza
lo hace cada uno por su cuenta

Micaela Chirif (Perú)

Una carta convertida en cosa

Cada vez, amiga, soporto menos
las emociones y sé que a veces tengo una expresión
capaz de entristecer el mediodía.
Con razón creo recordar otros días
cuya única sombra era
la que proyectaban los árboles,
y también recuerdo otras cosas.

Pero en fin, los recuerdos son pavadas.

Son como vendas, la momifican
a una, y soy como una momia
privada: últimamente tomo
la vida como es, como el carozo
que se sabe, entorpece la aceituna
y le da un alma laboriosamente amarga.

Últimamente murió mi madre
cuando ya era vieja.
He empezado a pensar en la vejez
como quien vaga en su catacumba privada
donde se aloja su propia momia privada
y ve pasar cada cosa como es.

Últimamente no soy del todo yo misma, claro,

and it always comes
we both become very sad
and begin to weep
but for the sake
   of delicacy
each of us does this alone

Micaela Chirif (Peru)

A Letter Transformed into a Thing

As time passes, my friend, I withstand emotions
less well, and I know that at times I wear an expression
capable of casting midday into gloom.
No wonder I think of remembering other days
on which the only shadow
was thrown by the trees,
and I remember other things too.

But well, memories are foolish things.

They are like bandages, they mummify you,
and I am like a private mummy:
recently I've been taking life as it is,
like the kernel that, as we know,
restrains the olive
and gives it a laboriously bitter soul.

Recently my mother died:
she was old by then.
I have begun to think of old age
as someone wandering in her private catacomb
where her own private mummy resides
and sees everything as it is go by.

Recently I haven't been myself, of course,

y veo pasar las cosas
hasta terminar con ellas
como un reflejo de mí
estacionado en los espejos.

Casi todas las cosas.

Estás tan lejos que pensé
hacer un movimiento de fondo
y escribir una carta a mi amiga.
Pero en esta oscuridad del yo
no puedo pegar un ojo
por miedo de no ver el cambio
en la forma de las cosas

y me he ido convirtiendo en una
de ellas, de esas cosas.

Pensé escribir una carta a mi amiga
que fuera materia sólida entre otras cosas
más inasibles o más gaseosas, sombras
más serias que lo perdido.

Menos una carta que una cosa.
Y en vez de enviarla recordarla
como un cambio de la cosa,
y que se hiciera entre las dos,
mi amiga y yo,
materia de metáfora.

Mirta Rosenberg (Argentina)

La canción de la sopa

En tiempos de mi abuelo las familias eran grandes
vivían en grandes casas —grandes o chicas, pero grandes,

and I see things happening
until I'm done with them
like a reflection of myself
lodged in mirrors.

Almost all things.

You are so far away that I thought
I'd make a basic move
and write a letter to my friend.
But in this darkness of the self
I cannot sleep a wink
for fear of not seeing the change
in the form of things

and I've changed into one
of them, one of those things.

I thought to write a letter to my friend
that was solid matter, among other things
more ungraspable or more gaseous, shadows
more grave than what has been lost.

Less a letter than a thing.
And instead of sending it, to remember it
as a change of the thing,
so that it became, between the two of us,
my friend and I,
a matter of metaphor.

Mirta Rosenberg (Argentina)

The Song of Soup

In my grandfather's day families were big
they lived in big houses – big or small, but big,

inclusive diminutas, pero grandes.

Comían alrededor de grandes mesas
mesas fuertes, cubiertas o no de mantel largo
pero bien establecidas en el piso.

Con cucharas enormes comían la sopa
en los grandes mediodías. La sopa extraída con grandes
cucharones
de unas enormes soperas.

Se reunían juntos después a oír la radio, a tomar café,
a fumarse un cigarrillo
sin grandes (ni pequeños) cargos de salud o de conciencia.

Mamá, bordando a veces y a veces tejiendo,
veía sucederse a los hijos y a los nietos
en un ininterrumpido y gran bordado.

Papá, la autoridad papá, llegaba todas las tardes a las 6
montado en un gran auto americano o en un gran caballo
o con un gran estilo
de caminar
para pasar la noche junto con los hijos y los nietos que el
tiempo no había interrumpido,
salvo aquél que enfermó, aquél que se fue
dejando un enigma y una sensación de vacío
—una enorme sensación de vacío—
flotando, con el humo de los cigarrillos,
sobre la sobremesa de la cena.
A veces, en esos momentos, papá, la autoridad papá,
dejaba de escuchar los sonidos de la radio y quería estar
solo consigo mismo, simplemente
no estar ahí, tal vez estar corriendo por alguna lejana
carretera con una rubia parecida a mamá cuando no era
mamá, montado en un gran auto americano o en un gran
caballo o
con un gran estilo de caminar aún no vejado por el tiempo.

even tiny, but big – .

They ate around big tables,
sturdy tables, with or without a wide tablecloth
but firmly set up on the ground.

With enormous spoons they ate their soup
in the big afternoons. Soup dished out with big
ladles
from enormous tureens.

They gathered together afterwards to listen to the radio, to drink coffee,
to smoke a cigarette
without big (or small) concerns about health or conscience.

Mother, sometimes embroidering, sometimes knitting,
would see children and grandchildren follow on
in a big, uninterrupted embroidery.

Father, the authority father, came home every evening at 6
riding in a big American car, or on a big horse
or with big style
walking
so as to spend the night together with his children and grandchildren
that time had not interrupted,
except for the one who fell ill, the one that went away
leaving behind an enigma and a sensation of emptiness
– an enormous sensation of emptiness –
floating, with the smoke from the cigarettes,
above the after dinner talk.
At times, on these occasions, Father, the authority father,
stopped listening to the sounds on the radio and wanted to be
on his own, simply
not to be there, perhaps racing along some distant
road with a blonde similar to Mother when she was not
Mother, riding in a big American car or on a big
horse or
walking with big style, not yet aged by time.

Mamá a su vez algunas sobremesas sentía un nudo
en la garganta, un nudo que después salía flotando de su
boca montado en un gran suspiro,
un enorme nudo que se enredaba en el vapor
de su taza de café, con unas
volutas que le robaban la mirada y la hacían desear
estar sola,
simplemente no estar ahí, escuchando los llantos
de las últimas hijas y los primeros nietos.

Así fueron los años, vinieron los cafés y los cigarrillos
y un día la gran casa se fue quedando sola, las enormes
soperas vacías, las cucharas mudas
de una enorme mudez que a hijas y nietos nos persiguió
a lo largo de miles de kilómetros de carretera, de cable de
teléfono, de grandes ondas que ya no se miden en kilómetros.

Incluso aquél que enfermó, el primero en partir
como cada quien que bebió de esa sopa fue alcanzado por la
mudez,
que se metió en su pecho por la gran boca abierta
de un enorme bostezo.

Entonces
compró una breve sopa instantánea
y entre sus mínimas volutas
se permitió un pequeño llanto.

No podía tomar la sopa.
en su diminuto departamento no había una sola cuchara,
una sola mesa bien fundada, algo
que vagamente pudiera parecerse a la felicidad
y sus rutinas.

Entonces pensó en los tiempos de su abuelo o del mío
o del tuyo, cuando las familias eran grandes

Mother, for her part, sometimes felt a knot in her throat during
after dinner talk,
a knot that afterwards would float from her
mouth astride a big sigh,
an enormous knot which became entangled in the steam
from her cup of coffee, in spirals
that absorbed her gaze and made her wish to be alone,
simply not to be there, listening to the crying
of the last daughters and the first grandchildren.

Such were the years, coffees and cigarettes appeared
and one day the big house was alone, the enormous
tureens empty, the spoons mute
with an enormous muteness that pursued us, the daughters and
grandchildren,
along thousand of kilometres of road, of telephone
cable, of the big waves that now are not measured in kilometres.

Even the one who was ill, the first to leave,
like all who drank that soup, was touched by muteness,
that entered his chest through the big open mouth
of an enormous yawn.

So
he bought an instant ready soup
and within its small spiralling
allowed himself a little sob.

He could not drink the soup,
in his tiny apartment there was not a single spoon,
or a single well-grounded table, something
that could vaguely resemble happiness
and its routines.

So he thought of the times of his grandfather, or of mine,
or of yours, when families were big

vivían en grandes casas —grandes o chicas, pero grandes,
inclusive diminutas, pero grandes
y veían sucederse a los hijos y a los nietos
en un ininterrumpido y gran bordado
con enormes hilos invisibles abrazándolos a todos
en el aire.

Gabriel Chávez Casazola (Bolivia)

Polaca

De un pasado dudosamente noble
como todo pasado noble. Modzelewska por padre,
Wyrzykowska por madre. Es huérfana y de quince años,
mil novecientos treinta y nueve:
pide pega en la industria intervenida.
El patrón frisa los cuarenta, arrancan
juntos a Viena por los rusos. Por los celos de Müller cae presa,
acusada a los nazis para casarlo con su hermana.
Son más de tres los meses. La liberan los gringos, camina días a
Salzburgo
y en la plaza tras una alarma ve correr a su jefe. —¡Papa!, chilla.
Se casan a escondidas para que nunca la bese en la boca.
Doméstica de su cuñado, duerme en la pieza de servicio
tal como en Chile. Donde trajo a Goethe
y un par de pilchas, para hacer del barquito de pesca
uno con capitán y marineros.
Un hijo. Viuda. Gatos. Perros. Pájaros
que huelen como ella o viceversa.
No está ni ahí con ver a sus nietos, le reclama mi padre.
Toco el timbre y no suena, grito y no respondo,
seis perros gordos y furiosos ladran sobre la reja.

Enrique Winter (Chile)

and would live in big houses – big or small, but big,
even tiny, but big –
and children and grandchildren would be seen to follow on
in a big and uninterrupted embroidery
with enormous invisible threads holding them all
in the air.

Gabriel Chávez Casazola (Bolivia)

Polish Woman

From a questionably noble background
like all noble backgrounds. Her father a Modzelewska,
her mother Wyrzykowska. An orphan at fifteen,
nineteen thirty-nine:
she asks for work in the occupied state industry.
The boss, close to forty, they flee together to Vienna
because of the Russians. Due to Müller's jealousy she falls prisoner,
denounced to the Nazis so he can marry her sister.
The months are more than three. The Yanks liberate her, she walks for days to
Salzburg
and in the square as a siren blares she sees her boss running: Papa! she yells.
They marry in secret so he'll never kiss her on the mouth.
A housekeeper to her brother-in-law, she sleeps in the servant's room,
just as in Chile. Where she brought Goethe
and a few old clothes to turn the fishing boat
into one with a captain and sailors.
A son. Widow. Cats. Dogs. Birds
that smell like her or vice versa.
You aren't even there for your grandchildren, complains my father.
I ring the bell and it makes no sound, shout and she doesn't answer,
six fat and furious dogs bark from over the railing.

Enrique Winter (Chile)

de 'Detrás los fragmentos'

1

No hubo guerreros
en mi familia
ni doctores ni poetas.

No tengo saga que contar
ni epopeya
sostenida con la espada
en el anca briosa de una yegua.

Sólo un puñado de historias
que ni registra siquiera
el nombre de los árboles
del río
o de los pájaros que amanecían
los días campesinos
en un pueblito de Italia
perdido con la muerte
y la memoria de mis abuelos.

Tengo por herencia
un resplandor del Adriático
y un enorme azadón
que puebla todas las cosechas.

Diana Bellessi (Argentina)

Mandado

Tendría unos nueve años
la tarde en que mi madre
me dijo andá a la frutería
de la otra cuadra y traeme

from 'Behind the Fragments'

1

There were no warriors
in my family
nor doctors nor poets.

I don't have a saga to recount
nor an epic
sustained by the sword
astride a spirited mare.

Only a handful of stories
which don't even mention
the names of the trees
of the river
or of the birds at daybreak
country days
in a small Italian village
lost with the death
and memory of my grandparents.

I have as inheritance
a gleaming of the Adriatic
and an enormous hoe
that occupies all the harvests.

Diana Bellessi (Argentina)

Errand

I was around nine years old
the afternoon my mother
told me to go to the greengrocer's
on the next block and bring her

un quilo de esas peras que Agustín
robó en Tagaste en el año 370.
Fue mamá ella misma esa vez
la que dijo quedate con el vuelto.

Edgar Dobry (Argentina)

Tratando de sepultar

Tratando de sepultar la narrativa de nuestros padres
se va la adolescencia.
Después pagamos para que la recopilen
y nos digan que podemos ser mejores.
¿Por qué sueño con perros?
¿Por qué me aburren las tardes
y no puedo hablar con mis amigos?
Mientras tanto la mujer cocina
y el marido se masturba en el baño.
La dicha se engendra
en el corazón de lo trivial
y a veces alguien muere,
a oscuras, en un cine.

Fabián Casas (Argentina)

a kilo of those pears that Augustine
stole in Thagaste in 370 AD.
That time, it was Mum herself
who said keep the change.

Edgar Dobry *(Argentina)*

Trying to Bury

Adolescence is spent trying to bury
our parents' story.
Later we pay to have it summarized
and they tell us we can be better people.
Why do I dream about dogs?
Why do the afternoons bore me,
and why can't I talk to my friends?
Meanwhile the wife cooks
and the husband masturbates in the bathroom.
Happiness is kindled
in the heart of the trivial
and occasionally someone dies
in the dark, in a cinema.

Fabián Casas *(Argentina)*

Jurar en vano

Mi padre miraba como si quisiera cortar algo con los ojos. Yo lo veía afeitarse: la espuma blanca como rabia de perro cediendo al paso de la cuchilla. Una vez se cortó escuchando un chiste en la radio; esa risa ensangrentada, y luego la toalla manchada sobre el lavamanos. Los ojos ocultaban sus intenciones en las grietas del espejo. El barco de Rimbaud sumergido en su blanco cuerpo ocular. Juró nunca heredarme algo: nada de bienes, nada de caricias de borracho, ni siquiera la alopecia, ninguna dipsomanía extraña. Sin embargo, ahora veo su cara cuando me afeito. Está apaciguado, distante, con la risa de sátiro escondida entre las rendijas de un espejo roto.

Alejandro Cortés González (Colombia)

La casa del loco

El padre loco,
vive en el bosque,
en la casa del loco.
En la casa del loco hay un violín,
hay paredes llenas de dibujos
garabatos, bestiarios y árboles imposibles.
El padre muerto no está muerto,
está loco,
pero al niño le han dicho que no tiene padre.
El pequeño
aferrado a una caja,
dentro de la caja
hay un encaje
—que no encaja—
hecho a mano
por las manos de su madre
quien nunca lo llamó hijo.

To Swear in Vain

My father used to look as if he wanted to cut something with his eyes. I would watch him shave: the white foam like rabid dog's drool giving way to the razor's passage. Once he cut himself listening to a joke on the radio; that bloodied laugh, and afterwards the stained towel on the washbasin. His eyes concealed his intentions in the mirror's crevices. Rimbaud's boat submerged in his white ocular body. He swore never to bequeath me anything: none of his goods, none of his drunkard's caresses, not even his alopecia, no bizarre dipsomania. However, I now see his face when I shave myself. He is appeased, distant, with that satyr's smile hidden between the cracks of a broken mirror.

Alejandro Cortés González (Colombia)

The Madman's House

The mad father
lives in the woods
in the madman's house.
In the madman's house there is a violin,
there are walls covered in pictures
doodles, bestiaries and impossible trees.
The dead father is not dead,
he is mad,
but they have told the child he doesn't have a father.
The little one,
clinging onto a box
inside the box
there is a piece of lace
which doesn't fit together
made by hand
by the hands of his mother
who never called him son.

El niño no tiene padre,
no tiene patria,
la patria no tiene padre,
es una patria bastarda.
Adivinando la puerta abierta
nervioso,
un perro muerto
al pie de la escalera
le da la bienvenida,
el corazón a punto de estallar.
En las paredes flores aladas,
hombres con cabeza de animal,
animales con cabeza de hombres
y pájaros como flores.
De las paredes blanqueadas
se desprenden esculturas de yeso
una mujer tendida sobre un león
y varios seres de bestiario.
El padre está muerto
el padre era un loco,
el padre era un artista,
pero en la América colonial
ser un artista era imposible.
En el árbol imposible
hay un nido imposible,
que guarda el huevo imposible
de un pájaro imposible,
con alas imposibles
para un vuelo imposible.
El loco, el padre,
vivió trece años de furor,
sumido en la negra melancolía
sin soportar la mirada de otros.
La razón volvió al loco
segundos antes de morir.
Sangre india y española
late dentro de un mismo ser
su madre una bruja

The child doesn't have a father,
he doesn't have a fatherland,
the fatherland doesn't have a father,
it is a bastard fatherland.
Guessing the door to be open
nervously,
a dead dog
at the foot of the stairs
welcomes him
his heart almost bursting.
On the walls winged flowers,
men with the heads of animals,
animals with the heads of men
and birds like flowers.
Sculptures in plaster fall away
from the whitewashed walls
a woman stretched out on a lion
and various beings from a bestiary.
The father is dead
the father was a madman,
the father was an artist,
but in colonial America
it was impossible to be an artist.
In the impossible tree,
there is an impossible nest,
that holds an impossible egg
from an impossible bird
with impossible wings
to make an impossible flight.
The madman, the father,
lived thirteen years of rage,
plunged in black melancholy
not standing the gaze of others.
Reason returned to the madman
seconds before he died.
Indian and Spanish blood
flow within a single being
his mother a witch

su padre un loco

Jessica Freudenthal Ovando (Bolivia)

Ronda infantil

De pestañas albinas
como espesor de polen a la luz
nace su propia alegría,
soplo de un estornudo.
Alérgica y albina
bien podría ser diosa
si al hincar con melindres lo que come
en el piel transparente le estallara lo púrpura,
se le hincharan los ojos,
si el golpe de la sangre fuera el de un sacrificio.
En este lugar sin estaciones, sin diosa antigua,
aquí donde no hay crímenes,
donde mejor que el crimen es la fábula,
ella cuenta lo que le cuenta una vecina,
un profesor de canto, un matrimonio,
el hombre de las cabras,
el joven novelista, la psicóloga . . .
Dicen ronda infantil de agudos que requiebran
y van más allá del canto
en proyecciones baratas de horror.
Dicen muñeca rota, pie de niña,
juguetería que cuelga entre las ramas;
de animales nocturnos dicen cópula.
En este lugar sin estaciones, sin diosa antigua
Y sin legítimos crápulas.

Alessandra Molina (Cuba)

his father a madman.

Jessica Freudenthal Ovando (Bolivia)

A Children's Round

From albino eyelashes
like thick pollen in the light
her own joy is born,
the blast of a sneeze.
Allergic and albina
she could well be a goddess
if amidst her squeamish bites
on her transparent skin a purple colour burst,
if her eyes swelled,
if the rush of her blood were sacrificial.
In this place without seasons, without an ancient goddess,
here where there are no crimes,
where the fable is better than the crime,
she tells what a woman neighbour tells her,
a singing teacher, a married couple,
the man who keeps goats,
the young novelist, the psychologist . . .
They recite a high-pitched children's round that compliments
and surpasses the singing
in tacky projections of horror.
They say broken doll, girl's foot,
toy shop hanging between the branches;
of nocturnal animals they say mating.
In this place without seasons, without an ancient goddess
and without genuine libertines.

Alessandra Molina (Cuba)

Escrito en la mesa de luz de un Hotel ★★★★

Por vergüenza de ser
pobre, me pasé media vida
escondiéndome
de mis amigos, no fuese que
murmuraran;
ahora ellos están
muriéndose
de todas esas
enfermedades nuevas,
raras,
ahora sí
los abrazo, pero ya no irradian
calor, sus caras están grises
– quiero decir, de un gris
oscuro – y ya no queda nada
de todo lo felices y geniales
que íbamos a ser.

Beatriz Vignoli *(Argentina)*

Instantánea

de mi padre

No bebía
tenía el renunciamiento de un pez en el Sahara
de una vaca castrada por los banderilleros de la feria.
Comunista,
pudo haber sido masón o cuáquero.
Igual le habrían cortado los nudillos,
igual habría partido su tazón con nadie.

Written on the Bedside Table of a Hotel ★★★★

For shame of being
poor, I spent half my life
hiding away
from my friends, to avoid
the gossip;
now they are
dying
from all these
new, rare
diseases,
now I
embrace them, but they no longer
radiate heat, their faces are grey
– I mean a dark grey –
and now nothing at all remains
of those happy and brilliant people
we were going to be.

Beatriz Vignoli *(Argentina)*

Snapshot

of my father

He didn't drink
he had the resignation of a fish in the Sahara
of a cow castrated by banderilleros at the fair.
A communist,
he could have been a Freemason or a Quaker.
They would have cut off his fingers at the knuckle anyway,
he would not have shared his bowl with anyone.

En deplorables noches montaba a mi madre
como quien coge un tren equivocadamente.
Ah la pradera donde fue comido por los buitres
(sus hijos)
Ah este sol implacable sobre mis ojos.

Damaris Calderón *(Cuba)*

Canción para Manuel

Apareciste un día con un saco de legumbres.

"Que me hiciste un poema dice tu madre"
dijiste, y quisiste escucharlo.

Leí conturbado y esperé tu sentencia,
tu respuesta.

Me hablaste en cambio
de lo hermoso que crece el maíz en hileras,
del arroyo y los pájaros,
del perro y la hierba,
de cómo el sol sobre el lago
es un puente de fuego entre los cerros.

Osvaldo Hernández *(El Salvador)*

American Bar

En el American Bar la tierra rodaba por mi cabeza
Mientras afuera el gran frío encrespaba de nieve los Andes
Para calentarme escribía en el American Bar
América no es Estados Unidos
América es una mujer chilena

On wretched nights he would mount my mother
like someone who catches a train by mistake.
Oh, the meadow where he was eaten by vultures
(his children)
Oh, this unrelenting sun in my eyes.

Damaris Calderón *(Cuba)*

Song for Manuel

You appeared one day with a sack of vegetables.

"Your mother says you made me a poem,"
you said, and you wanted to hear it.

I read uneasily and waited for your judgement,
your response.

You spoke to me instead
of how lovely the maize was, growing in rows,
of the stream and the birds,
of the dog and the grass,
of how the sun over the lake
is a bridge of fire between the hills.

Osvaldo Hernández *(El Salvador)*

American Bar

In the American Bar the earth rolled around my head
While outside the severe cold ruffled the Andes with snow
To get warm I used to write in the American Bar
America is not the United States
America is a Chilean woman

A la que le desaparecieron un hijo
Y los otros están en México
Para calentarme escribía
Afuera el gran frío, las tinieblas
La tierra rodando por mi cabeza en el American Bar.

Carlos Decap (Chile)

Función de la lírica

Mi padre agonizaba
en un sanatorio con TV por cable.
Puse el canal de ópera
Para amortiguar sus alaridos constantes.
Justo cuando Rigoletto abraza el cadáver
de su hija, debí tenerlo al viejo
para que no se cayera de la cama:
la doble simetría de la escena
me la volvió soportable.

Beatriz Vignoli (Argentina)

Desabrigo

Tuve un hijo.
Entre las ramas del bosque alemán
que rayan como ráfagas de grafito la ventana
de pronto adivino su perfil y siento su presencia.
Camina solo en una ciudad desconocida por mí,
entre dos barrios lúgubres, de inmigrantes.
Lleva un suéter muy grueso y muy gastado.
Y ha encendido un cigarro . . .

Who had one son disappear
And the others live in Mexico
To get warm I used to write
Outside the severe cold, darkness
The earth rolling around my head in the American Bar.

Carlos Decap (Chile)

Function of Lyric Poetry

My father was at death's door
in a hospital with cable TV.
I switched on the opera channel
to muffle his constant yelling.
Just when Rigoletto hugs the corpse
of his daughter, I had to grab the old man
to stop him falling out of bed:
the double symmetry of the scene
rendered it bearable.

Beatriz Vignoli (Argentina)

Exposed

I had a son.
Between the branches of the German forest
that scratch the window like splashes of graphite
I suddenly glimpse his profile and sense his presence.
He walks slowly in a city unknown to me,
between two sad, immigrant neighbourhoods.
He is wearing a thick and threadbare jumper.
And has lighted a cigarette . . .

En este mismo instante en que se me aparece su sombra
él me entrevé en este vagón oscuro
junto a una mujer dormida, escribiendo.
Escribiendo sobre él . . .

Siente mi turbación dolorosa
y la siente distante, fría, amortiguada
bajo la paja astrosa de la ausencia.
Tuve un padre apenas se murmura
a sí mismo cuando una rata
corriendo entre dos cloacas lo distrae.

Tuve un hijo apenas me murmuro y mi mujer despierta
y me dice quedito una rata, una rata
corriendo entre dos cloacas, en mi sueño . . .

Carlos López Beltrán (México)

Memento

Mi padre era doctor y olía a limpio.
Me gustaba el recuerdo de su olor
sobre la almohada
cuando se iba de viaje,
y miraba hechizado
cuando estaba en la casa
su brocha de afeitar.
Con sus cuchillas,
por tocarlas,
por medirles el filo que raspaba sus mejillas,
me corté muchas veces
las yemas de los dedos.
¡Esa sangre tan roja entre mis manos!
Por la mañana amaba
las huellas de sus pies en las baldosas

At the same moment that his shadow appears
he catches sight of me in this dark carriage
next to a sleeping woman. I am writing.
Writing about him . . .

He feels my pained bewilderment
and he feels it as distant, cold, numb
beneath the filthy straw of absence.
I had a father, he murmurs
just as a rat, running between two drains,
distracts him.

I had a son, I murmur, just as my wife awakes
and says, very softly: a rat, a rat,
running between two drains, in my dream . . .

Carlos López Beltrán (Mexico)

Memento

My father was a doctor and smelled clean.
I used to like the memory of his smell
on the pillow
when he was away on a trip,
and would stare spellbound
at his shaving brush
when he was in the house.
Touching his razors,
testing the blade that grazed his cheeks,
many times I cut
my fingertips.
That blood so red on my hands!
In the mornings I loved
his footprints on the tiles

y los rollitos de los calcetines
dejados en el suelo,
y sus muchas corbatas en el clóset
tras el frasco de agua de colonia,
Roger Gallet, que alguna vez regué.
Nunca consideré si era feo o buenmozo
por mucho que los otros mencionaran
su nariz de rabino y su cabeza calva.
No lo consideré,
pero cuando mis ojos veían su semblante
para mí era la calma.
Yo tocaba tambor en su barriga
y desde sus rodillas
en las lentas mañanas del domingo
rodaba
piernas abajo por las espinillas.
Mi hermana un día
lo hizo desmayar con un abrazo,
y él siempre a todos nos dejó aturdidos
con la ventosa enorme de sus besos
y con el viento de sus carcajadas.
Mi padre recitaba poemas de memoria
y me leía en voz alta el *Martín Fierro*
bajo un árbol umbroso de Rionegro.
Todos los sábados se ponía un sombrero
Y en su rosal se hacía jardinero.
«Nací en el siglo XIII y campesino,
no tengo otro abolengo.»
Como era liberal,
se decía cristiano y comunista
porque amaba a los pobres,
porque sufría con el sufrimiento.
Mi padre vacunaba por las selvas,
daba horas y horas y más horas de clase
en la universidad y también en las cárceles,
participaba en marchas de protesta
empuñando con furia sus pañuelos blancos
y publicaba artículos en los periódicos

and his rolled socks
left on the floor,
and the many ties in his wardrobe
behind the flask of Roger Gallet
cologne, which I once spilled.
I never thought about
whether he was ugly or handsome,
despite the others mentioning
his Rabbi's nose and his bald head.
I never thought about it,
but when my eyes settled on his face
I felt calm.
I played the drum on his belly
on slow Sunday mornings
and from his knees
rolled down the slope of his shins.
My sister one day made him
pass out with a hug,
and he always left us all bewildered
with the powerful suction of his kisses
and the gusts of his laughter.
My father recited poems from memory
and read *Martín Fierro* to me out loud
under a shady tree in Rionegro.
Every Saturday he would put on a hat
and play gardener in his rose garden.
"I was born a peasant in the thirteenth century,
I have no other lineage."
Because he was a liberal,
he called himself a Christian and a Communist
because he loved the poor,
because he suffered with suffering.
My father vaccinated in the jungle,
he gave hours and hours and more hours of classes
in the university and also in the jails,
he took part in protest marches
clutching his white handkerchiefs with rage
and he published articles in the newspapers

diciendo el nombre de los torturadores,
«capitán tal, sargento hijo de tal»,
denunciando secuestros,
asesinatos y desapariciones.
Yo lo quería tanto que, de niño,
había decidido morir si él se moría.
No lo cumplí de grande, hace unos años,
cuando no se murió sino que lo mataron.
Aunque era manso,
tal vez porque era manso lo mataron.
También era valiente y no envalentonado,
era manso y valiente
porque estaba en peligro y no sentía miedo
y su única arma eran las teclas
de una Olivetti azul
o el azul de la tinta de un bolígrafo.
Eso ha tenido un nombre: resistencia.
Nunca entendimos que lo hubieran matado
ni que el traje con sangre
que me entregaron en el anfiteatro
pudiera ser su traje son su sangre.
Nunca sangre tan roja entre mis dedos!
Había en los bolsillos un poema
de Borges, «Epitafio»,
una lista de muerte con su nombre,
y una bala incrustada
en el forro del cuello.
La bala fue una de las seis que lo mataron
y no la conservamos;
los nombres de la lista
fueron siendo borrados,
en los meses siguientes,
por los asesinos.
El poema decía:
«Ya somos el olvido que seremos».
Y es verdad. A veces lo olvidamos.
Yo voy a recordarlo el día que me muera.

Héctor Abad Faciolince *(Colombia)*

giving the names of the torturers,
"Captain such-and-such, Sergeant son-of-a . . ."
denouncing kidnappings,
murders and disappearances.
I loved him so much, as a child,
I had decided to die if he died.
I didn't fulfil this as an adult, a few years ago,
when he didn't die but was killed.
Although he was meek,
maybe because he was meek they killed him.
Also he was brave and not a braggart,
he was meek and brave
because he was in danger and was not afraid
and his only weapon was the keyboard
of a blue Olivetti
or the blue ink of a pen.
There's a name for that: resistance.
We couldn't grasp that they had killed him
nor that the suit with blood
that they handed me in the morgue
could be his suit with his blood.
Never blood so red on my fingers!
In his pockets was a poem
by Borges, 'Epitaph',
a death list with his name,
and a bullet embedded
in the lining of his collar.
The bullet was one of the six that killed him
and we didn't keep it;
the names on the list
went on being rubbed out
by the killers
in the months that followed.
The poem said:
"Already we are the oblivion we shall be."
And it's the truth. At times we forget him.
I will remember him on the day I die.

Héctor Abad Faciolince *(Colombia)*

Introduction to Part 3:
'The world we share.'

Taking a lead from Claude Lévi-Strauss' proposal that animals are 'good to think with'[1] (*bonnes à penser*) this section sets out to examine our human perception of animals and the natural world, and to reflect that we use animal imagery, and refer constantly to natural phenomena in order to account for both the world we have inherited and the world we make. But however poets choose to write about animals and the natural world, they inevitably end up writing about the human condition also.

In response to any expectations generated by the book's title, it seems fitting to begin and end Part 3 with a tiger poem. Pedro Serrano's 'Dark Ages' might have been composed specifically to illustrate Lévi-Strauss' argument. His tiger is one of smoke and mirrors, a 'crackling' beast, who 'licks the circus sands'. Freed from his cage, and set loose before faceless spectators, he sucks in the light of midday in order to shape the chaos of the night ahead: 'beatific, inscrutable.'

'At the Vadarkablar Stud Farm' is the first of two poems by Alejandro Crotto, a young Argentinian poet of the 'objectivist' school. Both poems (the other is 'Pigeons', p167) focus on animals and human dealings with them; respectively with breeding and with death. In the first, a stud stallion is led to mount a mare after she has been 'assessed' by an unwitting 'tester stallion'. Raw, visceral descriptions mark the poem, along with the poignant contrast between the conduct of the chosen pure-bred stallion, who approaches the expectant mare 'head-on with chest thrust out, unfurled and arrogant', and the 'other', the frustrated crossbreed, who is led away, until the next day, 'now placid, his muzzle in the water.'

Darío Jaramillo's sequence of reflections on 'Cats' (p153)

presents an alternative reading of basic physics, whereby 'The states of matter are four in number: / liquid, solid, gaseous and cat ... When spirit plays at being matter / it turns to cat.' The poet distances the mythical animal from its human neighbours, who, however – like the poet himself – are continually trying to find words to describe it, only to find that 'Cats are indifferent /to beings who speak.' However, the human need to find allegory within the animal kingdom is apparently insatiable.

Rómulo Bustos comments in a line from his first collection, *El oscuro sello de Dios*, that: 'You will always be your most intimate stranger'.[2] 'Of the hermit crab' (p161) is the closest any of the creatures in this section comes to being reduced to purely metaphorical status, while the enormous beached fish in 'Marbella scene' (p165) is actually 'God / swollen up and with spoiled scales', thus amplifying the ontological theme. In 'Story' (p187), the poet's third contribution to this section (Bustos' bestiary is amply populated) the reader is invited to ask, along with the poet, 'Why do I write?' – and is provided with an answer, lifted from a fairy tale, by way of a certain wolf: 'the better to know you'.

Eduardo Milán's horse (in the poem 'to say', p179) is a creature of a different universe from those in Crotto's carnal corral, a conceptual being lodged in a conceptual universe: 'to say the horse is to say it's black / it jumped over / the purest white reality'. The horse embodies (the verb could not be more inapt) *negation* of a theme: 'there is no now of word / there is no now of horse.' Similarly, Jorge Aulicino makes use of the possum as a figurative device in the extract from 'A somewhat difficult syntax' (p173), representing 'those who craved / the Holy Word, but who, once they have received it, / do nothing with it.' The possum's liability is that 'it never occurs to it to do anything but wander', a warning to the reader, perhaps, in his or her work of 'flaying, / weeding, bending, casting to the winds, storing or tossing.'

A sense of modest outrage permeates Igor Barreto's 'Rooster Thief' (p161). Despite the theft of his 'very special fowl', the speaker seems afraid to make any complaint to the perpetrator of the crime – who only lives 'down the dirt road' from his own house. However, the bird's absence, rather than stoking the victim's sense of loss, only serves to strengthen his love of the cockerel's call, since it is 'a bird that sings like the Angel Gabriel / scaring off the night's shadows.' Thus, paradoxically, the theft is vindicated, the 'debt settled.'

Pura López' poem, 'And the Anthurium, Undaunted' (p163), an unusually understated offering from this often complex poet, has two bumblebees, gorged on nectar, 'knock against the windows /again and again . . . unaware / of the magnet of mirage', while her fellow Mexican, Coral Bracho, in 'Goats' (p175) presents a stark, sun-drenched tableau of painterly precision: goats against a bright white rock, that 'holds them in its palm'.

Pedro Serrano's poem 'The Rabbit and the Top Hat' (p171), certainly not an 'easy' poem in the original Spanish, pays homage to Lewis Carroll, David Lynch (the severed ear at the opening of *Blue Velvet* making an intertextual cameo) and, perhaps, the Ecuadorean Jorge Carrera Andrade and his rabbit poem, 'La vida perfecta' (The Perfect Life).[3] This is a flesh and blood creature that 'come(s) pulsing forward' and 'bunny-hops towards the thickets / and the high spikes of the scrub' before entering a place where we cannot follow.

Environmental concerns are expressed overtly both in Deltoro's 'Spring' (p169), and Sergio Raimondi's 'What the Sea is'. In the former, the speaker's attention is roused by birds that 'sound . . . like a miracle' while concerned that 'in these songs / nests another catastrophe'. The birds should not be there, have been driven from 'the other direction', presumably by climate change. The poem's last line (and the title of the book from which it is taken: 'the trees that will forest the Arctic') contains a severe warning. Meanwhile, Raimondi's poem (p175) sweeps the reader along, just like a 'dragnet along the ocean floor', covering in its passage a mass of subject matter: the 'thirty-five hour shift, four hours' sleep' of trawlermen'; directives from bureaucrats with little or no knowledge of the sea; the obscene greed of factory ships; 'the tons of dead cuttlefish / due to the appearance of king prawn (worth five times more)'. And 'all that', as the poet has it.

Javier Bello's poem from 'The Glow of Emptiness' (p187), returns us to the equine theme broached by Crotto, but these horses equated with 'heavy words . . . enormous / words'. Not a poet afraid of grandiloquence, Bello's are 'enormous horses that drink from my hands // And in my hands let there be rust and death.' Meanwhile, Daniel Helder's 'Insignificance' is one of those gems that, as a translator, you occasionally find, and which translate themselves at first attempt. It all makes perfect sense; the conjunction of the cat, the sparrows in the orange tree, the truly cosmic realisation, and, finally, the insistence on choosing the right tin of tea: 'Not the white one, the red'.

Eduardo Milán completes the circle with 'The Tiger's Leap' (p191), a subtle and perplexing meditation on the metaphoric credentials of his poem's title: the leap is originally set up as a 'detachment from prose' but the leap within the poem itself takes us from the Roman circus, across imperial desert sands, neatly following the metaphor of the horse's step. But the leap within poetry can signal danger. Politics will intervene. Victims exist: there is no 'victory', only extermination.

1 Animals as 'good to think with': Claude Lévi-Strauss, *Totemism*, Penguin, 1969: 89.
2 'You will always be your most intimate stranger' (*Siempre serás tú tu más íntimo forastero*): cited also in the essay 'La poesía de Rómulo Bustos Aguirre' by Lázaro Valdelamar Sarabia, Universidad de Cartagena: https://pendientedemigracion.ucm.es/info/especulo/numero38/robustos.html
3 'The Perfect Life': a translation of Carrera's poem by Dudley Fitts can be found in Stephen Tapscott's *Twentieth Century Latin American Poetry* (University of Texas, 1996).

Dark Ages

El tigre salta
de la humareda a la fugacidad.
Cae en el aplastante corral con una pereza
que alude a la prisa de sus victimas,
no a su elasticidad.
Pasa rozando las rejas de su jaula
meneando la cola, golpeteando, taq', taq', taq', taq'.
Restallante lame las arenas del circo
y levanta espejuelas de polvo,
huellas de una estela aproximándose.
La razón de su observación
viaja en el suave ritmo de su vientre,
afelpado, glotón, elástico.
Da vueltas a los espectadores,
las orejas prestas, su olfato
en la agitación que se respira.
Pasa propicio por las mesas,
se enjundia, se estiliza.
Sume la cabeza entre los hombros,
crece en el riel que lo circunda.
Deja las uñas puestas
en el cuerpo animal que lo acecha.
Desde el espejo del mediodía
se apuntaba el final de la noche,
beatífica, hierática.

Pedro Serrano *(México)*

Dark Ages

The tiger leaps
from a cloud of smoke into transience.
Falls on the devastating corral with an idleness
corresponding to the haste of his victims,
not to his elasticity.
He brushes past the bars of his cage
swinging his tail, rattling, tac, tac, tac, tac.
Crackling, he licks the circus sands
and raises ripples of dust,
traces of an approaching wake.
The motive for his observation
journeys in the smooth rhythm of his stomach,
velvety, gluttonous, elastic.
He turns circles before the spectators,
ears cocked, instincts fixed
on the excitement in the air.
He walks by the tables, propitious,
exudes substance and style.
The head sinks between the shoulders,
swells in the rail that encircles him.
The claws are extended
in the animal body that awaits him.
In the mirror of midday
the night's end was taking shape,
beatific, inscrutable.

Pedro Serrano (Mexico)

En el Haras Vadarkablar

Hasta el corral de tierra y tablas
trajeron al retajo,
un criollo sin halo genealógico,
sin nombre inglés o propio o sangre pura,
a que probara conocer si estaba lista la alazana
alzada como un dios entre jejenes en la luz amarilla de la tarde
con tormenta de fondo; a ver si estaba honda y dispuesta,
veterinarios jóvenes de blancos guardapolvos entreabiertos
entraron el retajo lazo al cuello, y el caballo
meneaba cabizbajo entre resoplos la cabeza y de repente
la levantaba señalando a la alazana espléndida; y la yegua
tirante, sus ollares finísimos alerta, casi ciervo,
miraba de reojo mientras daba su grupa florecida,
y se hizo agua un poquito, se iba abriendo, parpadeaba
su sexo, y apartaba la cola, y el criollo
era potencia aproximándose creciente
hasta montar la yegua, y lo desviaron
las manos enguantadas, lo sacaron tirándolo del lazo y uno dijo
«está lista, buscalo al Equalize que por las dudas la maneo»
y mientras se acercaba por momentos de costado
luego enseguida pecho al frente,
desplegándose altivo, cabeceando
el aire que rompía al paso fino,
el padrillo valioso, se llevaron al otro hasta un corral
con bebedero hasta mañana, y el retajo
ya manso, hocico en agua,
temblaba en ráfagas oscuras
con mínimos relámpagos; no había viento,
se venía la noche.

Alejandro Crotto (Argentina)

At the Vadarkablar Stud Farm

Into the corral of earth and planks
they dragged the teaser stallion,
a crossbreed of no genealogical distinction,
not thoroughbred, no English name, not even his own,
to see if the chestnut mare was ready
raised high like a deity amid gnats in the yellow light of evening
with a storm on the horizon; to see if she was deep and eager,
young vets in half-open white overalls
brought in the stallion teaser, lassoed at the neck; and the horse
shook his head, between snorts, and promptly
raised it towards the splendid chestnut; and the mare,
straining, her superb nostrils alert, like a deer,
looked sideways and offered her flourishing rump,
dripping a little, opened herself, her sex quivering,
and lifted her tail, and the crossbreed
was sheer potency advancing and swelling
until he mounted her, and the gloved hands
pulled him away, tugging at the rope, and one said
"she's ready, fetch Equalize, and just to be sure I'll hobble her"
and as the precious stallion approached her, walking sideways,
and then head-on with chest thrust out,
unfurled and arrogant, tossing his head
and slicing the air with his fine step,
they led the other to a corral with a water trough,
until the next day, and the horse, now placid,
his muzzle in the water,
trembled in dark gusts
with tiny lightning flashes; there was no wind,
night was on its way.

Alejandro Crotto (Argentina)

Ajusco

Vaca, cuánta tristeza
en tus ojos ahora
que es lunes y el campo
es más inmenso y solo
y en torno a ti pululan
platos de cartón sucios
y latas de cerveza.

Pedazos de destierro
y calma se amontonan
en tu figura, vaca.
Miras alrededor
de ti, luego te agachas
hurgando en la basura
como un enorme perro.

Los restos de fogatas
parecen dentelladas
tuyas, no de los hombres
que incineran en ellas
antes de irse, último
rito de cohesión, vasos
de plástico y botellas.

La niebla cubre el cerro
y te rodea como
el mar a un promontorio,
y todo calla cuando
tu amplia maternidad,
de pronto, reclama entre
la bruma a tu becerro.

Fabio Morábito *(México)*

Ajusco

Cow, how much sadness
in your eyes now
that it is Monday and the field
is more immense and lonely
and around you shimmer
dirty paper plates
and beer cans.

Slabs of exile
and calm accumulate
in your figure, cow.
You look around
you, then lower your head
to rummage in the trash
like an enormous dog.

The remains of campfires
resemble the marks your teeth made,
not those of the men
who, before leaving,
burned in them plastic cups
and bottles as a last
rite of cohesion.

The fog covers the hill
and encircles you like
the sea a promontory,
and everything is quiet when
your ample motherhood,
of a sudden, claims your calf
amid the mist.

Fabio Morábito (Mexico)

Gatos

La luna dora los techos.
Inesperadas, aparecen las sombras de los gatos.
Son tan sigilosos
que son solamente sus sombras.
Ellos ven todo sin ser vistos
y todo debe estar quieto mientras se mueven
para que ellos puedan sentirse inmóviles,
los gatos, sus sombras.

★

Nube en forma de gato:
gato que come lunas,
sigiloso carnívoro del cielo,
disfrazado de nube
o embozado en lo oscuro,
gato que devora estrellas.
Agazapado, vigila las órbitas
y las engulle en la noche,
gato que come lunas.

★

Estados de la materia.
Los estados de la materia son cuatro:
líquido, sólido, gaseoso y gato.
El gato es un estado especial de la materia,
si bien caben las dudas:
¿es materia esta voluptuosa contorsión?
¿no viene del cielo esta manera de dormir?
Y este silencio, ¿acaso no procede de un lugar sin tiempo?
Cuando el espíritu juega a ser materia
entonces se convierte en gato.

★

Cats

The moon gilds the rooftops.
Unannounced, the shadows of cats appear.
They are so stealthy
they are only their shadows.
They see everything without being seen
and everything must be still while they move
so they can feel themselves to be unmoving,
the cats, their shadows.

★

Cloud in the shape of a cat:
cat that eats moons.
stealthy carnivore of the sky,
disguised as a cloud
or muffled in the darkness,
cat that devours stars.
Crouching, it surveys the heavenly spheres
and guzzles them in the night,
cat that eats moons.

★

States of matter.
The states of matter are four in number:
liquid, solid, gaseous and cat.
The cat is a special state of matter
although doubts remain:
Is this voluptuous contortion matter?
Is this way of sleeping not heaven-sent?
And this silence: might it emerge from a place without time?
When spirit plays at being matter
it turns into cat.

★

Sabiduría del gato:
hacer pereza todo el día sin llegar nunca al tedio.
Materialización del gato:
cuando el gato se convierte en materia, saca las uñas.
Astucia del gato:
fingir que es un animal doméstico.
Silencio del gato:
los gatos guardan todos los secretos de la noche.
Misterios del gato:
todo en el gato es misterioso.

★

Palabras para hablar de los gatos:
No hay palabras para hablar de los gatos.
Los palabras no abarcan a los gatos.
Los gatos son indiferentes
con los seres que hablan.
Un ladrido puede molestarlos
y un estruendo asusta a los gatos.
Pero los gatos no oyen las palabras.
no les interesa nada que pueda decirse con palabras.
¿Para qué las palabras si hay olfato,
para qué las palabras
si es posible el silencio?

Darío Jaramillo Agudelo *(Colombia)*

Libélulas

Libélulas, fantasmas de calor,
nacen cuando en los pastos altos
se vuelve sólida la angustia de diciembre.
Es en recuerdo de este origen que de día
baten las alas hasta lo invisible
y se lanzan al fuego por la noche.

Wisdom of the cat:
To be idle all day without ever being bored.
Materialisation of the cat:
when the cat becomes matter, it extends its claws.
Guile of the cat:
it pretends to be a domestic animal.
Silence of the cat:
cats keep all the secrets of the night.
Mysteries of the cat:
everything about the cat is mysterious.

★

Words for speaking about cats:
There are no words for speaking about cats.
Words do not encompass cats.
Cats are indifferent
to beings who speak.
A bark might disturb them
and a thunder-clap give cats a shock.
But cats do not hear words,
they are not interested in anything that can be said with words.
Why words when you can have smell?
Why words when
silence is possible?

Darío Jaramillo Agudelo *(Colombia)*

Dragonflies

Dragonflies, ghosts of the heat,
are born when December's anguish
thickens on the tall grass.
It is in memory of these origins that
by day they beat their wings into invisibility
and launch themselves at the fire by night.

Y todo por lo mucho que les pesa
la conciencia de casi no haber sido.

Daniel Samoilovich (Argentina)

Si alguien querría ser una tortuga

     sería yo:
hacer de una sección cónica
mi propia sede prehistórica
alojada en la espina dorsal.

Ser tortuga
     tiene algo de ideal:
desde joven luce arrugas
y en sentido literal
se hace mayor con los años
     – a más edad
más tamaño.
     Post-matrimonial,
sin lazos familiares
después de desovar,
igual a todas y cada una,
naturalmente hija de la luna,
     sin embargo
no hay cisma
entre ella misma y sus lares.

Entre tantos avatares,
     para mí
que estoy en mí
– puro apremio sin molicie –
poco cuenta que sea lenta
su marcha en la superficie:
     eso
me haría durar

And all for the weight their conscience bears
for barely having been.

Daniel Samoilovich (Argentina)

If anyone wanted to be a tortoise

      it would be me:
making of a cone-shaped section
my own prehistoric seat
lodged in the spinal column.

Being a tortoise
      has something ideal to it:
it flaunts wrinkles from first youth
and in a literal sense
it grows with the years
      – the older it gets
the bigger it gets.
      Post-matrimonial,
without family ties
after laying its eggs
each and every one equal,
by nature a daughter of the moon,
      however
there is no rift
between herself and her lairs.

Amid so many avatars,
      for me
the inner me
– all urgency and no softness –
it counts for little that progress
on the earth's surface is slow
      that
would make me last out

y capaz de entrar al mar,
 – que cubre dos tercios del mundo –
sabiendo que si me hundo
gano velocidad.

Mirta Rosenberg (Argentina)

Un perro mojado de rocío

El día entra en la casa
como un perro mojado de rocío.
(Jorge Teillier)

Si todo fuera silvestre y las aves
gorjearan sin molestar y la vecina
no arrojara sus puchos al jardín.

Y si la noche
              fuera un fulgor ebrio
donde escucho el silencio de Dios.
Si desatara la lengua de Dios
y pudiera pronunciar esa palabra
que tiembla cuando te veo aparecer

tal vez no vuelvas.
Y vendrían otras noches
como un perro mojado de rocío
a desbaratarlo todo.

Eduardo Chirinos (Perú)

and able to enter the sea
– that covers two-thirds of the world –
knowing that if I sink
I gain speed.

Mirta Rosenberg (Argentina)

A dog wet with dew

The day enters the house
like a dog wet with dew.
                    (Jorge Teillier)

If everything were wild and the birds
chirped harmlessly and the neighbour
didn't throw her cigarette butts into our garden.

And if the night
            were a drunken radiance
where I listen to the silence of God.
If I could untie the tongue of God
and could pronounce that word
that trembles when I see you appear

maybe you would not return.
And other nights would come
like a dog wet with dew
to spoil everything.

Eduardo Chirinos (Peru)

Del cangrejo ermitaño

Rara costumbre la del cangrejo ermitaño

Se le va la vida buscando caparazones de otros
moluscos, latas, recipientes vacíos
toda suerte de objetos cóncavos abandonadas por sus antiguos
huéspedes para instalarse en ellos

Es posible que todo se deba
a una compulsión turística por la novedad

O a un síndrome de inestabilidad casi metafísica

O a simple ejercicio peripatético de quien tiene
demasiadas patas que ejercitar

¿O habrá algo más de fondo en todo esto?

Quizás convenga preguntar
al secreto cangrejo ermitaño que habita
en cada uno de nosotros

Ese que, sin duda, acaba de escribir este poema

Rómulo Bustos Aguirre (Colombia)

Ladrón de gallos

Mi vecino floricultor
me ha robado un ave muy preciada.
Se trata de un gallo color tabaco
que pastaba en una jaula
al fondo del segundo patio de la casa.

Of the Hermit Crab

Strange ways, those of the hermit crab

He gets by in life looking for the shells of other
molluscs, tins, empty receptacles,
every kind of concave object abandoned
by their previous guests, and installs himself in them

It's possible that this is due to a touristic
compulsion for novelty

Or to an almost metaphysical insecurity syndrome

Or a simple peripatetic exercise for one
who has too many legs to exercise

Or might there be something more at the bottom of all this?

Perhaps it would be worth asking
the secret hermit crab that inhabits
each one of us

The one who, no doubt, has just written this poem

Rómulo Bustos Aguirre *(Colombia)*

Rooster Thief

My flower-growing neighbour
has robbed me of a very precious fowl.
I refer to a tobacco-coloured rooster
which grazed in a chicken coop
at the end of the house's back patio.

No hice ningún reclamo,
simplemente no me atreví.
Cada madrugada caminé furtivo
por la carretera de tierra
que bordea nuestras casas
y acercándome a la suya
escuché de nuevo cantar mi gallo.
Es un ave que canta como el Ángel Gabriel
espantando las sombras,
con cuatro inflexiones musicales bien marcadas.
Este modesto ritual
se prolongó por tres noches.
Tres veces aguardé el amanecer
anhelando escucharlo.
Mi vista y mi oído
se aguzaron de tal manera
en aquel último gesto
de pertenencia sobre el ave,
que sentí
que la deuda estaba saldada.

Igor Barreto (Venezuela)

Y el anturio, impávido

Dos abejorros
extraen el jugo,
dulce y amargo,
al centro
de las hojas color de rosa
de una flor que no es rosa.
Ahítos,
golpean los ventanales
vez tras vez,
seguros de emigrar,
con el tesoro adentro,

I didn't make any complaint,
I simply didn't dare.
Every daybreak I set out furtively
down the dirt road
that skirts our properties
and drawing close to his place
I once again heard my cockerel crow.
It is a bird that sings like the Angel Gabriel
scaring off night's shadows,
with four well defined musical inflections.
This modest ritual
went on for three nights.
Three times I awaited the dawn
longing to hear him.
My sight and hearing
sharpened in such a fashion
during that last gesture
over ownership of the bird
that I felt
the debt had been settled.

Igor Barreto (Venezuela)

And the Anthurium, Undaunted

Two bumblebees
extract the juice,
sweet and bitter,
at the centre
of these rose-coloured leaves
from a flower that is not a rose.
Gorged,
they knock against the windows
again and again,
certain of migrating,
their treasure within

allende el aire,
ignorantes del eclipse
de un sendero libre,
ignorantes
del imán
de un espejismo.
Con la sangre miel
en las entrañas,
parte ya de una médula
extática.
Y distinta.

Pura López Colomé *(México)*

Escena de Marbella

A Juan Marchena, cartagenero
del otro lado del mar

Junto a las piedras está Dios bocarriba
Los pescadores en fila tiraron largamente de la red
Y ahora yace allí con sus ojos blancos mirando al cielo
Parece un bañista definitivamente distraído
Parece un gran pez gordo de cola muy grande
Pero es sólo Dios
hinchado con sus escamas impuras
¿Cuánto tiempo habrá rodado sobre las aguas?
Los curiosos observan la pesca monstruosa
Algunos separan una porción y la llevan
              para sus casas
Otros se preguntan si será conveniente
Comer de un alimento que ha estado tanto tiempo
              expuesto a la intemperie.

Rómulo Bustos Aguirre *(Colombia)*

beyond the air,
unaware of the eclipse
of a free pathway,
unaware
of the magnet
of a mirage.
With honey blood
as their essence,
already part of a distinct
and rapturous
marrow.

Pura López Colomé (Mexico)

Marbella Scene

*To Juan Marchena, Cartagenina
from the other side of the sea*

Near the rocks, belly up, is God
The fishermen in a line heave at the net
And now he lies there, white eyes staring at the sky
He looks like a terminally distracted swimmer
He looks like a big fat fish with a very big tail
But it's only God
swollen up and with spoiled scales
How much time has he pitched across the waters?
The curious observe the monstrous catch
Some of them cut off a slab and carry it back
          to their houses
Others wonder if it would be advisable
to eat something that has spent so much time
          exposed to the elements.

Rómulo Bustos Aguirre (Colombia)

Las Palomas

Hay que ponerse rápido las medias
porque el piso de piedra está frío; en la cocina
desayunamos leche, pan con manteca y miel,
después salimos a cazar palomas
con nuestro rifle de aire comprimido,
mi hermano y yo con menos de once años
y con botas de goma, camisa gruesa a cuadros y balines
en el bolsillo —dos o tres,
los próximos a usar, van en la boca.
Vamos dejando huellas en la helada que empieza a deshacerse,
vamos alerta entre las ramas de los plátanos,
los altos eucaliptos, el nogal, las casuarinas,
los álamos del haras, la pileta,
un tiro cada uno, caminando,
señalando de a ratos las copas del otoño.

Después, detrás del lavadero, entre frutales,
las desplumamos y las destripamos:
sosteniendo en la izquierda el peso tibio
vamos sacando plumas con la otra,
las más largas y duras en la cola y el ala,
las fáciles del pecho, las cortitas
y oscuras de la espalda, las más suaves
en el flanco, debajo de las alas en la axila;
van quedando en los yuyos enredadas hacia el lado del viento,
pegadas en las manos, suspendidas del aire
cuando se arremolina de repente;
después vamos vaciando el cuerpo, mucho más chico
ahora en relación a la cabeza: primero el buche,
a veces con semillas de girasol intactas que se pueden comer,
apenas agrias, y metiendo con fuerza los dedos hacia arriba
donde termina el esternón, girándolos
dentro del cuerpo todavía caliente, agarrando y tirando para abajo,
arrancamos los largos intestinos y la panza, sacamos los pulmones
como una esponja rosa pegada a las costillas,
los riñones, el hígado, el quieto corazón,

Pigeons

Socks have to be pulled on quickly
because the stone floor is cold: in the kitchen
we breakfast on milk, bread and butter with honey,
then we go out hunting pigeons
with our small air rifle,
my brother and I, not yet eleven years old
with wellington boots, warm checked shirts, pellets
in our pockets – two or three,
the next ones up go in the mouth.
We walk on, leaving prints in the frost that has begun to melt,
walk on past the branches of the plane trees,
the tall eucalyptus, the walnut, causarinas,
the poplars of the stud farm, the pool,
one shot each, walking; from time to time
pointing out the autumn colours of the tree-tops.

Afterwards, behind the laundry, among the fruit trees,
we pluck and gut them:
holding in the left hand their lukewarm weight
while pulling out feathers with the right,
the longest and hardest in the tail and wings,
the easiest in the chest, the short
and dark ones on the back, the softest
on the flank, under the fold of the wing;
they get tangled in the weeds, facing the wind,
stick to our hands, hanging in the air
when it swirls suddenly;
afterwards we clean out the body, much smaller
now in relation to the head: first the crop,
sometimes with whole sunflower seeds which you can eat,
a little bitter, and forcing the fingers up to
where the sternum ends, twisting them
inside the still-warm body, grasping and pulling down,
we rip out the large intestine and belly, yank out the lungs
like a pink sponge sticking to the ribs,
kidneys, liver, stilled heart,

que los perros atrapan sin que toquen
el suelo; en la canilla lavamos las palomas
y les cortamos la cabeza, las atamos
subidos a un banquito de la pata a un alambre hasta la noche.

Las manos queman por el frío del agua,
brillan los cuerpos en el aire, al sol; la vida
es material, y la materia
es difícil, sagrada.

Alejandro Crotto (Argentina)

Primavera

Me suenan a milagro,
pero en estos cantos
anida otra catástrofe.

¿Qué hacen silbando aquí?

Vienen de abajo,
en dirección contraria
a las barrancas;

¿conquistando la cima?

Su aparición
parece buena señal
para la piel friolenta
y los frutales,
pero algo me dice
que son malas noticias.

Los pájaros de voz más grave
volarán hacia el norte
desplazando, a su vez, cantos nativos.

which the dogs snatch before they touch
the ground: we wash the pigeons under the tap
and cut off their heads, climb on a stool
and hang them from a wire by their feet until nightfall.

Our hands burn from the cold water,
the bodies glisten in the air, in the sun; life
is material, and matter
is difficult, sacred.

Alejandro Crotto *(Argentina)*

Spring

They sound to me like a miracle,
but in these songs
nests another catastrophe.

What are they doing whistling here?

They come from below,
in the other direction
from the ravines:

– conquering the summit?

Their appearance
seems a good sign
for the shivering skin
and the fruit trees,
but something tells me
they are bad news.

The birds with the deepest voice
will fly towards the north
displacing, in their turn, native songs.

Los seguirán los árboles
que poblarán el Ártico.

Antonio Deltoro (México)

El conejo y la chistera

Como en el jardín de Alicia
el conejo en el césped húmedo
salta y muelle su curvatura.
Suave alza las orejas de dos en dos,
husmeando en las olas de hierbas frágiles
y entre sus dientecillos va el pasto de este
confín luminoso.
No es una oreja quieta en la nada,
sino una alfombra en el centro de lo verde,
un nudo o borla marrón peluda
que avanza palpitando.
En sobresaltos se mece hacia los matorrales
y las altas agujas de la maleza
verdes y chatas como torres y almenas.
A través de unas puertas mágicas
se hunde entre los agapandos y lirios
como si entrara en un universo apretado,
adentro de la chistera de David Lynch.
Ya no lo sigo en ese mundo mágico
denso y oscuro,
aunque en una ráfaga súbita
pasa de nuevo frente a mí
como si fuera una serpentina
sin arrepentimiento ni mordaza,
repentino,
y así desaparece.

Pedro Serrano (México)

They will be followed by the trees
that will forest the Arctic.

Antonio Deltoro (Mexico)

The Rabbit and the Top Hat

As in Alice's garden
the rabbit on the damp lawn
jumps, its curvature springy.
Gently it raises its ears in tandem,
sniffing the waves of dainty herbs
and between its little teeth goes the grass
of this gleaming border.
It's not a motionless ear in the void,
but a rug in the middle of the green,
a knot or fleecy brown pompom
that comes pulsing forward.
Startled, it bunny-hops towards the thickets
and the high spikes of the scrub
green and flat like squat towers and turrets.
Through a few magic doors
it plunges between the agapanthus and iris
as though entering a universe crammed
inside David Lynch's top hat.
I lose track of it within that magic world,
dense and dark,
though in a sudden gust
it passes again in front of me
as if it were a streamer
with no lament or leash,
swiftly,
and so it vanishes.

Pedro Serrano (Mexico)

de *Cierta dureza en la sintaxis*

4

La comadreja representa a quienes estuvieron deseosos
de la palabra divina, pero que nada hacen con ella
cuando la han recibido. Y crían en las orejas.
La comadreja representa a quienes quisieron la gracia
y la gracia les fue dada, para nada.
No te muevas si encontrás a la comadreja
en la escalera o en el asiento de un taxi.
Reptará su pensamiento hacia lugares hollados,
porque, segura de la gracia y la palabra,
no se le ocurre qué hacer sino vagar
por donde hubo ciudades que los ejércitos
aplastaron con botas y llenaron de condones.
Más bien continúa construyendo el merecimiento
para que descienda la luz blanca o celeste sobre vos,
cuando realmente te distraigas en tu trabajo de desollar,
carpir, doblar, aventar, guardar o sacudir.
Aunque andes descalzo por los muelles ásperos
de tu propio pensamiento, habrás de distraerte profundamente
para no recibir en vano la amistad del reino,
para no deambular con la comadreja.

Jorge Aulicino (Argentina)

from *A Somewhat Difficult Syntax*

4

The possum represents those who craved
the Holy Word, but who, once they have received it,
do nothing with it. And they breed inside the ears.
The possum represents those who wanted Grace
and Grace was given to them, to no end.
Do not move if you find a possum
on the staircase or on a taxi seat.
Its thought will crawl towards well-trodden places,
because, assured of Grace and of the Word,
it never occurs to it to do anything but wander
where once there were cities that armies
crushed beneath their boots and filled with condoms.
Better for you to keep working on your worthiness
so that the white or celestial blue light falls on you,
when you get really distracted from your work of flaying,
weeding, bending, casting to the winds, storing or tossing.
Even though you walk barefoot on the rough wharves
of your own thought, you will have to be profoundly distracted
not to receive in vain the friendship of the kingdom,
not to go roaming with the possum.

Jorge Aulicino (Argentina)

Cabras

En la blancura persisten
las cabras quietas
y su centro de luz. Suavemente la piedra
las sostiene en la palma;
como una pincelada
a una mariposa.

Coral Bracho (México)

Qué es el mar

El barrido de una red de arrastre a lo largo del lecho,
mallas de apertura máxima, en el tanque setecientos mil
litros de gas-oil, en la bodega bolsas de papa y cebolla,
jornada de treinta y cinco horas, sueño de cuatro, café,
acuerdos pactados en oficinas de Bruselas, crecimiento
del calamar illex en relación a la temperatura del agua
y las firmas de aprobación de la Corte Suprema, circuito
de canales de acero inoxidable por donde el pescado cae,
abadejo, hubbsi, transferencias de permiso amparadas
por la Secretaría de Agricultura, Ganadería y Pesca; ahí:
atraviesa el fresquero la línea imaginaria del paralelo, va
tras una mancha en la pantalla del equipo de detección,
ignorante el cardumen de la noción de millas o charteo,
de las estadísticas irreales del INIDEP o el desfasaje
entre jornal y costo de vida desde el año mil novecientos
noventa y dos, filet de merluza de cola, SOMU y pez rata,
cartas de crédito adulteradas, lámparas y asiático pabellón,
irrupción de brotes de aftosa en rodeos británicos, hoki,
retorno a lo más hondo de toneladas de pota muerta
ante la aparición de langostino (valor cinco veces mayor),
infraestructura de almacenamiento y frío, caladero, eso.

Sergio Raimondi (Argentina)

Goats

In the whiteness
and its nucleus of light
the goats stand stock-still. Gently the rock
holds them in its palm;
like a brushstroke
a butterfly.

Coral Bracho (Mexico)

What the Sea Is

Sweep of a dragnet along the ocean floor,
maximum mesh size, seven hundred thousand litres of diesel
in the tank, sacks of potatoes and onions in the galley,
thirty-five hour shift, four hours' sleep, coffee,
agreements reached in offices in Brussels, growth
of ilex squid in relation to water temperature
and signatures of endorsement in the Supreme Court, circuit
of stainless steel channels through which the fish fall,
cod, *hubbsi*, transfer of permits protected
by the Ministry of Agriculture, Livestock and Fisheries; so;
a reefer ship crosses the imaginary parallel, goes
after a mark on the tracking system's screen,
the shoal oblivious to the notion of sea miles or chartering,
of unreal statistics from the Fisheries Research Institute
or the discrepancy between daily wage and the cost of living since
nineteen ninety two, hake's tail fillet, the shipping union and rat fish,
adulterated letters of credit, lamps and Asian flags,
outbreak of foot and mouth in British cattle herds, *hoki*,
return to the deep tons of dead cuttlefish
due to the appearance of king prawn (worth five times more),
storage infrastructure and cold, fishing ground, all that.

Sergio Raimondi (Argentina)

Las naturalezas muertas: mirlos, tordos y otras aves

no sabe el tordo, de plumaje opaco,
que se le emparenta con el mirlo,
mucho más vivaz y luminoso;
y el cuervo de los pantanos
cuando agita sus alas, moviendo el
pico largo y curvo,
no imagina tampoco la imagen
romántica del ave negra
pesando sobre el vestido de su propio nombre.

Hundir el pico, el cuello y los hombros
sobre la carne en descomposición
de una liebre echada irremediablemente
cortando la línea blanca de la carretera
como proyección nada más de la
ausencia del *Corvus corax*.

A falta del simbolismo de los cuervos
cedemos a la tentación tornasolada
del pequeño estafador de los parques – aves
carroñeras y oscuras, algunas;
otras más bien con
tendencias parasitarias
roba-nidos, falseadores de huevos –.
Para devorar cadáveres, por lo demás,
nos sobrevuela nuestro emblema patrio
– *Vulturgryphus* – con su cuello
peleado cumpliendo higiénica función:
evitar la acumulación de tripa y sangre,
y el consiguiente riesgo para la salud del cóndor.

– el despliegue absoluto de las alas
azabache sobre el fondo siempre
romántico e imaginario. Las aves tienen ese don
hipnótico de lo imposible: Lord Byron

Still Lives: Blackbirds, Thrushes, and Other Birds

the blackbird, with his opaque plumage, doesn't know
that he's linked by family to the thrush,
far brighter and more vivacious;
and the crow of the marshes
when it beats its wings, moving its
long curved beak,
has no notion either of the romantic
image of the black bird
weighing on the costume of its own name.

To sink the beak, the neck and shoulders
into the decomposing meat
of a hare irretrievably knocked down, breaking
the neat continuity of the road's white lines
like nothing more than a projection
of the absent *Corvus corax*.

Lacking crow symbolism
we give way to the iridescent temptation
of the little tricksters of the parks – dark
scavenger birds, some of them;
others more correctly with
parasitical tendencies
nest-robbers, counterfeiters of eggs –.
For the devouring of corpses, otherwise,
our national emblem flies over us
– *Vultur gryphus* –its bare
neck fulfilling a hygienic function:
avoiding the accumulation of blood and guts,
and the consequent health risk to the condor.

– the total unfurling of jet black
wings over the always romantic and imaginary
background. Birds have this hypnotic
gift of the impossible: Lord Byron

derramando sangre sobre el catre de campaña en
Grecia; una cierta lectura de Rimbaud,
su soliloquio burgués, armas, concubinas y especias
como horizonte, el aire caliente de las barricadas,
tatuada La Comuna en sus sienes enfermizas; los
pájaros de Diómedes que abrazan a los griegos en sus
islas, memoria de los días de su gloria contra Troya;

viejos militantes
viendo fotos de la UP, las protestas o la última
Guerra Civil de nuestras vidas.

Camilo Brodsky (Chile)

decir ahí

decir ahí es una flor difícil
decir ahí es pintar todo de pájaro
decir ahí es estar atraído
por la palabra áspera
cardo
y por el cardenal cardenal
decir ahí es decir todo de nuevo
y empezar por el caballo

el caballo está solo
ahora está solo
no hay ahora oscuro
no hay ahora de silencio
no hay ahora de palabra
no hay ahora de silencio contra la pared
el caballo está solo es decir está negro
saltó por encima de la blanca
purísima realidad

shedding blood over his camp bed in Greece;
a certain reading of Rimbaud,
his bourgeois soliloquy, weapons, concubines and spices
as a horizon, the warm air of the barricades,
the Commune tattooed on his sickly temples;
the birds of Diomedes which embrace the Greeks on
their islands, a memory of their days of glory against Troy;

old militants
looking at photos of the UP, the protests or the final
Civil War of our lives.

Camilo Brodsky *(Chile)*

to say

to say there is a difficult flower
to say there is to paint everything bird
to say there is to be attracted
by the rough word
thistle
and by bristle bristle
to say there is to say everything again
and to begin with the horse

the horse is alone
now it is alone
there is no dark now
there is no now of silence
there is no now of word
there is no now of silence against the wall
to say the horse is alone is to say it's black
it jumped over
the purest white reality

el caballo está ahí
fuga
por las hendiduras del día
florescencia
como la luna fluye

el caballo salta por encima de su sombra
salta por encima de su silencio
salta por encima de la realidad
salta por encima
de un universo todavía negro
antes de la suma
antes de la cima
de los colores:
montaña verde sobre cielo azul

la silueta del caballo es colorada
colorada de sol cuando se oculta
ahora se oculta
ahora se hunde en el caballo
moneda de sol
no hay ahora de silencio
no hay ahora de palabra
no hay ahora de caballo

Eduardo Milán (Uruguay)

the horse is there
it runs away
through the cracks in the day
florescence
just as the moon flows

the horse jumps over its shadow
jumps over its silence
jumps over reality
jumps over
a universe that remains black
before the summing up
before the summit
of colours
green mountain over blue sky

the horse's silhouette is red
the red of the hidden sun
now it is hidden
now it sinks into the horse
a coin of sun
there is no now of silence
there is no now of word
there is no now of horse

Eduardo Milán *(Uruguay)*

Lección de supervivencia

Nada hay de bello en el pepino o carajo de mar.
Es, en verdad, un animal sin gracia,
como su nombre.
En el fondo de los grandes océanos,
inmóvil, blando, amorfo,
permanece
condenado a la arena,
y ajeno a la belleza que encima de su cuerpo
despliega el mar.

Se sabe que
cuando el pepino de mar huele la muerte
en el depredador que lo amenaza,
expele
no sólo su intestino
sino el racimo entero de sus vísceras,
que sirven de alimento en su enemigo.

Como un limpio ritual
huye el pepino de aquello que amenaza con dañarlo.

Para sobrevivir queda vacío.

Liviano ya de sí y libre de otros
muda de ser.

Y poco a poco
sus entrañas
            se recomponen.
Y vuelve a ser, en letargo de sal,
una entidad en paz que vive a su manera.

Piedad Bonnett *(Colombia)*

Lesson in Survival

There is nothing beautiful about the sea cucumber.
It is, in truth, an animal without grace,
like its name.
At the bottom of great oceans,
unmoving, soft, amorphous,
it remains
condemned to the sand,
set apart from the beauty that the sea displays
above its body.

It is known that
when the sea cucumber gets a whiff of death
in the predator that threatens it,
it expels
not only its intestines
but the entire cluster of its gut,
which serves as food for its enemy.

In a clean ritual
the sea cucumber flees from whatever threatens to harm it.

To survive, it stays empty.

Relieved of itself and free of others
it mutates its being.

And little by little
its innards
       recompose.
And it returns to being, in salty lethargy,
an entity at peace that lives in its own way.

Piedad Bonnett (Colombia)

El Viejo licántropo

A Lilith, la que aúlla en la noche

El viejo licántropo se pasea en Bucarest
Hay un alfil sobre la torre del castillo
una flor amarilla en su solapa
Negra la noche la sangre negra
Se juega el tres de bastos
y la lluvia es cosa de ranas
Los príncipes de la tierra
deciden otra vez
Se equivocan hasta en el color de
sus sombreros
¿Amanecerá en Bucarest?

La hora no es conocida por sincera
ni por seria
y si acaso me preguntas
qué gano cortándole la pata
al batracio
te señalo al pobre licántropo
que otra vez da vueltas a la plaza

Ella
mientras tanto
para matar el invierno
inventa palabras
pinta de blanco sus labios
descubriendo el dulce placer de
la licantroginia
Descorcha una manzana
y tiembla de frío
mientras piensa
que la meta
no es el lobo

Mauricio Molina (Costa Rica)

The Old Lycanthrope

To Lilith, who howls in the night

The old lycanthrope takes a stroll in Bucharest
There is a bishop on the tower of the castle
a yellow flower in his lapel
Black the night and black the blood
He plays the three of clubs
and the rain is the stuff of frogs
The princes of the land
decide once again
They are mistaken even about the colour of
their hats.
Will day break in Bucharest?

The hour is not known to be honest
nor serious
and just in case you ask me
what I gain cutting off the leg
of the batrachian
I will point out to you the poor lycanthrope
who once again is walking in circles around the square

She
meanwhile
invents words
to kill the winter
paints her lips white
discovering the sweet pleasure of
lycanthrogyny
She uncorks an apple
and trembles with cold
while thinking
that the goal
is not the wolf

Mauricio Molina (Costa Rica)

de *El fulgor del vacío*

XI

Quiero palabras grandes como caballos grandes, palabras
Pesadas, candados en los bolsillos de enfrente, palabras
enormes, el cielo después del relámpago, palabras, polvo
para cubrir las huellas.

Quiero palabras grandes como cenizas grandes. No seré tan alto
para pronunciarlas, no seré tan sabio para decirlas despacio,
no seré tan valiente para ofrecer a la noche esas huesas, las
dejaré beber junto a los animales que viven en mis manos,
animales arteros que vigilan mi frente.

Quiero palabras calladas, susurros, palabras descalzas para tejer
y salir de casa, pero que sean grandes para cubrir el vacío
que queda en las heridas del sueño.

Quiero palabras grandes, enormes caballos que beban de mis
manos.

Y en mis manos haya óxido y muerte.

Javier Bello (Chile)

Cuento

Me pregunto: ¿Por qué escribo poesía?
Y desde algún lugar del misterioso bosque
(de ese otro cuento que en vano estoy tratando
        de escribir en este poema)
responde el lobo
moviendo socrático la peluda cola:

from *The Glow of Emptiness*

XI

I want big words like big horses, heavy words,
    padlocks in my front pockets, enormous
    words, the sky after lightning, words, dust
    to cover the traces.

I want words like big flakes of ash. I will not be tall enough
    to pronounce them, I will not be wise enough to say
    them slowly, I will not be brave enough to offer the night
    those graves, I will leave them to drink alongside the animals
    that live in my hands, cunning animals that guard my brow.

I want quiet words, whispers, barefoot words to weave and
    leave home, but which are big enough to cover
    the hole that is left in the wounds of the dream.

I want big words, enormous horses that drink from my
    hands.

And in my hands let there be rust and death.

Javier Bello (Chile)

Story

I ask myself: why do I write poetry?
And from some place in the mysterious forest
(in that other story that I am trying in vain
    to write with this poem)
the wolf replies
moving his bushy tail Socratically:

– Para conocerte mejor.

***Rómulo Bustos Aguirre** (Colombia)*

Intrascedencia

Un momento.
Y despacio, shhh...
Que el gato no despierte.
Que los gorriones en el naranjo
no se espanten.
Hierve el agua, cierro el libro,
mayo ha vuelto a la ventana.
¿Alguien quiere una taza de té?
¿Alguno de ustedes desea
una taza de té?
En el segundo estante,
a la izquierda, hay dos latas,
una roja y otra blanca.
150 millones de kms
ha recorrido este rayo de sol
que trasluce el vidrio
y las cortinas
y se fija en la madera del piso.
Dentro del rayo, en la no-gravedad,
el polvillo gris enloquecido
hormiguea.
La blanca no, la roja.

***D.G. Helder** (Argentina)*

– The better to know you.

Rómulo Bustos Aguirre (Colombia)

Insignificance

One moment.
And slowly, shhh...
Don't wake the cat.
Don't frighten the sparrows
in the orange tree.
The water's boiling, I close my book,
May has returned to the window.
Does anyone want a cup of tea?
Would any of you like
a cup of tea?
On the second shelf,
to the left, there are two tins,
one red and one white.
This ray of sunlight
that shines through the glass
and the curtains
has travelled 150 million kms
to alight on the wooden floor.
Inside the sunbeam, in the non-gravity,
crazed grey dust specks
swarm.
Not the white one, the red.

D.G. Helder *(Argentina)*

El salto del tigre

El salto del tigre, metáfora
de un desprendimiento de prosa
que salta a verso contra la adversidad
que está circunscribiendo, trazando un círculo.
Lince, tigre, león, saltan desde acá.
Protejo la palabra circo, al precioso
trofeo de mi infancia arrebatado a Roma:
en mi palabra no se come carne humana.
El círculo de la prosa va pasando en viaje inverso
por la arena imperial, pasto para
la caballería del presente, memorioso pasto
para la caballería que lo pisa, ciega.
El paso del caballo es metáfora antigua,
una herramienta, un instrumento corroído
para el roído corazón de la metáfora –imagínate
una nuez, al corazón roído en su nuez–,
nadie creíble canta la victoria de aplastar
víctimas, nadie creíble canta la victoria,
no hay victoria: hay exterminio, letra muerta.
Técnica pobre, destiempo referido
a las actuales, ricas de aniquilamiento,
tanto que un tanque no de agua, no de oxígeno,
sí de guerra, israelí, otra vez
a volver masa, a deshacer como materia
para pasta que se reenvía a un amorfo,
informe origen donde amor, que tiene forma,
no cuenta, para que nada cuente –palestinos.
Salta el tigre, desprendimiento.

Eduardo Milán (Uruguay)

The Tiger's Leap

The tiger's leap, metaphor
for detachment from prose
which leaps to verse in the face of misadventure
circumscribing, tracing a circle.
Lynx, tiger, lion, they jump from here.
I protect the word 'circus', the precious
childhood trophy snatched away from Rome:
in my word human flesh is not eaten.
The circle of prose goes around on an reverse journey
across the imperial sand, pasture for
the cavalry of the present, a pasture with a memory
for the cavalry that tread there, blindly.
The horse's step is an ancient metaphor,
a tool, a rusty instrument
for the chewed-up heart of the metaphor – imagine
a walnut, a heart chewed to the kernel –,
Nobody believable sings of the victory of crushing
victims, nobody believable sings of victory,
there is no victory: there's extinction, inert words.
Poor technique: bad timing in relation to
current times, rich in annihilation,
so that a tank of neither water nor oxygen
but a tank used in battle, Israeli, once again
turns to dough, melting as matter
into paste that is returned to formlessness,
shapeless origin where love, which has a form,
doesn't matter, so that nothing matters – Palestinians.
The tiger leaps, detachment.

Eduardo Milán (Uruguay)

Introduction to Part 4:
'What we do and and where we go.'

Originally designated to contain poems dealing with social and political themes, along with exile and travel, this section soon began to attract all the waifs and strays of the anthology – the poems that could not find a home in the other five, more cohesive parts. It also began to garner – as if by magnetic force – a few pieces concerned with the self-reflexivity of the poet.

The opening piece, by Darío Jaramillo, relaying news about an absent person, is notable for its epistolary style, and its long, rolling cadences. The reasons for the man's absence are never given, and the slightly elevated language and incantatory style creates a strange juxtaposition with the content, which describes a life of sensual dissolution, and the profound sense of loss or lack with which the 'absentee' seems infused, wherever he may be. The theme of exile is sustained in Juan Manuel Roca's surrealist collage 'What happens in the poem' (p199), and further developed, in a very different way, in the same poet's parable of the dispossessed, 'Landscape with Beggars' (p227).

Frank Báez' marvellously irreverent couplet, 'Miaow' (p201) provides a caustic response to the opening lines of Allen Ginsberg's 'Howl', while Báez' other contribution to Part 4, 'The Beach Poets' (p223) offers a eulogy for surfers, claiming: 'At thirty, like the Romantic poets, they retire. / Some of them die by drowning. Others are attacked by sharks and lose / their legs or arms. / Others become lawyers.'

Ariel Williams' prose poem sequence, *Discourse of the Teller of Worms*, manages, in its laconic delivery, to unravel the way in which a culture (or, by extension, any social group) insists on maintaining its explanatory devices: it posits instead an inversion of causality ('If it rained it's because there's mud') alongside an ironic insistence of 'method': 'I need a method. / I go to drink wine in the bar. Inside there are several / who would give this definition of themselves: I am /one glass after another.'

Part Four contains two poems by the Mexican Tedi López Mills, the first, 'Fiestas' (p211), being the story of the speaker's' 'friend with the lame dog' (a character who features in the poet's collection *Amigo del perro cojo*, 2014), and a person endowed with a speculative imagination but limited social skills, 'who doesn't know how to arrive at places / . . . and usually loiters, / . . . waiting by the entrance until someone familiar / greets him'. The second poem by López Mills, 'The subtle war' (p251) is an impressionistic travelogue inspired by a reading of the poet Arnaut Daniel, whose narrator can 'hear the age in the horse's trot, / the ancient madness, the bitter air' and fears they might 'lose the gift of speech / and lose a way of return.'

'The days keep taking away the things I loved. / With secret steps, behind my back / they vanish', mourns Jorge Fernández Granados in his poem 'Things' (p213). This contemplation of loss brought to mind Elizabeth Bishop's Villanelle 'One Art', and ends in wistful lament: 'I think my life / has been a going about /misplacing useless / and beloved things / in places I have forgotten.'

With Sergio Raimondi's 'English words regarding the effect of fire' (p215), I will need to digress on a specific problem of translation. The British built railways all over South America, and occasionally left behind written evidence of their passing. The poem centres on the mistranslation of a sign prohibiting the crossing of the tracks, erected beside a level-crossing keeper's cabin in southern Argentina: 'Es prohibido' (in line 3 of the original) should read 'Está prohibido'. In Spanish there are two verbs for 'to be': *ser* is ontological, whereas *estar* is (to simplify) to do with being in a certain place at a certain time, a distinction which causes endless problems for language learners.

By analogy, Spanish speakers find it difficult to discern between the inflexions of certain English adjectives, such as 'bored' and 'boring' or 'tired' and 'tiring', so I improvised a solution by mistranslating 'forbidden' as 'forbidding' – the kind of mistake that might be made in a reverse situation, by a Spanish speaker of English. The crucial line in the poem, however, refers back to the mistranslation of the verb 'to be'; that the English built 'from the foundations up / with the same will as their architecture: functional and with a calling towards eternity', a nice reflection on the grandiosity of Empire.

While on the theme of the British, Marcelo Guajardo Thomas, in 'Cochrane' (p233) remembers the famous admiral of that name, in which the exiled hero of the Napoleonic wars considers the prospect of commanding the newly formed Chilean navy, with its 'useless rotting ships / their unstoppable desire to form a republic'.

Travel is the theme of several of the younger poets in this section. The speaker in the second of Marina Serrano's two poems (p219), provides a searing self-appraisal, questioning the outcome (and/or the purpose) of a journey made by a couple, 'people who radiate strength, and are so stupid / we don't even understand failure'. Travel is also the subject of Wendy Guerra's 'Reverse Journey', in which the narrator's plans for escape (from Cuba) falter as she 'secretly board(s) the raft / to absorb the sorcery of the sun in peace', and later 'trace(s) the thousand forms of an exploratory circumnavigation'. Catalina González, in 'Journey' (p247), details a realization of breakdown (or break-up), declaring 'this world is worn out for us', and 'at customs we have lost /something irretrievable'. Enrique Winter, a fellow-traveller, on a 'journey that will last several months' just about survives the ordeal, on a bus that is 'a country where everyone is passing through, / somewhat haggard and evil-smelling / where no one makes love, neither on the seats nor in the WC'.

Roberto Appratto offers two poems about poets (p235 & p249), or more exactly, about the difficulty of being a poet; a topic that might only be of interest to other poets, were its principal concerns not universal. Meanwhile, the Honduran Juan Ramón Saravia castigates Wall Street and the worship of wealth in his poem (with the self-explanatory title) 'How some cures end up being worse than the illness itself' (p251).

Part Four closes with 'Cage of Verdicts' by Javier Bello, a didactic poem which, from its start, warns the speaker's son of the perils of travel: 'Beware of journeys, my son, / beware of journeys and trains, / and of the lurching of ships in the battle for dawn.' Mid-way, the poem ventures into unexpected territory: 'Don't leave your hat outside the house, / don't leave your gloves far from the break of day, / because ants will strike you with their antennae' ... and we come to realize that the journey of the poem itself is a meditation on death, because 'on journeys death comes along, talking in your ear, /because on trains death travels seated / and on ships death stands up.'

1 Arnaut Daniel: a twelfth century Occitan troubadour, beloved of Ezra Pound, called 'il miglior fabbro' (the better craftsman) by Dante, a term of praise borrowed by T.S. Eliot in his dedication of 'The Wasteland' to Pound.
2 Elizabeth Bishop's Villanelle 'One Art', a meditation on loss, that begins with the lines: 'The art of losing isn't hard to master; / so many things seem filled with the intent / to be lost that their loss is no disaster'.
3 'the famous admiral of that name': Thomas Cochrane, 10th Earl of Dundonald, Marquess of Maranhão. After achieving fame and glory in the Napoleonic wars, he was dismissed from the Royal Navy in 1814 following a conviction for fraud on the London Stock Exchange. He helped organize and lead the nascent navies of Chile, Brazil and Greece during their respective wars of independence. (Adapted from Wikipedia).

Razones del ausente

Si alguien les pregunta por él,
díganle que quizá no vuelva nunca o que si regresa
acaso ya nadie reconozca su rostro;
díganle también que no dejó razones para nadie,
que tenía un mensaje secreto, algo importante que decirles
pero que lo ha olvidado.
Díganle que ahora está cayendo, de otro modo y en otra parte
    del mundo,
díganle que todavía no es feliz,
si esto hace feliz a alguno de ellos; díganle también que se fue
    con el corazón vacío y seco
y díganle que eso no importa ni siquiera para la lástima
    o el perdón
y ni él mismo sufre por eso,
que ya no cree en nada ni en nadie y mucho menos en él mismo,
    que tantas cosas que vio apagaron su mirada y ahora,
    ciego, necesita del tacto,
díganle que alguna vez tuvo un leve rescoldo de fe en Dios,
    en un día de sol,
díganle que hubo palabras que le hicieron creer en el amor
y luego supo que el amor dura
lo que dura una palabra.
Díganle que como un globo de aire perforado a tiros,
su alma fue cayendo hasta el infierno que lo vive y que ni siquiera
    está desesperado
y díganle que a veces piensa que esa calma inexorable
    es su castigo;
díganle que ignora cuál es su pecado
y que la culpa que lo arrastra por el mundo la considera apenas
    otro dato del problema
y díganle que en ciertas noches de insomnio y aun en otras en que
    cree haberlo soñado,
teme que acaso la culpa sea la única parte de sí mismo
    que le queda
y díganle que en ciertas mañanas llenas de luz
y en medio de tardes de piadosa lujuria y también borracho de vino

Reasons for his Absence

If anyone asks after him,
tell them that perhaps he'll never come back, or else
on returning no one will recognise his face;
tell them also that he left no one any reasons,
that he had a secret message, something important to tell them
but he's forgotten what it was.
Tell them that he is falling, in a different way, and in another
    part of the world,
tell them he is still not happy,
and if that makes some of them happy, tell them also that he left
    with his heart empty and dry
and tell them that this doesn't matter, not even for pity
    or pardon's sake
and that he himself doesn't suffer on this account,
and that now he doesn't believe in anything or anyone, far less in himself,
    that from seeing so many things, his sight dwindled, and now,
    blind, he needs touch,
tell them that once, on a sunny day, he had the faint glimmer
    of a faith in God,
tell them that once there were words that made him believe in love
and that later he learned love lasts
as long as it takes to say a word.
Tell them that like a balloon punctured by gunshot,
his soul plunged toward the hell within, and he isn't even
    in despair
and tell them that sometimes he thinks this inexorable calm
    is his punishment;
tell them that he doesn't know what sin he has committed,
and that he considers the blame he drags around the world
    just another aspect of the problem
and tell them that on certain insomniac nights and even on others
    during which he believes he has dreamt it,
he is afraid that the blame might be the only part of himself
    that is left
and tell them that on certain luminous mornings
and in the middle of afternoons of merciful lust and also on rainy nights

en noches de lluvia
siente cierta alegría pueril por su inocencia
y díganle que en esas ocasiones dichosas habla a solas.
Díganle que si alguna vez regresa, volverá con dos cerezas
    en sus ojos
y una planta de moras sembrada en su estómago y una serpiente
    enroscada en su cuello.
Y tampoco esperará nada de nadie y se ganará la vida
    honradamente,
de adivino, leyendo las cartas y celebrando extrañas ceremonias
    en las que no creerá
y díganle que se llevó consigo algunas supersticiones, tres fetiches,
ciertas complicidades mal entendidas
y el recuerdo de dos o tres rostros que siempre vuelven a él en la
    oscuridad
y nada.

Darío Jaramillo Agudelo (Colombia)

Lo que ocurre en el poema

En este poema
Entra un gato persiguiendo una madeja
Y se trepa en un armario.
Hay un hombre que riega en las almohadas del sueño.
Un frasco azul de negra tinta china.
Entra un perro rojo como si fuera en cuadro de Gauguin.
En este poema, un matemático loco
Cuenta en un ábaco el número de muertos
Censados en el año de la peste.
La deseada mujer del puesto de toronjas
Se desnuda y baila la danza del vientre
En torno a mi mesa empapelada.
Entre las rectilíneas carrileras del poema
Hay un tesoro a punto de ser encontrado,

       drunk with wine
he feels a certain puerile joy in his innocence
and tell them that on these blissful occasions he talks to himself.
Tell them that if some day he returns, he will come with two cherries
       for eyes
and a blackberry bush seeding in his stomach and a snake
       coiled around his neck.
And nor will he expect anything from anyone and he will earn his living
       honourably,
as a fortune-teller, reading the cards and celebrating strange ceremonies
       in which he will not believe
and tell them that he made off with some superstitions, three fetishes,
a few misunderstood instances of complicity
and the memory of two or three faces that always come back to him
       in the darkness
and nothing.

Darío Jaramillo Agudelo (Colombia)

What Happens in the Poem

In this poem
A cat enters, chasing a skein of wool
And climbs into a wardrobe.
There is a man watering dream pillows.
A blue flask of black china ink.
A red dog enters as if in a painting by Gauguin.
In this poem, a mad mathematician
Counts on an abacus the number of dead
Registered in the plague year.
The coveted woman from the grapefruit stall
Takes off her clothes and performs a belly dance
Around my paper-strewn table.
Between the unbending tracks of the poem
A treasure is about to be found,

Un milagro a punto de ocurrir.
En este poema regresan al país los desterrados.

Juan Manuel Roca (Colombia)

Maullido

No he visto las mejores mentes
de mi generación y ni me interesa.

Frank Báez (República Dominicana)

de *Discurso del contador de gusanos*

1.

Soy alguien que camina. Es la única definición que puedo dar de mí. Caminar es avanzar un paso después de otro. Eso es lo único que hay. Por un barrio, por unas calles, por unas afueras: un paso arriba de un pedazo de tierra y algunas piedras, un paso saltando una raya que separa dos baldosas. Y otro paso. Al final a veces llego a casa. Casa no es el lugar adonde vivo.
Veo unos postes de luz con sus filas tan bellas de cables. Detrás está el cielo azul del final de la tarde. Detrás de ese cielo no hay una Mirada. Nadie que diga "Estás ahí".
Necesito un método.
Voy a tomar vino en el bar. Ahí hay varios que darían esta definición de sí mismos: soy un vaso después de otro vaso.

A miracle is about to take place.
In this poem the exiles return home.

Juan Manuel Roca (Colombia)

Miaow

I haven't seen the best minds
of my generation and nor does it bother me.

Frank Báez (Dominican Republic)

from *Discourse of the Teller of Worms*

1.

I am someone who walks. It is the only definition I can give of myself. To walk is to advance one step after another. It's the only thing there is. Across a neighbourhood, down the streets, through the suburbs; one step above a scrap of earth and some stones, one step skipping the line that divides two paving stones. And another step. At the end sometimes I arrive home. Home is not the place where I live.
I see some lampposts with such beautiful lines of cable. Behind is the blue sky of late afternoon. Behind that sky there is no Gaze. Nobody who says: "There you are!"
I need a method.
I go to drink wine in the bar. Inside there are several who would give this definition of themselves: I am one glass after another.

2.

Si llovió es porque hay barro. Se va secando, pero está en el aire. Un método. Antes tenía uno. Encendía un cigarrillo después de cada momento del día. No era un mal método. Pero ahora el día no tiene momentos. No hay, entonces, método. Me atraviesan unos gusanos de color lila. Salen por el ano. Hace un tiempo, los llamaba "pensamientos". No los pensé yo, pero vinieron a mi cabeza. No sé de dónde vienen, pero sé por dónde se van. Parecen pasto, pero son gusanos. Parecen dedos de alguien muerto. Ahogado por ejemplo. Dicen que los ahogados se ponen de color azul o lila. Pero no son dedos de ahogado, son gusanos. La diferencia está justamente en que comen. Pasan unos autos por la calle oscura: con sus luces, sacan pedazos de cosas de la noche. Como unas piernas que asoman de una pollera. El ventanal vacío de una casa. Una señora barriendo la vereda, invisible debajo del cielo negro.

3.

¿Y qué sé yo si no es una bruja la que me puso acá? En este lugar que es una ciudad mediana. Que está en otro lugar al que le dicen "mundo". Qué sé yo si no hay un hechizo detrás de todas estas cosas bastante tristes. Dos álamos muertos, sin hojas. Un nene con la cara sucia, solo en la vereda. ¡Es todo un momento! Esa pregunta. Podría valer un cigarrillo. Pero ya no fumo. Me quedé sin método. Sí, puedo caminar, y así parece que algo avanza hacía algún lado. Yo, por ejemplo. Voy para allá. Un pedazo de cosa que se cree un

2.

If it rained it's because there's mud. It starts to dry out, but it's in the air. A method. Before, I had one. I used to light a cigarette after every moment of the day. It wasn't a bad method. But now the day does not have moments. There is, therefore, no method. Some lilac-coloured worms pass through me. They exit through the anus. Once upon a time, they were called "thoughts". I didn't think them, but they came into my head. I don't know where they come from, but I know where they go. They look like grass, but they are worms. They look like the fingers of a dead person. A drowned person, for example. They say that the drowned turn a shade of blue or lilac. But they are not the fingers of a drowned person, they are worms. The difference is precisely that they eat. Some cars pass down the dark street: with their lights, they pick out bits of things of the night. Like legs sticking out from a skirt. The big empty window of a house. A lady sweeping the pavement, invisible beneath the black sky.

3.

And how do I know it isn't a witch who put me here? In this place which is a medium-sized city. Which is in a different place from what they call "world." How do I know sorcery is not behind all these rather sad things. Two dead poplars, without leaves. A kid with a dirty face, alone on the pavement. It's quite a moment! That question. It could be worth a cigarette. But I quit smoking. I was left without a method. Yes, I can walk, and so it appears that something is advancing towards some place. I, for exampe. I am going over there. A

Yo. Que pierde gusanos lila por el culo. Y qué sé
yo si la bruja no me engaña haciéndome creer que
soy yo. Y entonces soy de todos modos yo.
Porque *me* engaña. A *mí*.
Pero para eso tiene que haber una bruja.

Ariel Williams (Argentina)

Argel

Saavedra: que, a pesar mío, sin saber lo que era,
me vi el marchito rostro de agua lleno.
Ofrecióse a mis ojos la ribera.
                              Cervantes

El polvo de vientos barrió las calles
ahí donde estaba tu cuerpo en la ciudad,
aunque tallada a lluvia en las fachadas
de los hoteles,

se llevó tus especias, tu pelo, tu bálsamo,
tus pechos que ya iban en pleno tránsito
del barro, del más no poder, la podredumbre,
la muerte, al fin;

fue injusto ya que tú no sabías nada del Universo,
la mierda, el rock, los sueños; te barrieron
no más al margen como papeles o preservativos o
colillas de cigarros, baba, cenizas, semen, todo
eso que el viento quiere, se nutre, se hincha;

ya las calles de la ciudad quedaron tan vacías,
tan sin ti, tan sin maravilla,
que me dije nos dijimos todos, ¿para esta ausencia
tantas millas ganas ardor dolor sueño?

Se había declarado el Estado de Sitio,

A piece of stuff that is believed to be an I. From whose arse drop lilac worms. And how do I know the witch is not tricking me into believing that I am me. And therefore I am by all means me. Because she tricks *me*. *Me*!
But for that there has be a witch.

Ariel Williams (Argentina)

Algiers

Saavedra: in spite of myself, without knowledge of what it was,
I saw my own wizened face covered with tears.
My eyes were surprised by a new shore.
Cervantes

The dust storm swept the streets,
where your body was, there in the city,
although carved by rain in the facades
of hotels,

took away your spices, your skin, your balm,
your breasts that were in the process of emerging
from clay, carried from the no-longer-able, putrefaction,
death, finally;

it was unfair since you knew nothing of the Universe,
shit, rock, dreams; they swept you away
to the margin like papers or condoms or
cigarette butts, saliva, ashes, semen, all
that the wind loves, is nourished by, rallies round;

and the streets of the city were left so empty,
so without you, so without wonder,
that I told myself we all told ourselves: for this absence
so many miles wishes heat pain dream?

It had been declared the State of Siege,

las calles vacías, los lumínicos brillaban para
la muerte; los cuerpos eran la danza de la
muerte por los bulevares atestados de objetos.

Ahora el mundo se poblaba
de animales
sustitutos de tu cuerpo.

Todo esto era en Argel, la ciudad más triste
del Universo; no puede haber ciudad feliz
repleta de prisioneros y putas: por todas las partes
penaban las ánimas, y nosotros, cautivos del
deseo de seguir vivos por nuestros cuerpos,
nos perseguimos por los bulevares atestados de
objetos, máscaras, sombras chinas, fantasmagorías,
la guerra era a muerte, cuerpo a cuerpo,

inacabable como si todo transcurriera en un
juego de video:
el deseo nos estallaba contra los ojos,
como sol.

Tomás Harris (Chile)

de 'La vida nueva'

En el fondo de un pozo
cuya boca ha sido tapada desde afuera,
sin un resquicio que permita la entrada de la luz
un hombre, solo, con una botella de agua.
Debe meditar, si puede, sobre la impermanencia de las cosas
pero en cambio elige adivinarse las uñas de los pies.
Ha fracasado en todo: ni el amor,
ni la pura poesía en estado salvaje,
ni el ideal paupérrimo de una vida dedicada al arte.
Tiene cuarenta años y no puede mirar hacia adelante,

the empty streets, the lights were shining for
death; the bodies were the dance of
death through the boulevards packed with objects.

Now the world was populated
with animals
substitutes for your body.

All this was in in Algiers, the saddest city
in the Universe: there cannot be a happy city
full of prisoners and whores: everywhere
tormented souls, and we, captives of
out of desire to keep living for our bodies' sake,
we chased each other through boulevards packed with
objects, masks, shadow puppets, phantasmagoria,
the war was to the death, body to body,

interminable, as if all were taking place in a
video game:
desire slammed against our eyes
like sun.

Tomás Harris (Chile)

from 'The New Life'

At the bottom of a well
whose entrance has been sealed
with not even a crack to let in light
a man, alone, with a bottle of water.
He needs to meditate, if he can, on the impermanence of things
but instead chooses to guess where his toenails are.
He has failed in everything: not love,
nor poetry in its pure wildness,
nor the humblest ideal of a life dedicated to art.
He is forty years of age and cannot see a way forward,

tampoco hacia atrás. (El pasado
es una cortina de humo sobre todas las cosas;
su sola noción opaca los usos del presente,
en cierto modo lo desanda.)
En el fondo del pozo, el hombre,
que es chino y está a punto de morir pero no (y él lo sabe),
imagina que enciende un fósforo;
siente en la yema de los dedos la aspereza
de la pólvora: el fulgor repentino
que lo fascinó en su infancia
es ahora, en el pozo, un sueño sin dimensión.
(Un fantasma sin cara, él mismo sin su aspecto.)
En el fondo del pozo el hombre podría ser cualquiera,
sumirse en la historia colectiva
como quien cava una fosa común.
Ser víctima o verdugo: ha perdido los límites. Desconoce
el peso permanente que arrastra sobre sí.
Él quisiera dejarse deslizar por la vía más fácil:
hacer de sus sentidos afilados un aquí y un ahora.
Pero sólo conoce aquello que lo espera: el hambre, la sed.
Como un monje suicida o destinado a la automomificación,
el hombre —que antes tuvo una esposa, a la que amaba—
querría tener ahora, en el pozo, una campana.
Una campana de tañido minúsculo para anunciar
que todavía sigue vivo.
En sus horas de miedo dice palabras sueltas,
destajos de un poema
que no sabe o no quiere recordar. Pasa la yema del pulgar
por los labios resecos. Supone que sería más fácil dejar de respirar.
En el fondo del pozo el hombre quisiera ser juez
de su propia vida
e inclinar el platillo hacia el lado de los inocentes,
los que sin más que su paciencia resignada esperan
las tramas infinitas.
Pero sabe que de algún modo es culpable
de estar allí sentado, solo,
en la extrema oscuridad.

Teresa Arijón (Argentina)

any more than he can see the past. (The past
is a curtain of smoke over everything;
its only idea is to darken the uses of the present,
to leave it somehow undone.)
At the bottom of the well, the man,
who is Chinese and about to die, yet not (and he knows it),
imagines that he lights a match;
he feels the roughness of the gunpowder
on his fingertips: the sudden flash that fascinated him as a child
is now, in the well, a measureless dream.
(A phantom without a face; him, but without his features).
At the bottom of the well the man could be anything,
could plunge into collective history
like one who digs a communal grave.
He could be a victim or a tyrant: he has lost any boundaries. He is unaware
of the permanent weight dragged above him.
He would like to be left to glide along the easiest way:
to make of his sharpened senses a here and now.
But he knows only what is awaiting him: hunger, thirst.
Like a suicidal monk or one destined to self-mummification,
the man – who before had a wife, whom he loved –
would like now to have a bell, in the well.
A bell with a miniscule chime to announce
that he is still alive.
In his fearful hours he utters flowing words,
piecemeal from a poem
that he doesn't know or doesn't want to remember. He passes the tip
of his thumb over his parched lips.
He suspects it would be easier to stop breathing.
At the bottom of the well the man would like to be the judge
of his own life
and tip the scales in favour of the innocents,
those who, without anything more than their resigned patience, wait for
infinite plans.
But he knows that in some way he is to blame
for being seated there, alone,
in utter darkness.

Teresa Arijón (Argentina)

Fiestas

Alguien en un cóctel de fin de año
le comentó a mi amigo del perro cojo,
la copa entre las manos, el pelo cuidadosamente
revuelto, la sonrisa mítica y profesional,
que la historia en realidad nunca se repite,
reproduce semejanzas por inercia,
porque no conoce otras estructuras,
pero que los hechos en sí son siempre únicos
y uno debe aprender a distinguirlos
sin los vicios del pasado o algo así,
dijo esta persona antes de trasladarse
hacia un grupo risueño, menos aburrido
o taciturno que mi amigo del perro cojo
que no sabe llegar a los lugares
como si fuera una costumbre
y suele detenerse, ver de reojo su reloj,
esperar junto a la entrada hasta que un conocido
lo saluda y le señala algún asunto más o menos
esencial como el juego político tras bambalinas
o las cifras estancadas o la sequía venidera
antes de seguir por otro camino, hacia el jardín
con su toldo donde un cuarteto de jazz
filtra sus melodías suavemente y el pasto
es una alfombra que no guarda polvo
y la gente se felicita, se abraza,
y mi amigo entonces examina el piso, piensa
en los puentes de medianoche que vio en un sueño,
rotos a la mitad con sus piedras tiradas
en el agua de los ríos donde un casco
flota junto a un niño muerto en la ciudad
de los arcos nítidos y blancos,
piensa en la historia más pequeña
donde casi nunca se demora la época
ni marca pautas un conflicto sino que hay simples
edificios alrededor de una plaza y lo decisivo
sucede en otra parte sin las campanas rituales

Fiestas

Someone at a New Year's party,
glass in his hands, hair scrupulously untidy,
smile mythic and professional,
commented to my friend with the lame dog,
that history, in reality, never repeats itself,
it reproduces similarities through inertia
because it doesn't know other models,
but that events in themselves are always unique
and one must learn to distinguish between them,
without vices from the past, or something like that,
this person said before moving away
towards some smiling group, less boring
or taciturn than my friend with the lame dog
who doesn't know how to arrive at places
as if it were a habitual matter, and usually loiters,
looking at his watch from out the corner of his eye,
waiting by the entrance until someone familiar
greets him and brings up some more or less essential
matter like the political game behind the scenes
or the stagnant numbers or the approaching drought
before filing out by another route, towards the garden
with its awning where a jazz quartet's
melodies strain smoothly and the lawn
is a carpet that doesn't gather dust
and the people congratulate and hug one another,
and so my friend examines the ground, thinks
about the midnight bridges that he saw in a dream,
broken half way across with their stones scattered
in the water of the rivers where a helmet
floats next to a dead child in the city
of precise white arches,
thinks about the smallest story
in which the era barely ever lingers
nor conflict marks a pattern but where there are simple
buildings around a square and what matters
takes place elsewhere without the ritual bells

o la nieve imaginaria que se embarra
un segundo en la banqueta,
piensa en sí mismo mi amigo
y siente su espíritu en un rincón,
cómo se restriega contra los huesos,
cómo lo incita a bajar hacia el jardín de los demás,
a compartir esa euforia del recuerdo impreciso
para que todos exclamen:
¡qué imagen tan interesante! No dejes de escribirla
y mi amigo del perro cojo, ya lleno de valor,
les dirá que en su mente las palabras
son como vidrios, miran y dejan mirar,
calcan a veces paisajes, una barda
sin yedra pero envuelta por la bruma,
la vida nunca se imita, pule sobre todo
los detalles, señala con ironía mi amigo
del perro cojo como si hablara
con una persona o varias, bajo el toldo
o en la orilla mientras la música
se diluye y junto a la puerta una figura
se despide con la cara oblicua,
o eso afirman los que estuvieron.

Tedi López Mills *(México)*

Las cosas

Se van yendo las cosas
en un ritual tranquilo.

No sé si desaparecen
o sólo cambian de lugar.
Pero cada vez son menos
las cosas y parecen perderse
alrededor de mí
en una blanca neblina.

or the imaginary snow which muddies
the pavement for a second,
he thinks about himself, my friend,
and feels his spirit is cornered,
how it rubs up against his bones,
how it incites him to go down to the garden of others,
to share that euphoria of an imprecise memory
so that everyone can exclaim:
what an interesting image! *Don't forget to write about it!*
and my friend with the lame dog, by now full of courage,
will tell them that in his mind words
are like pieces of glass, they look and allow looking,
sometimes trace landscapes, an enclosing wall
without ivy but wrapped in fog,
life never imitates itself, mostly it polishes
the details, my friend with the lame dog
points out ironically, as if talking
to one person or several, beneath the awning
or on the bank while the music
dissolves and next to the door a figure
says goodbye with his face at an angle,
or that's what those who were there claim.

Tedi López Mills (Mexico)

Things

Things keep leaving
in a quiet ritual.

I don't know if they disappear
or only change place.
But the things are fewer all the time
and they seem to get lost
around me
in a white mist.

Esa luz de tarde las protege.

Los días se van llevando las cosas que he querido.
Con pasos secretos, a mi espalda
se desvanecen. Las cosas
pequeñas, provisionales. Las cosas
que supuse que eran mías.

Y cada vez me siento
más solo, pero más ligero.
Un emigrante, digamos,
que va perdiendo su equipaje
pero no lo lamenta.

Creo que mi vida
ha sido un ir dejando cosas
extraviadas, inútiles
y queridas
en lugares que he olvidado.

Jorge Fernández Granados (México)

El verbo inglés ante la acción del fuego

La casilla del guardabarrera de Bahía Blanca Sur
tiene dos pisos: ladrillo abajo y arriba chapa y madera.
Abajo, sobre lo rojo, hierro: "Es prohibido
transitar por las vías". Los ingleses
construyeron sus frases desde los cimientos
con voluntad igual a la de sus arquitecturas:
funcionales y con vocación de eternidad,
pero aquí la localía impone sus límites,
menos por la acción razonada de los ciudadanos
que por la inercia convulsa de los paisajes.
Y alta ardió ayer la casilla, y cenizas quedaron

That evening light protects them.

The days keep taking away the things that I have loved.
With secret steps, behind my back
they vanish. Little things,
provisional things. The things
I supposed were mine.

And with each loss I feel
more alone, but lighter.
A migrant, let's say,
who loses his luggage
but isn't sorry.

I think my life
has been a going about
misplacing useless
and beloved things
in places that I have forgotten.

Jorge Fernández Granados (Mexico)

English words regarding the effect of the fire

The level-crossing keeper's cabin in Bahía Blanca Sur
has two storeys: brick downstairs, wood and sheet metal upstairs.
Downstairs, on the brick, in iron: "It is forbidding
to cross the tracks." The English
put together their phrases from the foundations up
with the same will as their architecture:
functional and with a calling towards eternity,
but here the locale imposes its limits,
less by the rational action of its citizens
than by the tumultuous inertia of its landscape.
The hut burned up yesterday, leaving in ashes

de la madera que cruzó el océano, y las chapas,
en el momento culminante del calor,
volaron sobre los cascos de los bomberos.
Luego encontraron entre las insistentes paredes
pedazos de vidrio y un hombre asado.
Si existieran, sería posible conjeturar
que el humo espeso y tentador, en volutas
negras revueltas subiendo hasta sus mesas,
habría complacido a los dioses del lugar.

Sergio Raimondi (Argentina)

Novelista

Será posible entonces que todo cobre sentido de repente,
como si agarraras diez años de tu vida y batiéndolos rápido
los volcaras en el formato preexistente de una novela?
No es tan fácil, parecen repetir, una y otra vez,
hombres que miran desde la ventana de un bar.
Ellos también se hicieron la misma pregunta antes,
mucho antes de que en vos naciera el germen
de esta fuerza que te obliga a caminar en redondo.
Algunos, tras responder negativamente,
dedicaron otra década a amaestrar un perro,
cultivar tomates en el jardín de su casa o convertirse
en coleccionistas de un objeto antiguo y anodino.
Cuando más tarde volvieron con ímpetu a la carga
buscaban mentalmente moldes donde verter su vida:
diez años acá, cinco allá, veinte en una frontera.
Sin embargo, el problema no era de forma sino de fondo.
No estaba, como el vino, añejándose en una bodega profunda
la experiencia, esperando el momento del descorche;
había escapado, quién sabe bien cuándo y por qué orificio,
dejando en su lugar como un inmenso depósito
donde flota, sin llegar a evocar nada, un perfume familiar.

Miguel Petrecca (Argentina)

the wood that crossed the ocean, and the sheet metal,
at the moment of the fire's greatest heat,
flew above the helmets of the firemen.
Later they found between the persistent walls
pieces of glass and a roasted man.
One might conjecture – if they existed –
that the dense and tempting smoke, in black
revolving spirals rising to their tables,
would have pleased the gods of the place.

Sergio Raimondi (Argentina)

Novelist

So, will it be possible for everything to suddenly make sense,
as if you were to grab ten years of your life, beat them rapidly
and spill them out in the pre-existing format of a novel?
It's not so easy, they seem to repeat, again and again,
the men who look out from the window of a bar.
They asked themselves the same question before,
long before the seed of this force that makes you
walk in circles was born in you.
Some, after responding negatively,
dedicated another decade of their lives to training a dog,
cultivating tomatoes in the garden of their house or
becoming collectors of old and anodyne objects.
When later they returned with gusto to the task,
they searched mentally for a mould into which to spill their life:
ten years here, five there, twenty on the borderline.
However, the problem was not one of form but of substance.
Experience wasn't ageing in a deep cellar like a wine,
waiting for the moment to be uncorked;
it had escaped (no one knows exactly when or through what orifice)
leaving in its place a vast tank, in which – without touching
or evoking anything – floated a familiar perfume.

Miguel Petrecca (Argentina)

Nunca decías sí

Sea vuestro lenguaje: "Sí, sí"; "no, no": que
lo que pasa de aquí viene del Maligno
                    Evangelio de Mateo

Nunca decías: sí.
Sólo un silencio mientras yo creía.
Porque te dijeron que un sí, debía ser un sí,
y todo lo que se dice de más
está bien para matar el tiempo, para convencer gente,
¿pero los no?
Los no deberían haber sido no,
y fueron banquinas inundadas,
halos de soberbia
que decantaron hasta ser otros, distintos.
Yo siempre tuve un sí para las cosas, y los sueños,
pero como caída en la zozobra,
en la penumbra, el aburrimiento y la desesperanza,
sólo me quedan los no
que son no, con tanta crudeza
como el más contundente bloque de cemento fraguado
en el gélido invierno de Rawson.

Marina Serrano (Argentina)

¿Qué fuimos a ver, Simón...?

¿Qué fueron a ver al desierto?
¿Una caña agitada por el viento?
                    Evangelio de Mateo

¿Qué fuimos a ver, Simón, al otro lado del océano,
al otro lado de las nubes, arriba y debajo,
sino hombres que nos esperaban tranquilos
deteniéndonos con el esfuerzo mínimo que requiere
tensar un hilo de globo, patear hormigas,

You never said yes

But let your communication be, Yea, yea; Nay, nay: for whatsoever is more than these cometh of evil.
                              Gospel according to Matthew

You never said: yes.
Only silence, while I believed.
Because they told you a yes must mean yes,
and anything else one says
was fine for killing time, to convince people,
– but the no's?
The no's should have been no's,
but were a flooded roadside,
haloes of pride
that spilled into being something else, other.
I always had a yes for things, and dreams,
but as if fallen in despair,
into the half-light, boredom and hopelessness,
I am left only the no's,
that mean no, as bare
as the most solid block of set cement
in Rawson's frozen winter.

Marina Serrano (Argentina)

What did we go to see, Simón...?

What went ye out into the wilderness to see?
A reed shaken with the wind?
                    Gospel according to Matthew

What did we go to see, Simón, on the other side of the ocean,
on the other side of the clouds, up and down,
but men who waited for us quietly
detaining us with the minimum required force
to tighten the balloon string, to stamp on ants,

levantar un insecto entre los dedos
y dejarlo caminar mientras la mano gira
brindando un nuevo horizonte tan efímero y cercano
como una cinta cerrada en sus dos puntas,
cinta de Moebius.
¿Fuimos, Simón,
adultos analfabetos de la gracia que no entendían nada,
nada de nada, los arrebatos de sí mismos?

Los reyes de los barrios marginales,
el kapanga de Villa Dálmine, el barrabrava de Boca
y los negros murgueros
cayeron detenidos por las manos predicadoras,
impotencia funcional de rodillas, tétrada de Celso.

Luego volviendo al sitio de origen
de su emperramiento e ignorancia, llenos de excusas,
contando lo poco que faltó, lo injusto,
hicieron alarde de un golpe fuerte, porque así somos, Simón,
gente que desborda fuerza, y es tan bruta
que no comprende siquiera el fracaso.

Marina Serrano (Argentina)

Sí hay sueño americano

Me gusta disimular,
voy sin maquillaje,
el pelo en la cara,
con cualquier ropa
para andar por alguna calle
y llegar a un edificio.

Allí soy retribuida por no hacer nada

to lift an insect between the fingers
and let it walk while your hand turns
offering a new horizon so ephemeral and close
like a ribbon joined at both ends
a Moebius strip.
Were we, Simón,
adults devoid of grace who understood nothing,
nothing at all, not even our own rage?

The kings of the marginal districts,
the *kapanga* of Villa Dálmine, the *ultras* of Boca
and the black *murgueros*
all fell into preaching hands,
the functional helplessness of knees, the Celsus tetrad.

Later, returning to the place of origin
of our pig-headedness and ignorance, full of excuses,
telling how close we got, how unfair it was,
bragging about a mighty blow, because that's what we're like, Simón
people who radiate strength, and are so stupid
we don't even understand failure.

Marina Serrano (Argentina)

Sure, there's an American Dream

I like pretending,
I go out without make-up,
hair in my face,
wearing whatever clothes
to walk down some street
and arrive at a building.

There I am remunerated for doing nothing

y hablar con personas que no conozco
a pesar de reconocer sus voces.

Las conversaciones transcurren rápido,
mecánicas, más repasadas
mientras pasa el tiempo.

Con ansias de que suceda algo,
después de la jornada,
regreso a casa.
Encuentro ¡al fin!
caras conocidas en la televisión.

Paula Piedra *(Costa Rica)*

Los Beach Poets

Ahora aprovecho para contarles la leyenda
de los beach poets.
Un puñado de genios que viven en las playas
haciendo poesía con las olas:
escribiendo odas, sonetos y elegías en las páginas del mar.
Los beach poets no necesitan ir a la universidad,
ni trabajar, ni pertenecer
a la federación nacional de surfistas.
Les basta con tener oído para el océano.

Los beach poets reman y se suben
en las tablas con disciplina espartana,
dispuestos a domar la manada de salvajes y estruendosas olas.
Cuando meteorología anuncia un huracán
son los primeros que llegan a las playas.
Los bomberos y la defensa civil con megáfonos
les ruegan que salgan.

and talking with people I don't know
despite recognising their voices.

The conversations are over quickly,
more skimmed over, mechanically,
while time passes.

Eager for something to happen
after the working day,
I return home
and there – finally! –
I find familiar faces on the television.

Paula Piedra *(Costa Rica)*

The Beach Poets

Now I will take the opportunity of telling you the legend
of the beach poets.
A handful of geniuses who live on the beaches
making poetry with the waves:
writing odes, sonnets and elegies on the pages of the sea.
Beach poets do not need to go to university,
nor to work, nor belong
to the national federation of surfers.
It is enough for them to have an ear for the ocean.

The beach poets paddle and mount
their boards with a Spartan discipline,
ready to tame the tumult of wild and deafening waves.
When the weather forecast announces a hurricane
they are the first to arrive at the beaches.
Firemen and civil defence gendarmes with megaphones
beg them to leave.

A los treinta, al igual que los poetas románticos, se retiran.
Algunos mueren ahogados.
Otros son atacados por tiburones y pierden
sus piernas o sus brazos.
Otros se hacen abogados.
Pero créase o no sus obras perduran.
Y noche y día, si uno se acerca lo suficiente al mar
puede escuchar como este ola tras ola las recita.

Frank Báez (República Dominicana)

Esta será la única mentira en la que siempre creeremos

a fuerza de admitirla tantas veces.
Hoy
alguien intentará leer el ojo de un vecino
con el fin de saber si la tristeza
(esa muchacha indócil que va escupiendo amor)
es una amiga sádica de siempre
o un pez muerto nadando en la garganta.
Sería difícil disfrazar la felicidad
(a ella siempre le quedaría corrido el maquillaje).
Pero de todos modos tendrás que perdonarme
que no te ladre amor junto al oído.
Podrían despertarse muchos muertos que están bajo nosotros.
Es una historia triste
jugar a ser perfectos.

Damaris Calderón (Cuba)

At thirty, like the Romantic poets, they retire.
Some of them die by drowning.
Others are attacked by sharks and lose
their legs or arms.
Others become lawyers.
But believe it or not, their works endure.
And night and day, if you come close enough to the sea
you can hear wave after wave reciting them.

Frank Báez *(Dominican Republic)*

This will be the only lie in which we'll always believe

as a result of accepting it so many times.
Today
someone will attempt to read into a neighbour's eye
to learn if sadness
(that headstrong girl who goes around spitting love)
is the sadistic friend we've always known
or a dead fish swimming in the throat.
It would be hard to disguise happiness.
(Her make-up would always remain smudged).
But in any case you'll have to pardon me
if I don't bark love in your ear.
So many dead beneath our feet might awaken.
It's a sad story
playing at being perfect.

Damaris Calderón *(Cuba)*

Diez tequilas

A la calle salí en llamas y sin mí,
lo que restaba eran jirones de miradas:
el mundo era mis ojos
y mis ojos
yo,
buscando a la vez
dispuesto a ser hallado,
zancadas allá abajo,
resuello y resonancia,
caudal que va sin rumbo y que desea
desembocar.
¿Qué mar espera al hombre desbordado?,
pero el instante no pregunta,
avanza y se mantiene,
se yergue a toda altura,
iza
sus estandartes
que en esta noche azul
siguen ondeando.

Julio Trujillo (México)

Paisaje con mendigos

Las buenas gentes se preguntan
Por qué los mendigos interponen,
Entre sus ojos y los nardos,
Su amasijo de harapos. Si no reciben
Su cuota de maná es por su feroz costumbre
De llagar el paisaje y la mirada.
Más antiguos que su oficio,
Los mendigos vienen de antiguas catacumbas
O de remotas catedrales que levantan sus cúpulas
Entre hospicios y hospitales.

Ten Tequilas

I went out into the street in flames
and without myself,
what was left were shreds of gazes:
the world was my eyes
and my eyes
me,
seeking and at the same time
willing to be found,
striding down there below,
gasp and echo,
a flow without direction that wants
to debouch.
What sea awaits the man who brims over?
But the instant doesn't ask questions,
it advances and remains standing,
straightens up to full height,
hoists its colours
that in this blue night
keep flying.

Julio Trujillo (Mexico)

Landscape with Beggars

The good people wonder
Why a tattered rabble of beggars
Block their prospect of the lilies.
If they don't receive their ration of manna,
It's due to their savage custom
Of blighting the landscape and the view.
More ancient than their profession
The beggars emerge from ancient catacombs
Or from remote cathedrals that raise their domes
Between hospices and hospitals.

Al cruzar hieren y enferman el paisaje
Y las gentes se abren a su paso
Como si partieran en dos un mar
Que tiñen de dicterios y quebrantos.
Un séquito de olor y un séquito de perros
Van tras las hordas miserables. Los alcaldes
Los miran con ojos acuosos
Mientras cucharean una sopa densa como lava.
Los sacerdotes los buscan como alimento
De un reino de otro mundo
Y les describen las canteras del infierno,
Aunque parezcan habitarlo desde siempre.
Son de otra raza, de otro país,
Los mendigos son oscuros forasteros
Que viven en las fronteras invisibles del lenguaje.
Entre ellos y nosotros una moneda nos escarnece,
Un oscuro comercio de penurias
Bajo la tienda de abalorios de un pariente de Dios.
Los días festivos escrutan buques fantasmas:
No encuentran a quien extender yacijas o escudillas
Y sólo amontan en los atrios migajas de milagro.
Algo de espantapájaros hay en su oficio,
Algo de cetrería en sus ojos,
En su manera de mirar el pan de las palomas.
Un hombre ebrio y compungido me dijo a la salida del bar:
Podrían mandarlos a la guerra, servir de barricadas.
Los mendigos no saben dónde ir
Cuando ordenan que acuartelemos las sombras malheridas
Los guías de turismo, para no inquietar a los viajeros,
Advierten que son actores de reparto
De una película que ruedan en las calles.
Quizá hayan salido de un mal sueño, de una factoría,
De un muelle, de una mina, de una casa usurpada.
Del mal sueño traen la mirada arisca de quien huye,
De la fábrica conservan un color de presidario,
Del muelle el vicio de cargar fardos de nada,
De la mina unos ojos duros y pugnaces,
De la casa usurpada en eco llegado de tierras de Nadie.

As they go by they wound and poison the landscape
And the people give way at their passing
As if they were parting a sea
Which they stain with taunts and devastation.
A procession of smells and a procession of dogs
Go past with the wretched hordes. Town mayors
Watch them with watery eyes
While spooning out soup as thick as lava.
The priests seek them out like food
From a kingdom in another world
And describe to them the quarries of hell,
Although they seem to have lived there forever.
They are of another race, another country,
The beggars are dark strangers
Who live on the invisible frontiers of language.
Between them and us a coin makes mock,
A dark commerce in scarcity
Beneath the trinket shop of a relative of God.
On festive days they stare at phantom ships:
They extend their bowls and rough beds to no one
And in the atriums they only pile up scraps of miracles.
There is something of the scarecrow about their trade
Something of falconry about the eyes,
In the way they look at the doves' bread.
A drunk and downcast man told me at the exit to the bar:
They could send them off to war, to serve as barricades.
The beggars don't know where to go
When we are ordered to confine the wounded shadows.
The tourist guides, so as not to worry travellers,
Inform them that the beggars are extras
For a film being shot on the streets.
Perhaps they have emerged from a bad dream, from a factory,
From a dockside, from a mine, from a squat.
From the bad dream they bring the surly gaze of those who flee,
From the factory they retain the complexion of a prisoner,
From the docks the vice of loading bales of nothing,
From the mine hard and aggressive eyes,
From the squat an echo carried from the land of Nobody.

Escarnio y mofa, dos perros fieles, los acompañan.

Juan Manuel Roca (Colombia)

La caída

Si te dicen que caí
es que caí.
Verticalmente.
Y con horizontales resultados.
Soy, del ángulo recto
solamente los lados.
Ignoro el arte monumental del sesgo,
esa torsión ornamental del héroe
que hace que su caer se luzca como un salto.
Ese rizo del mártir que, ascendiendo
se sale de la víctima
y su propio tormento sobrevuela
no es mi especialidad. Yo, cuando caigo,
caigo.
No hay parábola
ni aire, ni fuerza de sustentación.
Un resbalón: espero. Al suelo llego
por la ruta más breve.
Un alud, una piedra,
una viga a la que han dinamitado.
No hay astucias del cuerpo en mi descenso.
Se sobrevive: el fondo
del abismo es más blando
para quien no vuela, sólo cae.
Si te dicen que caí,
no vengas
a enseñarme aerodinámica revisionista.
No me cuentes de los que cayeron venciendo.
No vengas a decirme
que no crees que haya sido un accidente.

Ridicule and Mockery, two faithful dogs, are their companions.

Juan Manuel Roca (Colombia)

The Fall

If they tell you that I fell
it's because I fell.
Vertically.
And with horizontal results.
In a right angle I am
only the sides.
I am ignorant of the monumental art of slanting
the hero's ornamental torsion
that passes off his fall as a jump.
That loop of the martyr who, ascending,
casts off the role of victim
and soars above her own anguish
is not my specialty. Me, when I fall,
I fall.
There is no parabola
no air, no lift force.
A slip: I wait. I land on the floor
by the shortest route.
An avalanche, a stone,
a beam that has been dynamited.
There is no bodily guile in my descent.
It outlasts itself: the bottom
of the abyss is softer
for one who does not fly, only falls.
If they tell you that I fell
don't come
and teach me revisionist aerodynamics.
Don't tell me of those who fell in victory.
Don't come and tell me
that you don't believe it was an accident.

En lo único que creo es en el accidente.
Lo único que sabe hacer el universo
es derrumbarse sin ningún motivo,
es desmoronarse porque sí.

Beatríz Vignoli (Argentina)

Cochrane

Me han traído para que lidere la batalla naval
por una independencia que no es la mía
me han recibido con un mes de parranda y jolgorio
mientras el enemigo avanza por un mar en llamas

Pienso en sus inútiles barcos de hojarasca
su irrefrenable deseo de formar una república y ellos
me han expuesto malamente una obra de Shakespeare
y ofrecido algunas mujeres de la región

A lo lejos
bajo un cielo enrojecido y brillante
los oscuros ciudadanos de la nueva república
flotan sobre el agua negra.

Marcelo Guajardo Thomas (Chile)

Mester de servidumbre

Por carecer de flechas,
Los mendigos
Arrojaban
A los nobles

The only thing I believe in is the accident.
The only thing the universe knows how to do
is fall over for no reason,
is collapse, just because.

Beatriz Vignoli *(Argentina)*

Cochrane

They have brought me here to lead the sea battle
for an independence that is not my own
they have welcomed me with a month of partying and merriment
while the enemy advances across a sea in flames

I think of their useless rotting ships
their unstoppable desire to form a republic and they
have put on for me, badly, a play by Shakespeare
and offered me some women from the region

In the distance
beneath a reddening and brilliant sky
the dark citizens of the new republic
float on the black water.

Marcelo Guajardo Thomas *(Chile)*

Craft of Servitude

For want of arrows,
The beggars
Cast
Their own wounds

Sus propias heridas.
Pero había
Una raza de pordioseros
Más mísera aún:
Robaba heridas ajenas
Y las vendía
En la plaza del mercado.
Con tan burdas armas
Los pobres cruzaron
La noche medieval.

Juan Manuel Roca (Colombia)

Es la voz de tu conciencia la que te habla

Es la voz de tu conciencia la que te habla
y te dice: no has de sufrir.
Has de pensar en ti sobre todas las cosas,
es decir en mí: sin distraerte
con las ansiedades y los sentimientos de pérdida
que te acechan a cada paso. Escucha:
Es la voz de tu conciencia la que te pide
concentración y seriedad
para pensar en tu vida.
Ésta es la voz de tu conciencia que te exige,
desde ahora,
escribir un poema por día.
Un poema.
no es una broma
ni una exageración: un poema por día
te ayudará a limpiar tu espíritu
para no sufrir. Repito: no has de sufrir
por los problemas amorosos, sino
amar a ese poema que escribirás
para no sufrir. La voz de tu conciencia
vuelve a hablar: escúchame: no te pierdas

Before the nobles.
But there was
An even more wretched
Class of mendicant:
They stole the wounds of others
And sold them
In the marketplace.
With such makeshift weapons
The poor passed
The medieval night.

Juan Manuel Roca (Colombia)

It's the voice of your conscience speaking to you

It's the voice of your conscience speaking to you
and it tells you: you don't have to suffer.
You should put yourself– which is to say *my*self –
first: without becoming distracted
by anxieties and the feelings of loss
that stalk your every step. Listen:
It's the voice of your conscience asking for
concentration and seriousness
to think about your life.
It's the voice of your conscience demanding
that from now on,
you write a poem every day.
One poem.
it's not a joke
nor an exaggeration: a poem a day
will help you clean your spirit
so as not to suffer. I repeat: you don't have to suffer
from concerns of the heart, but
love instead that poem that you will write
so as not to suffer. The voice of your conscience
speaks again: listen to me: don't lose yourself

en los trajines del día. No duermas tanto.
No vayas al cine
sólo para pasar el rato.
Debí haberte hablado antes. Debí
haberte prevenido contra todo eso,
pero esperaba que actuaras
por ti mismo. De modo
que me mantuve en silencio. Hoy,
con una voz ronca, tal vez por desuso,
pero fuerte,
he decidido hablar, y por eso me estás escuchando:
¿Me estás escuchando?
hablo con una voz pausada, serena, para decirte
que te quedes así,
sentado, si es posible, en actitud de cumplir
estrictamente mis palabras: es en presente,
es en imperativo, que te digo que te concentres,
que te mantengas alejado del alcohol
y de las malas compañías; que estés solo,
profundamente solo,
aun en presencia de los otros,
que no harán sino molestarte
con textos imprecisos, torpes, mal puntuados,
la expresión indirecta y borrosa de sus almas;
la voz de tu conciencia te dice que no los escuches,
que limpies tus oídos,
que te pongas de una vez
a escribir el poema. Ése es el llamado.
el poema permanece en ti como una fuerza invisible,
el ritmo de un contrabajo que va y viene
sobre las inclinaciones de tu espíritu, hasta el otro día,
en que escribirás otro poema,
como si nunca hubieras escrito antes:
con una pose ingenua ante la salida libre,
indómita, de tus palabras. Yo las guiaré, yo,
la voz de tu conciencia, capaz de ver el dolor
y la imperfección en lo que has hecho.
me dirás que es tu vida, pero es también la mía;

in the hustle and bustle of the everyday. Don't sleep so much.
Don't go to the cinema
only to pass the time of day.
I should have spoken to you of this before. I should
have warned you about all this,
but I was hoping you would act
on your own behalf. For that reason
I kept my silence. Today,
with a hoarse voice, perhaps due to disuse,
but strong,
I have decided to speak, and therefore you are listening to me:
Are you listening to me?
I am speaking in a slow, calm voice so as to tell you
to remain as you are,
sitting, if possible, in a posture that guarantees
strict obedience to my words: this is in the present tense,
it's an imperative, that I tell you to concentrate,
that you keep away from alcohol
and from bad company; that you be alone,
profoundly alone,
even in the presence of others,
who will only bother you
with imprecise, inept, mispunctuated texts,
the indirect and blurred expression of their souls;
the voice of your conscience tells you not to listen to them,
that you wash out your ears,
that you commit yourself once and for all
to write the poem. That is the call.
The poem remains in you like an invisible force,
the rhythm of a double bass that comes and goes
above the inclinations of your spirit, until the next day,
when you will write another poem,
as though you had never written before:
With an ingenuous stance before the free, irrepressible
release of your words. I will guide them, I,
the voice of your conscience, able to see the pain
and imperfection in what you have made.
You will tell me that it's your life, but it's also mine;

tengo derecho, por tanto, a decirte que te calles.
La voz de tu conciencia exige, perentoria,
el respeto del silencio,
del ejercicio espiritual
de un poema por día, y lo seguirás aun cuando
los demás te indiquen otro camino:
serás un hombre si puedes desoírlos y hacer
solamente lo que te estoy diciendo:
no pienses en otra cosa; sobre todo,
no pienses en eso. La voz de tu conciencia
piensa por ti
para que no confundas el ritmo de tu vida
con el de tu corazón. Te lo dice, sólo por hoy,
esta voz, que advierte el desorden
en el uso inútil, operático,
de la fantasía, de la memoria,
de la ensoñación.
Deja que tu pasado,
a menudo abrumado por el dolor,
por la incertidumbre,
por la entrega absoluta a causas imposibles,
se evapore. Por eso te dice, una vez más,
la voz de tu conciencia que te quedes así, quieto,
y no sufras. Escribe tu poema, firme, sólido,
impasible, galvanizado en tu soledad, y estarás bien.
Ahora, con un gesto desprendido y generoso,
Con una sonrisa de aceptación, sin otra cosa que tu propia fuerza,
Escribe lo que te dictaré: empieza así:

Roberto Appratto (Uruguay)

I have the right, therefore, to tell you to shut up.
The voice of your conscience demands, absolutely,
respect for silence,
for the spiritual exercise
of a poem a day, and you will follow it even when
others point out to you another way:
You will be a man if you can ignore them and do
only what I am telling you:
Don't think about anything else; above all,
don't think of that. The voice of your conscience
thinks for you
so that you don't confuse the rhythm of your life
with that of your heart. I'm telling you, just for today,
this voice, that warns of the disorder
in the useless, melodramatic use
of fantasy, of memory,
of daydreaming.
Let your past,
so often burdened by pain,
by uncertainty,
by the absolute surrender to impossible causes,
evaporate. And so the voice of your conscience
tells you, once again, to remain like this, calm,
and not to suffer. Write your poem, steady, solid,
unemotional, galvanised in your solitude, and all will be well.
Now, in an unselfish and generous gesture,
With a smile of acceptance, with nothing more than your own will,
Write what I will dictate: it begins like this:

Roberto Appratto (Uruguay)

El espejo

Por ahora, el grito,
la contundente arista de la piedra,
el visceral odio y las plañideras formas de la ira.

Después – ya lo sabemos –
el lavatorio de manos,
la contrición,
levantar los vidrios y formar de nuevo
el indolente espejo de la fábula.

Fabricio Estrada (Honduras)

Camino al revés

De vez en cuando camino al revés:
es mi modo de recordar.

Si caminara sólo hacia delante,
te podría contar
cómo es el olvido.

Humberto Ak'Abal (Guatemala)

El viaje inverso

Hago y deshago la maleta
hago y rehago todo con intención de partir
Llamo a los amigos   les cuento que me escapo
y luego subo disimuladamente a la balsa
a recibir en paz los sortilegios del sol

The Mirror

For now, the yell,
the blunt edge of the rock,
the visceral loathing and mournful expressions of rage.

Later – as we now know –
the washing of hands,
contrition,
picking up the pieces of glass and shaping once more
the indifferent mirror of the fable.

Fabricio Estrada (Honduras)

Walking Backwards

From time to time I walk backwards:
it's my way of remembering.

If I were to walk only going forward,
I could tell you
what forgetting is.

Humberto Ak'Abal (Guatemala)

Reverse journey

I pack and unpack my bag
I do and undo everything with the intention of leaving
I call my friends   tell them I'm escaping
and later secretly board the raft
to absorb the sorcery of the sun in peace

Un anillo de bodas perdido en el estómago de un pez
Y otra vez las valijas para el viaje impostergable
Veo y veo ese inmóvil trozo de mármol
que son las botas de mi monumento personal
Mira cómo viajan mis lágrimas sobre la valija
los sigues con el dedo índice
y llegarás hasta al centro de mis dudas
Pesco en el mismo mar que desborda el agua de mis ojos
Veo cómo sube mi valija incompleta
mi brújula atormentada
y el dibujo de un niño con el mapa de Cuba
Trazo las mil formas de un bojeo exploratorio
Sacar el pie   para probar la temperatura exacta de las aguas
retroceder un poco   y partir luego
a la regata interminable y conclusiva
Alguien me empuja en broma y casi caigo ahogada
pero conservo un asombroso estado de equilibrio
Hago el viaje al interior
divisando iluminada que yo dicto
el último renglón de mis ideas.

Wendy Guerra *(Cuba)*

La ley de la calle

Qué bueno cuando asamos conejos imaginarios
y qué bueno la canoa que recogía
nuestros cuerpos quemados y exhaustos,
y qué bueno disparar un rifle de precisión
imaginario, pero oler pólvora de verdad.

Sin embargo estoy en una ciudad.
Hay una moneda en el fondo de un charco
y una mujer se detiene detrás de mí.
La veo en la vidriera donde

A wedding ring lost in the stomach of a fish
And again the luggage for the non-deferrable journey
I keep seeing that unmoving piece of marble
that are the boots of my personal memorial
Look how my tears course down the suitcase
you track them with your index finger
and you will arrive at the centre of my doubts
I fish in the same sea that overflows in the water from my eyes
I see my half-packed suitcase come on board
my tormented compass
and the child's drawing of a map of Cuba
I trace the thousand forms of an exploratory circumnavigation
Dip a foot in   to test the exact temperature of the waters
withdraw a little   and then leave
for the interminable and conclusive regatta
Someone pushes me for a laugh and I almost fall and drown
but I sustain an amazing state of equilibrium
I make the journey to the interior
realizing in an epiphany
that I dictate my ideas' last line.

Wendy Guerra (Cuba)

The Law of the Street

How fine it is when we roast imaginary rabbits
and how fine the canoe that picked up
our sunburnt and exhausted bodies,
and how fine it is too shoot an imaginary
precision rifle, but to smell the powder in reality.

However, I am in a city.
There is a coin at the bottom of a puddle
and a woman stops behind me.
I see her in the shop window where

también se reflejan
ciertas nubes.

Jorge Aulicino (Argentina)

Batalla del Ebro

Estoy en ningún lugar y voy a ninguna parte
Escucho una vieja canción de The Police
Mientras escribo y miro unas tablas lustrosas
De negro como nuestro futuro
Estoy esperando que suceda algo
Como hace tantos años
Estoy perdiendo la batalla del Ebro
Este es el momento culminante
Me fumo el último cigarro
Bebo la penúltima copa
Luego volveré a ser el anónimo ciudadano de siempre
Escribo para no estar solo
Mientras afuera la ciudad ensordece
Como un río lleno de piedras

Carlos Decap (Chile)

Profundo en el mapa

Hay valles en el mapa que se acogen a ley de amnistía
y tallan con humo su memoria ósea
y no dejan rastro.
Hay valles en el mapa que construyen un nombre
y sobre el nombre erigen una importancia
y sobre ésta se visten de gala
y se inclinan con sed.

are reflected also
a few clouds.

Jorge Aulicino (Argentina)

Battle of The Ebro

I am nowhere and going no place
I am listening to an old song by The Police
While I write and stare at some shiny boards
Black like our future
I am waiting for something to happen
Like so many years ago
I am losing the battle of the Ebro
This is the decisive moment
I smoke the last cigarette
Drink the penultimate glass
Later I will return to being the same anonymous citizen
      as always
I write so as not to be alone
While outside the city is deafening
Like a river filled with stones

Carlos Decap (Chile)

Deep in the map

There are valleys on the map that appeal to the law of amnesty
and they carve their bony memory with smoke
and do not leave a trace.
There are valleys on the map that make a name for themselves
and above the name they fashion self-importance
and above that they dress for a dinner party
and they bow with thirst.

Hay valles en el mapa
como el suyo
que no son de luz ni olvido
y arrastran su ilusión hasta alguna cima
sólo para resbalar por la cota contraria
y volver a saborear el gusto a barro original.

En su valle y ahora
se sufre leve de mareo matutino
y todo está pronto a parirse en algún lecho tibio.

Hay
en la cantera más profunda del valle
un cartel cegado que reza:

mi vida
por dos cuencas que sepan ver.

Verónica Zondek (Chile)

Viaje

Hemos sometido nuestros cuerpos
a los rigores del instante
y este mundo se ha agotado
para nosotros.

El frío nos ha llevado al hastío,
el verano amenaza con devorarnos.

Sería mejor cambiar todo el equipaje
pero la memoria es caprichosa,
en las aduanas hemos perdido
algo irremediable.

Catalina González Restrepo (Colombia)

There are valleys on the map
like his
that are not of light or oblivion
and they drag their illusion toward some peak
only to bounce down the other side
and return to relish the taste of original clay.

In his valley and now
one suffers mild morning sickness
and everything is ready to be born in some warm place.

There is
in the deepest quarry of the valley
a blind sign that says:

my life
for two hollows that know how to see.

Verónica Zondek (Chile)

Journey

We have subjected our bodies
to the rigours of the moment
and this world is worn out
for us.

The cold has made us weary,
summer threatens to devour us.

It would be better to change all the luggage
but memory is fickle,
at customs we have lost
something irretrievable.

Catalina González Restrepo (Colombia)

El piso sucio y la luz prendida

Ningún servicio es tan básico, ni la luz ni el agua
y si de noche la ciudad pestañea sus brillos
tanto mejor se ve a oscuras. El ojo se acostumbra a todo.
El viaje en bus durará algunos meses
se habituará a dormir sentado, al pan con jamón y al café,
a ser discreto como un lago
y no como esta lluvia sobre el techo de cinc.
Un poco de baba sobre la almohada
que diga "aquí durmió"
repetirá temas siempre variables
como el clima y su opinión del país extranjero,
porque usted está en contra de la belleza que se note
– que parezca agarrable como un plato:
Andrés lava su auto en un pasaje
de Lima, Monterrey o de Santiago,
su esposa es güera o rubia como un sable –.
El bus, en cambio, es un país donde están de paso todos,
un poco trasnochados y malolientes
donde nadie hace el amor ni en los asientos ni en los baños.

Enrique Winter (Chile)

Todos los poetas esconden algo

Todos los poetas esconden algo
Cuando avanzan hacia la mesa de lectura
Con unos papeles bajo el brazo. Lo saben antes de empezar
Y lo afirman con gestos expresivos, elevando la voz ante las hojas.
Los que sólo ven la superficie no entienden el énfasis
Con que señalan un estado de las cosas o se sitúan en otro tiempo
Pequeñas escenas con un sentido muy preciso, pero invisible.
Eso que esconden es un trato exclusivo, personal, con el mundo.

The floor dirty and the lights on

No service is so basic, neither electricity nor water
and if at night the city blinks its lights
so much better for seeing in the dark. The eye becomes
    accustomed to everything.
The bus journey will last several months
and you will get used to sleeping sitting down, to bread and ham and coffee,
to being discrete like a lake
and not like this rain on the zinc roof.
A little dribble on the pillow
that says "you slept here"
you will reiterate ever-variable topics
such as the weather and your opinions of the foreign country,
because you are against conspicuous beauty
– that seems graspable like a plate:
Andrés washes his car in an alley
in Lima, Monterrey or Santiago,
his wife is fair-haired or blonde like a sable –.
The bus, by contrast, is a country where everyone is passing through,
somewhat haggard and evil-smelling
where no one makes love, neither on the seats nor in the WC.

Enrique Winter (Chile)

All poets hide something

All poets hide something
As they advance towards the readers' table
With some papers under their arm. They know it before starting
And affirm it with expressive gestures, raising their voice before the sheets of
    paper.
Those who only see the surface do not understand the emphasis
With which they indicate a state of affairs or situate themselves in another
    time
Small scenes with a very precise meaning, but invisible.

La conexión secreta con una forma de poesía que se dicen a sí mismos.

Roberto Appratto (Uruguay)

De cómo algunas curaciones resultan peor que la enfermedad misma

Como un castigo a la idolatría de la riqueza
Moisés echó al fuego al becerro de oro
lo pulverizó
lo disolvió en agua
y lo dio a beber a todo su pueblo
a partir de entonces
ningún profeta pudo explicar
por qué
    cuando menos se esperaba
la gente caía en éxtasis
repitiendo
en un idioma hasta entonces desconocido
OH WALL STREET
OH WALL STREET
OH WALL STREET

Juan Ramón Saravia (Honduras)

La Guerra sutil

Yo soy Arnaut, el que amasa la brisa
y caza la liebre con el buey
y nada contra la tempestad.
                Arnaut Daniel

What they are hiding is an exclusive and personal contract with the world.
The secret connection with a form of poetry that they tell themselves.

Roberto Appratto (Uruguay)

How some cures end up being worse than the illness itself

As a punishment for the worship of wealth
Moses cast the golden calf into the fire
he pulverized it
dissolved it in water
and gave it to all his people to drink
from then on
not a single prophet could explain
why
    when least expected
the people would fall into an ecstasy
repeating
in a language at that time unknown
OH WALL STREET
OH WALL STREET
OH WALL STREET

Juan Ramón Saravia (Honduras)

The Subtle War

I am Arnaut who gathers up the wind,
and chases the hare with the ox,
and swims against the torrent.
                Arnaut Daniel

Vuelvo de lo que vi ayer,
el paisaje de ríos
que cambian de nombre
entre una ruta de álamos
y reducen su estancia en cada meandro
donde un muro de piedra amarilla
ocupa el tramo de agua con su reflejo.

Vuelvo de lo que vi,
la amapola atravesada
por la voz del cuchillo al amanecer
junto a una pileta
en cuyo centro oscuro
un perro hundió el hocico
y buscó después la orilla
con una pata lenta
que se iba resbalando en el lodo.

Vuelvo con el recuerdo aún reciente
de cruzar el camino de la liebre;
de haber conjurado la guerra sutil
en un feudo visto de reojo,
el simulacro de una pascua torpe
entre las tejas caídas,
los restos de una torre,
prensada por el tronco de la yedra.

Oigo la época en el trote del caballo,
la antigua locura, el aire amargo.
Aquí te vi pasar;
en la tierra ocre
marcaste los surcos en un verso
que se torcía suavemente para ella,
la mujer compuesta,
una sola y muchas,
mil prendas y un anillo
que comba el regazo,
un listón alrededor del cuello

I return from yesterday's sights,
the landscape of rivers
that change name
between a track of poplars
the time spent between them lessening with each bend
where a wall of yellow rock
occupies the stretch of water with its reflection.

I return from what I saw,
the poppy pierced through
by the voice of the knife at daybreak
next to a pond
in whose dark centre
a dog buried his snout
and then searched the bank
with a slow paw
that had him sliding in the mud.

I return with the still recent memory
of crossing the hare's path;
of having conjured up the subtle war
in a region seen out of the corner of my eye,
the sham of a hopeless Easter
amongst the fallen tiles,
the remains of a tower,
gripped by the trunk of the ivy.

I hear the age in the horse's trot,
the ancient madness, the bitter air.
Here I saw you go by;
on the ochre earth
you marked the furrows of a verse
which twisted smoothly for her,
the composite woman,
one alone and many,
a thousand dresses and a ring
that swings upon her breast,
a ribbon around the neck

que huele a flor de castaño
bajo las ramas verdes
en que pierdo el habla
y pierdo una forma de regreso.

Oigo un nombre indistinto,
un nombre metálico,
breve como martillazo;
lo oigo rodear cuesta abajo
entre la hojarasca.
No hay nadie aquí que escuche:
tú eres quien quise ser.

Tedi López Mills (México)

La jaula de la sentencia

I
Cuídate de los viajes, hijo mío,
cuídate de los viajes y de los trenes
y del tambaleo de los barcos en la batalla del amanecer.

Cuídate de los trenes
y de la tierra donde baila sepultada una llama,
cuídate de los barcos y de los fuegos fatuos
como escondes tus rodillas del tormento de la tempestad.

Nunca entenderás el recorrido de los animales
por las veredas y los parques,
los animales malos que se comen la sed.
Nunca entenderás los ojos de los perros
que desaparecen tras el silbido de los cazadores.
No me digas que no has visto
los animales negros que tienen cara de anciano.
No me digas que no has visto
los caballos cansados que cruzan con sus patas la verdad.

with the scent of the chestnut flower
below the green branches
in which I lose the gift of speech
and lose a way of return.

I hear an indistinct name
a metallic name,
abrupt like a hammer blow;
I hear it moving down below
amongst the fallen leaves.
There is no one here who listens:
you are who I wanted to be.

Tedi López Mills (Mexico)

Cage of Verdicts

I
Beware of journeys, my son,
beware of journeys and trains
and of the lurching of ships in the battle for dawn.

Beware of trains
and of the earth where a buried flame dances,
beware of ships and of fatuous fires
as you hide your knees from the torment of the storm.

You will never understand the coming and going of animals
through the lanes and the parks,
the bad animals that gobble up thirst.
You will never understand the eyes of dogs
that vanish after the hunters' whistle.
Don't tell me that you haven't seen the black animals
that have the face of an old man.
Don't tell me that you haven't seen
the tired horses that trample the truth.

Ten cuidado de los viajes,
ten cuidado de los trenes y de las potencias malignas
y de perderte entre tus propias aguas.

No dejes tu sombrero fuera de la casa,
no dejes tus guantes lejos del amanecer,
porque las hormigas te golpearán con sus antenas hasta causarte daño,
porque las piedras arderán en tus zapatos negros,
para que aprendas a no jugar con las líneas de tus manos,
para que recuerdes, hijo mío,
que el norte de las brújulas se come la cabeza de tu propio animal.

Cuídate de los viajes,
cuídate de los viajes y de los trenes
y del tambaleo de los barcos en los mares sin ley,
porque en los viajes va la muerte hablándote al oído,
porque en los trenes va la muerte sentada
y en los barcos va la muerte de pie.

Javier Bello (Chile)

Be careful on journeys,
be careful on trains and with malignant forces
and beware of straying in your own waters.

Don't leave your hat outside the house,
don't leave your gloves far from the break of day,
because ants will strike you with their antennae, hurting you,
because stones will burn in your black shoes,
so that you learn not to play with the lines of your hand,
so that you remember, my son,
that the north of the compass racks the brains of your own animal.

Beware of journeys,
beware of journeys and of trains
and of the lurching of ships in the lawless seas,
because on journeys death comes along, talking in your ear,
because on trains death travels seated
and on ships death stands up.

Javier Bello (Chile)

Introduction to Part 5:
'What we are and how we love.'

'Poem of the First Time', by the Colombian John Galán Casanova – his two surnames unfairly predisposing him towards a career as a love poet – seemed a fitting opening to the section dealing with love, sex and the body (a triad whose components, however confusingly, demand to be treated together). In this poem, Galán considers the emotions stirred by 'Offering oneself before the sight and touch / of one who, until that time, / we have only had dealings with in a clothed state', and explores the strange detachment experienced in undressing the object of our desire. That the initial state of wonder diminishes, that 'Afterwards will come the usual procession: caresses, caution, delirium, boredom' does not, in the end, surprise, nor that the memory of the occasion becomes merely a 'tattoo of the instant'. Such intensity can never be sustained, a fact confirmed by Galán's second piece, 'Poem of the last time' – which closes part 5 – in which 'Desire has now become / the memory of desire.'

Wendy Guerra addresses her 'Eskimo's word' (p265) both to the beloved and the frozen landscape, which she must, for reasons that are not given, now leave: 'I will put on a Western accent and wear summer clothes'. Her character is 'in exile from the ice', but 'will watch the thaw as though it were my sexual water / at the end of the night I will not give to the stranger what is yours'. These are paradoxical lines, coming from a Cuban writer who has claimed to be living in 'inner exile' within her own country,[1] while achieving considerable success throughout the rest of the Spanish speaking world.

Diego Maquiera's poetry – 'ludic' and 'baroque', according to no less a figure than Enrique Lihn[2] – and infused with colloquial diction, was widely read in the Chile of the 1980s, his personae often dissolute or outsider figures, influenced by gangsters and folk (anti-) heroes. Here, in one of his best known poems (p269), we are introduced to 'The Tyrantess', who considers herself 'the Greta Garbo of the Chilean cinema'; who is 'very refined and horny' and will 'reminisce about my shags with Velázquez' (yes, Velázquez the painter of *Las Meninas*). Even defeat is sweet, for while 'those who are outside will destroy me / still I am the old woman who screwed them all / still I am of a ferocious vulgarity'.

Tres, by the Argentine poet Osvaldo Bossi (p275), relates, in short fragments, the history of a love triangle involving a gay man, his lover, and the lover's wife. In an interview, Bossi has claimed that 'The other is always an enormous mystery',[3] and one might argue that the figure of the 'other' is multiplied twice over in a relationship such as the one described in this arresting poem, beginning with the lines 'A man who loves a man / who loves a woman is trapped . . . he gives of himself / in an extravagant emptiness, touches / emptiness with his fingers'. Varieties of sexual self-expression are further explored in 'Snort', by the Nicaraguan poet Tania Montenegro (p285). According to one critical reading, the word 'ñatazo' – the poem's title in Spanish – comes from the verb 'ñatar', apparently from the English 'to sniff', both of them onomatopoeic renderings – like the subtitular "¡Oh Gsik!" – of the inhalation of cocaine. The poem begins with the lines: 'She loves a number of men / who are that and more . . . She loves women hidden in masculine bodies, / therefore feels like a male lesbian, / and since she also likes men, she feels homosexual.' There is something intentionally self-limiting in the terminology here: the poet acknowledges this, and paraphrases: 'she likes women, and enjoys himself being Her Self'. The poem, in its way, shows how language encourages us to follow traditional, or fossilized responses to gender and sexuality, separating 'the body' from a simplistic rationalization of female/male dualism, and using the emotional climate of a shared drug experience to break down accepted rules of gender delineation.[4] Explorations of gender fluidity, such as here, and in the work of Maggie Nelson, aspire towards a less reductive approach to sexuality.[5]

Aleyda Quevedo's 'Luckily the Moon' (p287) warrants inclusion as the only poem in the collection that addresses masturbation, the speaker celebrating 'the festivals of Lesbos by moonlight, / assisted by a bone of red china'; while the sinister image of a single red shoe lingers in the imagination long after finishing Luis Felipe Fabre's 'Image of the unknown woman' (p277), which ends with the cryptic lines: 'A shoe that is a question / whose answer is another shoe'.

Lust and sensual pleasure can be prickly topics to address in a poem: both Carmen Ollé's 'Bars' (p279) and Diana Bellessi's 'Equatorial cruise' (p283) comment on the pleasures of the flesh from a woman's point of view. In the former, one of the drinkers in the bar 'loves / the bottle like a woman's thigh – in great gulps', while 'the other one' – the dangerous one, 'robs kills lies' and when passing the speaker's table, his 'his great silky spider eyes' slide to her lap, and she claims: 'at last I feel as if I've travelled.' Bellessi celebrates meeting, and losing ('cheerfully, without regret') a lover who 'talked to me about slow pink / squid / that swim together / in the golden depths of the Caribbean'. Her female speaker, a 'vagabond between different nationalities' has a series of erotic encounters with men 'who appear and disappear with equal levity throughout the course of the book'.[6] Desire is also a theme of Catalina González' poem 'Nourishment' (p295), the lovers' absence from each other making them 'like birds that keep their wings folded / while their hearts beat / in hot chests'.

Both Eduardo Chirinos ('The wound', p287) and Daniel Samoilovich (Porto Dos Ossos', p299) tell of loss, the former by means of the scar, which 'remembers the wound, speaks to it / very slowly'; the latter with the notion of night entering the sea, via an imaginary swimmer, 'through the black wake / left by his invisible strokes'. In not dissimilar vein, the two brief, tightly-woven poems by Jorge Fondebrider are subtly laced with pathos: in the first, 'All the things you are' (p281), the speaker sits on the bed in a significant other's room, 'to see through the window the things that you see / when you come home / alone.' In 'How love becomes the memory of love' (p283), the protagonist realises he is speaking in the past tense of the woman he loves, and that no matter how deep the trace of her might be, the memory is now a sequence of historic verbs: 'She was, she did, she said, she went.'

With his poem 'Reason for all things' (p303) Eduardo Espina's turbulent diction, rich in wordplay, offers delightful challenges to the translator. The final utterance, 'Love, it's the only necessary impossibility' comes across as a slamming on of brakes after a reckless literary seduction, when 'the skin alone gives in to the outcome'.

1. Article about Wendy Guerra in *El País* newspaper (Spain), 27 December 2014: 'La gente acostumbrada a verla en pantalla le pregunta por la calle si se ha marchado a vivir fuera de Cuba, a lo que ella responde que vive en el *inxilio*.'
2. Enrique Lihn, Chilean poet (1929-88). From review of *La Tirana* in the literary magazine *Apsi*, Santiago, IX, no. 137, February 1984): http://poetaenriquelihn.blogspot.com.es/2009/03/un-lenguaje-violento-y-chilensis-la.html
3. From interview with Osvaldo Bossi in online magazine *Boquita pintada*: http://blogs.lanacion.com.ar/boquitas-pintadas/arte-y-cultura/el-poeta-gay-que-adora-pecarae/
4. Ilse Guzmán and Carla Rodríguez, in *Herencia*, Vol. 19 (2), 2006: 79-88, who also write: 'By accepting other sexualities, language is reconstructed. It is for this reason that the reader of 'El ñatazo' is not only confronted by a series of images that they will try to decipher in vain, but also an obscure and grammatically confusing construction' http://revistas.ucr.ac.cr/index.php/herencia/article/viewFile/10024/9429
5. See, for example, Jenny Turner on *The Argonauts* (Graywolf, 2015) in *London Review of Books*, Vol. 37 No. 20, 22 October 2015, pp. 11-14, in which the reviewer discusses Nelson's radical, questioning, approach to gender.
6. Quotations from Javier Bello's article, 'Diana Bellessi: Inmóvil Transparente', University of Chile website: http://web.uchile.cl/publicaciones/cyber/19/jbello.html

Poema de la primera vez

Hay algo irrecuperable
en descubrir a un desconocido.
Ofrecerse ante la vista y el tacto
de quien hasta entonces
sólo nos ha tratado vestidos
entraña un acto de desprendimiento
poco común.
Si la ocasión permite
hacerlo sin vehemencia,
hay algo de paternal y fraterno
en desatar los cordones,
desajustar los broches
y bajar las cremalleras.
De este modo
las prendas van quedando en el suelo
como espigas segadas por el deseo.
Suele sobrevenir entonces
un instante en que la caja negra se abre
y retiene para siempre
un olor, un gesto, algún escorzo del cuerpo.
Luego vendrá lo de costumbre en estos casos:
las caricias, las precauciones, el delirio, el hastío,
el amor, la obsesión, las despedidas.
Cualquier cosa puede suceder
y llegar a borrarse.
Pero queda el tatuaje del instante
en que nos fue dado
robar el fuego
del aliento del desconocido.

John Galán Casanova (Colombia)

Poem of the First Time

There is something irretrievable
in discovering a stranger.
Offering oneself before the sight and touch
of one who, until that time,
we have only had dealings with in a clothed state
involves a rare act
of detachment.
If the occasion permits,
do it without fervour,
there is something paternal or fraternal
in untying laces,
releasing clasps
and unfastening zips.
In this fashion
articles of clothing settle on the floor
like ears of wheat reaped by desire.
And then, without warning, there is an instant
in which the black box opens
and retains for ever
a smell, an expression, some perspective of the body.
Afterwards will come the usual procession:
caresses, caution, delirium, boredom,
love, obsession, farewells.
Anything can happen,
and then be erased.
But the tattoo of the instant remains
in which we were allowed
to steal fire
from the breath of the stranger.

John Galán Casanova *(Colombia)*

Palabra de esquimal

Por ti dejaré la nieve y esquiaré en la arena
no escribiré grafittis sobre el hielo
tendré acento de occidente y ropas de verano
mis dientes no ablandarán otra piel que la tuya
mi olor se diluye en tu lavanda limpia
así como el esturión pierde el caviar perderé mi nombre
olvidaré el rito del iglú la mujer y la presa
miraré el deshielo como agua de mi sexo
no regalaré al extraño lo que es tuyo al final de la noche
quedaré en tu cama toreando al fuego
borraré de mi boca el cebo y el pescado
dejaré en libertad los perros del trineo
intentaré olvidar el exilio del hielo
invernaremos juntos mientras duela el invierno.
sobre el confin del iceberg   viajando en la isla blanca
sobreviven   una lágrima helada de mi madre
y el murmullo suplicante de tu padre
tal vez la amnesia sea lo mejor
aunque todo parezca cosa de otro mundo
cazaremos juntos;
palabra de esquimal.

Wendy Guerra (Cuba)

El regreso de Lolita

I

Yo soy Lolita
Así los Lobos esteparios
me desenreden
las trenzas con sus dientes,
y me lancen
caramelos de cianuro y goma.

Eskimo's Word

For you I will leave the snow and will ski in the sand
I will not write graffiti on the ice
I will put on a Western accent and wear summer clothes
my teeth will not soften anyone's skin but yours
my smell dissolves in your fresh lavender
just as the sturgeon loses its caviar I will lose my name
I will forget the ritual of the igloo the woman the catch
I will watch the thaw as though it were my sexual water
at the end of the night I will not give to the stranger what is yours
I will stay in your bed fighting the flames
I will wipe from my mouth both bait and fish
I will set free the sleigh dogs
I will try to forget exile from the ice
we will hibernate together while the winter hurts
on the edge of the iceberg travelling on the white island
they survive   my mother's frozen tear
and your father's imploring murmur
perhaps amnesia would be best
although everything seems like stuff of another world
we will hunt together:
eskimo's word.

Wendy Guerra (Cuba)

The Return of Lolita

I

I am Lolita.
Even if the wolves from the steppe
tear my braids
with their teeth,
and toss me
chewy cyanide sweets.

Intuí mi nombre aquel día del puerto
con los náufragos
¿recuerdas?.

Y aquel combate
con Vladimir, el implacable.
Sé que soy Lolita,
lo supe cuando me entregó
sus manos laceradas de escribirme.

II

Por eso cuando apareciste suplicante
a contarme tus temores,
te dejé tocarme,
morder mis brazos y rodillas,
te dejé mutilar entre mis piernas
los temores de Charlotte.

Sabía que tu vieja espada
cortaría una a una mis venas,
mis pupilas,
y me burlé cien veces
de tu estupidez de niño viejo
llorando entre mi vientre,
y cuando todos los náufragos del mundo
volvieron a mi puerto
a entregarme dádivas
que yo pagaba, con calostro y carne
tú saltaste tras mi sombra,
mientras yo huía,
mientras yo bailaba.

Por eso soy Lolita,
la nínfula de moteles y anagramas
que vuelve con la maleta al hombro
a retomar tras años el pasado.

Siomara España (*Ecuador*)

I realised my name that day at the harbour
with the people from the shipwreck.
Do you remember?

And that struggle
with the relentless Vladimir,
I know I'm Lolita.
I knew it when he offered up
his hands lacerated with writing me.

II

That is why when you appeared, pleading,
telling me your fears,
I let you touch me,
bite my arms and knees,
I let you mutilate Charlotte's fears
between my legs.

I knew that your old sword
would cut my veins one by one
and my pupils,
and a hundred times over
I mocked your ageing child's stupidity
crying within my womb,
and when all the shipwrecked of the world
came back to my harbour
to offer me gifts
that I paid for with colostrum and flesh
you leapt across my shadow
while I fled,
while I danced.

That's why I'm Lolita
nymphet of motels and anagrams
who returns, bag on my shoulder
to repossess the past from across the years.

Siomara España (Ecuador)

de *Hija de perra*

Afuera daba vueltas un farol rojo y el letrero se caía a pedazos como de boite de mala muerte, como si fuésemos a estrellarnos contra la muerte, el hombre sacó una pequeña llave. Ladraban los perros, y el hombre nos condujo hasta un cuartucho que no volveríamos a ver, encendimos la TV y unos porros, luego me fumé un cigarro detrás de otro, uno detrás de otro y te contemplé hablar y hablamos del cuartucho, de la cojera del hombre, nuestra propia cojera, de la noche que corría con una prisa extraña, las nubes pasaban rápidas, azulosas, violáceas, como golpes de la vida, como si nos fuésemos a golpear contra la vida, el hombre trajo dos cafés que se enfriaron sobre el velador, en un rincón del cuarto quedaban los restos de una fiesta que otros dejaron, qué ganas de tomarme un trago, te dije, tú te acercaste lentamente, al contrario de las nubes, al contrario de la noche que corría aprisa, al contrario de los perros que no dejaban de ladrar, de vez en cuando se callaban, y se callaban hasta que las luces de un automóvil se estrellaban contra los vidrios y encendían el cuartucho que dejaba ver tu cuerpo y luego venían las sombras que te cubrían, lejos de casa, tan lejos de casa y en la radio con las pilas medio muertas la Janis cantaba bye, bye, baby.

Malú Urriola (Chile)

La Tirana

(Me sacaron por la cara)

Yo, La Tirana, rica y famosa
la Greta Garbo del cine chileno
pero muy culta y calentona, que comienzo
a decaer, que se me va la cabeza
cada vez que me pongo a hablar
y hacer recuerdos de mis polvos con Velázquez.

from *Bitch's Daughter*

Outside a red light was swinging and the sign fell apart like the sign of a deadbeat nightclub, as if we were crashing into death, the man took out a small key. Dogs were barking and the man drove us to a hovel we would never see again, we switched the TV on and lit up a few spliffs, later I smoked one cigarette after another and I watched you speaking, and we spoke about the hovel, about the man's lameness, about our own lameness, of the night as it hurried along with a strange urgency, the clouds were passing swiftly, bluish, violet, like life's blows, as if we were about to knock against life, the man brought two coffees that turned cold on the bedside table, in a corner of the room were the remains of a party that others left behind, what I'd give for a drink, I said to you, you came over to me slowly, unlike the clouds, unlike the night that hurried along swiftly, unlike the dogs that wouldn't stop barking, once in a while they quietened down, and they quietened down until a car's headlamps slammed against the window panes and lit up the hovel allowing your body to be made visible and then the shadows came that covered you, far from home, so far from home and on the radio with dying batteries Janis sang bye bye baby.

Malú Urriola (Chile)

The Tyrantess

(They recognised my face)

I, The Tyrantess, rich and famous
the Greta Garbo of Chilean cinema
but very refined and horny, beginning
to look the worse for wear, whose head spins
whenever I begin to talk
and reminisce about my shags with Velásquez.

Ya no lo hago tan bien como lo hacía antes
Antes, todas las noches y a todo trapo
Ahora no.
Ahora suelo a veces entrar a una Iglesia
cuando no hay nadie
porque me gusta la luz que dan ciertas velas
la luz que le dan a mis pechugas
cuando estoy rezando.
Y es verdad, mi vida es terrible
Mi vida es una inmoralidad
Y si bien vengo de una familia muy conocida
Y si es cierto que me sacaron por la cara
y que los que están afuera me destrozarán
Aún soy la vieja que se los tiró a todos
Aún soy de una ordinariez feroz.

Diego Maquiera (Chile)

de 'Delicias de la noche'

V

Viví así una temporada de cruda actividad
hasta que una crisis de nervios me llevó
al manicomio; allí, experimenté, con los
locos, torturas más sutiles y crueles. Sin
embargo, no he logrado aplacar mi perversidad
y ahora he llegado a la
urbe de siniestros símbolos que me acoge
como a un espectro más.

Edwin Madrid (Ecuador)

I don't do it as well as I used to before
Before, it was every night and at full throttle
Not now.
Now it's more usual for me to go into a church
when there's no one there
because I like the light that certain candles cast
the light that they cast on my tits
when I'm praying.
And it's true, my life is terrible
My life is immoral
And even though I come from a very well known family
And even though they recognised my face
and those who are outside will destroy me
Still I am the old woman who screwed them all
Still I am of a ferocious vulgarity.

Diego Maquiera (Chile)

from 'Pleasures of the Night'

V

I pursued my wild ways like that, for a spell,
until a nervous breakdown led me
to the madhouse: there, alongside the crazy people,
I underwent more cruel and subtle tortures. However,
I have not succeeded in placating my perversities
and now I have come to
the city of sinister symbols, that welcomes me
just like any other ghost.

Edwin Madrid (Ecuador)

Pequeña canción realista

Las manos toman, las manos dejan
caer cosas, para que otras manos
las tomen. En el vago aire pálido,
las cosas se desplazan bajo el imperio
de los dedos, la suave curvatura de las palmas;
ya que impotentes y quietas las cosas
sienten las cadenas del mundo y envejecen
cuando se les olvida. Eso es todo.
En los pasillos llenos de estatuas
marmóreas, bajo la fe incorruptible
de las leyes, los pobres hombres
viejos y encorvados suponen que hay
fantasmas, y que las cosas andan, y que acatan
las manos misteriosas órdenes. Y que todo
se mueve según el leve vals
que desde los parlantes de los edificios
canta, suave. Pero del lado de acá,
en que la primavera aún no detiene
el viento helado, y ese par de ebrios
se aprestan a morir a cuchilladas
apenas salgan del bar, las manos,
por inercia, hastiadas toman cosas,
las dejan caer, y otras manos las toman,
para alguna vez dejarlas caer
también. Llega el momento en que caen
las manos; y son cosas. Son tomadas,
y en un rincón oscuro, alguien hace
quizás qué cosas con ellas.

Carlos Henrickson (Chile)

Little Realist Song

Hands take things, let things
fall, so that other hands
take them. In the vague feeble air,
things are moved about beneath the empire
of the fingers, the smooth curvature of the palm;
because impotent and silent things
feel the chains of the world and grow old
when they are forgotten. That's all.
In the corridors filled with marble
statues, beneath the incorruptible faith
of the law, poor and bowed
old men suppose that there are
ghosts, and that things go on, and that the hands
comply with mysterious orders. And that everything
moves according to the gentle waltz
playing softly from the buildings'
loudspeakers. But on this side,
where the spring still does not restrain
the icy wind, and that pair of drunks
prepare for death by stabbing
as soon as they leave the bar, the hands,
out of habit, worn out, take things,
let things fall, and other hands take them,
so that for once they drop
also. The moment arrives in which the hands
fall; and they are things. They are taken,
and in a dark corner, someone makes
who know what things with them.

Carlos Henrickson (Chile)

Fragmentos de *Tres*

Un hombre que ama a un hombre
que ama una mujer, está acorralado;
pende en lo alto como una hora
bella e inútil; se a da a sí mismo
en un extravagante vacío, toca
el vacío con los dedos.

★

Sublime es el reposo de quien
dejó caer el peso de un terrible deseo
sobre el más fuerte; ese
que tuerce el curso de los ríos
y hace del agua estancada una fuente
donde él se detendrá, se detendrá
una sola, una sola vez.

★

Cuando mi amado entra
al cuerpo de ella, es a mí
a quien tan hondamente
llega; me quita la respiración,
arrasa y mira a los ojos.
Pero cuando por mi propia
carne él entra, es a ella
a quien toca: desnuda, la puedo
sentir del otro lado, suspirar.

★

Estás fuera de mí, por eso
sufro. Tenés un rostro, un cuerpo:
él lo besa todas las noches ¿qué hacer
para recuperarte? Él no hace nada,
te guarda para sí, es tan mezquino
su amor . . .

Fragments from *Three*

A man who loves a man
who loves a woman is trapped;
he hangs aloft like a beautiful
and useless presence; he gives of himself
in an extravagant emptiness, touches
emptiness with his fingers.

⋆

Sublime the repose of he who
lets the weight of a terrible desire
fall on the stronger one; he
who twists the course of rivers
and makes of stagnant water a fountain
where he pauses, pauses
once and once only.

⋆

When my beloved enters
her body, it is me to whom
he most deeply comes;
my breath struck from me,
I am laid waste, he looks in my eyes.
But when he enters my own
flesh, it is she he touches;
naked, I can feel her
on the other side, sighing.

⋆

You are outside me, for this
I suffer. You have a face, a body:
he kisses it every night. What can I do
to retrieve you? He does nothing,
keeps you for himself, so miserly
his love . . .

★

Dice que solamente a mí
él ama, y que mi espíritu lo rodea
como una cuerda, por eso dice,
él quiere aventurarse, lejos . . .
Nunca estuvo más lejos de su cuerpo
como ahora que lo tiene.

★

Cuando él te ve, te mira a lo hondo,
me ve a mí, se olvida. Olvido
es una manera de ver también,
por lo otro. Quien mira a una mujer
¿se olvida de sí, o se acuerda?

Osvaldo Bossi *(Argentina)*

Imagen de la desconocida

a partir de un poema de Juan Carlos Bautista

Un zapato rojo de tacón alto

que es, en sí mismo,
el fantasma de su par ausente.

Un zapato perdido a mitad de la noche,
perdido, entre un paso
y otro, a mitad de la calle.

Un zapato del que se puede deducir una mujer
súbitamente coja
y probablemente trágica.

★

He says that he loves
only me, and that my spirit encircles him
like a rope, that's why, he says,
he wants to venture far . . .
He never was so far from his body
as now, when he has it.

★

When he sees you, he looks deeply,
seeing me, he forgets. Forgetting
is a way of seeing also,
by means of the other. Who looks at a woman;
does he forget himself, or remember?

Osvaldo Bossi *(Argentina)*

Image of the Unknown Woman

after a poem by Juan Carlos Bautista

A red high-heeled shoe

which is, of itself,
the ghost of its absent pair.

A shoe lost in the middle of the night,
lost, between one step
and the next, in the middle of the street.

A shoe from which may be deduced a woman
suddenly limping
and probably tragic.

Más que un zapato: una pista para resolver un crimen.

Un zapato que es una pregunta
cuya respuesta es otro zapato.

Luis Felipe Fabre (México)

Bares

Vivir es alegre – los he oído reír cada vez
más fuerte – y seguían cada vez más alegres –
la noche se apiada de mí porque no siento
vergüenza.
Y una más pide el más ronco – que traga sin ser
procaz – porque es suave y delicado – adora la
botella como una nalga de mujer –
a grandes sorbos.
Aquél sí es de los peligrosos: roba mata miente
y es astuto – pero cuando pasa próximo a mi mesa
sus grandes ojos de arañas sedosas se deslizan
como un tigre en mi regazo – Por fin siento
que he viajado –

Carmen Ollé (Perú)

More than a shoe: a clue towards resolving a crime.

A shoe that is a question
whose answer is another shoe.

Luis Felipe Fabre (Mexico)

Bars

To live is a joy – I've heard them laugh louder
and louder – and they carried on even happier –
the night takes pity on me because I feel no
shame.
And another, asks the most raucous one– who drinks without
becoming
lewd– because he's smooth and subtle – loves
the bottle like a woman's thigh –
in great gulps.
Yes, that other one is dangerous: he robs kills lies
and he's clever – but when he next goes past my table
his great silky spider eyes slide
like a tiger's to my lap – At last I feel
as if I've travelled –

Carmen Ollé (Peru)

Despertarte

Despertarte a mitad de la noche
y ver en el otro lado de tu cama
a tu mujer llorando
es una experiencia importante.
Quiere decir, entre otras cosas,
que mientras paseabas por los cuartos
iluminados de tu cerebro
algo se estaba gestando cerca tuyo.
Un error con el cual mantenés
una particular relación de intimidad.
Porque aunque no firmemos nada,
ni corramos apurados bajo la lluvia de arroz
pensamos que es para toda la vida
y así seguimos.
Botes, que durante la noche,
quedan amarrados al muelle,
golpeándose entre sí,
según el viento.

Fabián Casas (Argentina)

All the Things You Are

Pagué todas tus cuentas, regué todas tus plantas,
las llaves que pediste ya las hice.
Después busqué la forma de tus pies en los zapatos,
y me senté en el borde de tu cama
a ver por la ventana lo que ves
cuando volvés a casa
sola.

Jorge Fondebrider (Argentina)

To Awaken

To awaken in the middle of the night
and see on the other side of the bed
your woman crying
is an important experience.
It means, among other things
that while you were passing through
the lighted rooms of your mind
something was gestating beside you.
A mistake with which you maintain
a particular intimacy.
Because even if we don't sign anything
nor run hurriedly beneath a rain of rice
we think that it's for life,
and so we carry on.
Boats, which during the night
stay fastened to the quay
bumping against each another,
according to the wind.

Fabián Casas (Argentina)

All the things you are

I paid all your bills, watered your plants,
had the keys you asked for cut.
Afterwards I sought out your feet's contours in your shoes,
and sat on the edge of your bed
to see through the window the things that you see
when you come home
alone.

Jorge Fondebrider (Argentina)

De cómo el amor se vuelve recuerdo del amor

Difícil es luchar con el corazón.
y es el alma la que debe
pagar sus deseos.
          Heráclito de Efeso: Fragmento 85.

Entre dos tazas de té
Hablo en pasado de la mujer que quiero.
Hago de ella un rastro en la conversación.
No importa qué profunda sea su huella.
El resultado es el mismo:
Ella era, ella hizo, ella dijo, ella fue.

Jorge Fondebrider (Argentina)

Crucero ecuatorial

VII

Comimos pescado
y un racimo de mangos dulces, anaranjados.
Después apareció el muchacho esbelto
parecido a un novio que tuve a los diecisiete años.
Esa noche hicimos el amor,
mientras me hablaba de los calamares lentos
rosados
que nadan juntos
en la profundidad dorada del mar Caribe.
Allí nos hicimos el amor.
Era biólogo marino y temía,
me parece, perder dignidad, estatus.
Se escabulló del dormitorio temprano
y estaba frío después del desayuno. No quiso
fumar mariguana con nuestro amigo negro

How love becomes a memory of love

It is difficult to fight with the heart,
and it is the soul that must pay
for its desires.
             Heraclitus of Ephesus: Fragment 85.

Between two cups of tea
I speak in the past tense of the woman I love.
I lay down a trace of her in the conversation.
It doesn't matter how deep that trace might be.
The result is the same:
She was, she did, she said, she went.

Jorge Fondebrider (Argentina)

Equatorial Cruise

VII

We ate fish
and a few sweet orange mangoes.
Afterwards the slim boy appeared
he looked like a boyfriend I had at seventeen.
That night we made love,
while he talked to me about slow pink
squid
that swim together
in the golden depths of the Caribbean.
There too we made love.
He was a marine biologist and he was afraid
– it seemed to me – of losing dignity, status.
He slipped out of the bedroom early
and was cold towards me after breakfast. He didn't want
to smoke marijuana with our black friend

que venía de Tanzania. Lo perdí alegremente,
sin nostalgias. Cuando cruzamos las salinas
yendo a Santa Marta desde Río Hacha,
y vi las espaldas, las cabezas envueltas
de los peones guajiros paleando sal a media mañana,
se me hizo un nudo en el pecho,
y en él guardé, como quien lo hace en un pañuelo,
la camiseta colorada del gigante negro,
los calamares flotando en la oscuridad dorada.

Diana Bellessi (Argentina)

El ñatazo

Oh Gsik!

Ella ama a varios hombres
que son eso y más.
Él más provoca reacciones encontradas en todos,
algunos se sienten halagados con la observación
uno se niega totalmente a aceptarlo.
Ella ama a las mujeres escondidas en cuerpos masculinos,
por eso se siente lesbiano,
como también le gustan los hombres, se siente homosexual,
y, como es un hombre en el cuerpo equivocado
se siente lo que llaman transexual y bisexual.
Pero es feliz en el cuerpo femenino porque como en el fondo se
siente 'hombre',
le gustan las mujeres,
y se disfruta a sí mismo sintiéndose Sí Misma,
Sí Misma se ama toda.

Piensa:
Él es una aguja cosida a la lengua, el manjar de una cena para dos.
Él entra y sale sin entrar, sale y entra sin entrar…
y sin entrar – entra.

from Tanzania. I lost him cheerfully,
without regret. When we crossed the salt flats
on the way to Santa Marta from Río Hacha,
and I saw the backs and covered heads
of labourers shovelling salt at midday,
it gave me a knot in my chest,
and I kept it there, as one keeps things in a handkerchief,
the red shirt of the giant black man,
the squid floating in the golden darkness.

Diana Bellessi (Argentina)

Snort

Oh Gsik!

She loves a number of men
who are that and more.
He, meanwhile, provokes contradictory reactions in everyone,
some feel flattered by the observation,
one refuses utterly to accept it.
She loves women hidden in masculine bodies,
therefore feels like a male lesbian,
and since she also likes men, she feels homosexual,
and since she is a man in the wrong body,
feels what is called transsexual and bisexual.
But she is happy in her female body because since in essence
she feels herself to be a 'man',
she likes women,
and enjoys himself being Her Self.
Her Self loves herself completely.

She thinks:
He is a needle sewn to the tongue, the delight of a dinner for two.
He enters and withdraws without entering, withdraws and enters
without entering . . . and without entering – enters.

Él acalora sin calor.
Él duele y desaparece.
Y entonces llega Ella.
Sí Misma baila con Ella espalda con espalda
y pantorrilla con pantorrilla.
Ellas se miran y enloquecen.
Él sonríe.

Tania Montenegro (Nicaragua)

La herida

A scar remembers the wound.
                              Mark Strand

La cicatriz
            se acuerda de la herida, le habla
muy despacio. Soy flor, le dice
hace años plantaste una palabra

que alguien quiso escuchar. Pero te fuiste.

Y me dejaste hablando sola.

Eduardo Chirinos (Perú)

Por fortuna la luna

me distingue.
Mas no puedo olvidar a aquel soldado
de miembro enorme y velludo
que lo llevaba descubierto

He arouses heat without heat.
He hurts and vanishes.
And then She arrives.
Her Self dances with Her back to back
and calf to calf.
She and Her Self look at each other, go crazy.
He smiles.

Tania Montenegro (Nicaragua)

The wound

A scar remembers the wound.
                            Mark Strand

The scar
           remembers the wound, speaks to it
very slowly. I am a flower, it says
years ago you planted a word

that someone wanted to hear. But you went away.

And left me talking to myself.

Eduardo Chirinos (Peru)

Luckily the moon

honours me.
But I cannot forget that soldier
with his enormous hairy member
which he openly displayed.

Celebro en mi habitación
las fiestas en Lesbos a la luz de la luna
acompañada de un hueso de porcelana roja
largo suavísimo y limpio
que activa mis vías nerviosas
sin lastimar mi virginidad.

Aleyda Quevedo Rojas (Ecuador)

Mirándola dormir

todo hombre es su propio sol
en la media noche del hastío
cuando los grillos chillan
como fuego endemoniado
y las estrellas
están más distantes que nunca

bajo la luz del aguardiente
todo hombre
         apaga
la lumbre interior de la nada
mientras mira dormir
a la mujer que le cedió el destino
no la que le inventó la ilusión
todo hombre
que como yo se emborracha
junto a la mujer
que nos huye en sueños
evade la necesidad del otro
hace de su fracaso
un tintineo abstracto
y se bebe en silencio su perdición

Osvaldo Sauma (Costa Rica)

In my room I celebrate
the festivals of Lesbos by moonlight,
assisted by a bone of red china,
long, clean and very smooth
which stimulates the nerve tracts
without harming my virginity.

Aleyda Quevedo Rojas (Ecuador)

Watching her sleep

every man is his own sun
in tedium's midnight
when the crickets shriek
like fire possessed
and the stars
are more distant than ever

under the light of strong liquor
every man
        snuffs out
the inner glow of nothingness
while he watches the woman sleep
who conceded to him her destiny
sleeping
not the one who invented the illusion
every man
who, like me, gets drunk
at the side of the woman
who flees us in dreams
avoids the need for the other
makes of his failure
an abstract tinkling
and drinks his perdition in silence

Osvaldo Sauma (Costa Rica)

Odiseo

No sé adónde voy
ni de dónde vengo
ni a qué viene esto
si pienso sólo en una mujer parada
en una calle
la vida es simple
si sólo se piensa en una mujer parada
en una calle
yo pienso en una mujer parada
en una calle
no pienso adónde va ella
ni de dónde viene
ni a qué vienen estas preguntas
no se debe preguntar adónde va ella
ni de dónde viene
ni a qué viene esto o lo otro
la vida es simple
si sólo se piensa en una mujer
parada en una calle

Miguel Ildefonso (Perú)

Peligro de extinción

Un insecto camina en la tensión del té
despacio
teje y comienza a rodearnos:
Peligro de Extinción

Coinciden los colores
la rapidez del vuelo
y su fugaz azul
vidrio soplado

Odysseus

I don't know where I'm going
nor from where I come
nor what this amounts to
if I think only of a woman standing
in a street
life is simple
if you only think of a woman standing
in a street
I think of a woman standing
in a street
I don't think about where she is going
nor from where she comes
nor what these questions amount to
you shouldn't ask where she is going
nor from where she comes
nor what this or that amounts to
life is simple
if only one thinks of a woman
standing in a street

Miguel Ildefonso (Peru)

Danger of extinction

An insect walks on the surface of the tea
slowly
weaves about and begins to surround us
Danger of Extinction

The colours match
the swiftness of flight
and its fleeting blue
blown glass

(Habrá que revisar este sistema de creencias
la fragilidad del argumento
la mercantilización de los sueños)

Densidad
que reconoce indicios en lo leve
Partículas de Prácticas Infantiles

El cuerpo (voraz)
necesita volver cada tanto a ese lugar de frutas:
       el enrojecimiento o el temblor de las manos, por ejemplo

Es el ritmo el que ha ido envejeciendo
[los ojos y narices agotados
llorosos por la luz, o por la cercanía de una sustancia tóxica]

Lo inaceptable es perder los sentidos
—deja que entre el sol aquí, que nos caliente el cuarto.

Ana Franco *(México)*

Como Perceval

(Chrétien de Troyes)

Una gota de sangre en la nieve
es la imagen que amo
por sobre todas las otras.

Yo me desnudo allí,
me invento,
ignorando con elegancia fingida
todo lo que no es esa violencia.

Como la sonrisa cruel e innecesaria
que se le brinda a un adversario derrotado

(We will have to revise this system of beliefs
the fragility of the argument
the commercialization of dreams)

Density
recognises signs in all that is light
Particles of Infantile Practices

The body (voracious)
needs to return every so often to that fruitful place:
    blushing or trembling of the hands, for example

It is rhythm that has been ageing
[eyes and nose exhausted
tearful due to light, or the proximity of a toxic substance]

Unacceptable for the senses to vanish
– let the sun in here, so that the room warms us.

***Ana Franco** (Mexico)*

Like Percival

(Chrétien de Troyes)

A drop of blood in the snow
is the image I love
above all others.

I undress there,
I invent myself,
disregarding, with feigned elegance,
everything apart from that violence.

Like the cruel and unnecessary smile
afforded a defeated enemy

o como cuando vienes con la boca
todavía húmeda
y yo te miro pasar con desapego.

La gota de sangre en la nieve
es como lo que espero
acodada en la lividez de este silencio.

Alicia Torres (Venezuela)

Alimento

Revisamos nuestros buzones
esperando siempre la última carta,
vivimos para recibir.

Somos como pájaros que guardan las alas
mientras sus corazones laten
en pechos calientes.

– Yo cargo tus palabras en la cartera
como una limosna extra –.

No podemos dormir,
soñamos con anillos en cada dedo,
que mides mi torso con tus manos
y descubres la piel
antes de que se marchen los invitados.

Catalina González Restrepo (Colombia)

or like when you come with your mouth
still moist
and I, detached, watch you pass by.

The drop of blood in the snow
resembles the thing I wait for
leaning out across this pallid silence.

Alicia Torres *(Venezuela)*

Nourishment

We check our mailboxes
always hoping for the latest letter,
we live to receive.

We are like birds that keep their wings folded
while their hearts beat
in hot chests.

– I carry your words in my purse
like an extra gift of alms –.

We cannot sleep,
we dream of rings on every finger,
you measure my torso with your hands
and uncover my skin
before the guests leave.

Catalina González Restrepo *(Colombia)*

Muchacho de corazón amarillo

me imaginas durmiendo entre tus cartas
             recordando la lujuriosa ruta
                de nuestros orgasmos
                desnudo y prendido de tu cuello
       haciéndote revelaciones
       para que me digas que crees en la felicidad
si estoy atado a tu cuerpo
              nutriéndome de tus pechos
                    como rómulo y remo
muchas gracias de veras
           pero ya no soy el muchacho de corazón amarillo
mirando confundido la sombra
           de tus nalgas en las fiestas
esa frágil marioneta
          que se movía a medianoche por la cocina
                llevándote café en la tetera blanca
ni siquiera soy el vagabundo
          que te escribía poemas
                 en las puertas de los baños públicos
nunca más seré
una patata frita en la sartén de mi suegra
                aunque para ella no deje de ser el ebrio
atropellado por la húmeda luz de un camión
               ahora estoy sufriendo
la magnificencia de la gracia del señor
                 vivo al margen
                         a la orilla de tu sed
en Aqiev
esa región invisible de la muerte
             donde apolo y afrodita
             son perfectamente humanos
donde la lluvia se quiebra en los siete colores del sol
y las mujeres se tienden en las riberas
              como si nunca hubieran pertenecido
                  a estas cuevas o avenidas.

Edwin Madrid *(Ecuador)*

Boy with a yellow heart

you imagine me sleeping amidst your letters
        remembering the luxurious pathway
           of our orgasms
      naked and clinging to your neck
    disclosing revelations
    for you to tell me that you believe in happiness
if I am attached to your body
        nurturing myself on your breasts
           like romulus and remus
I thank you, truly,
     but now I am not the boy with a yellow heart
looking confusedly at the shadow
    of your buttocks at parties
that fragile puppet
    who moved around the kitchen at midnight
        bringing you coffee in the white teapot
I'm not even the vagabond
    who was writing you poems
        on the doors of the public baths
no more will I be
a fried potato in the skillet of my mother-in-law
      even though for her I will remain the drunk
run down by the damp light of a lorry
    now I am suffering
the magnificence of the lord's grace
         I live on the margins
            on the shore of your thirst
in Aqiev
that invisible region of death
      where apollo and aphrodite
      are perfectly human
where the rain breaks in the seven colours of the sun
and women lie down on the riverbanks
      as if nothing had belonged
      to these caves or avenues.

Edwin Madrid (Ecuador)

Porto dos Ossos

La angustia del amor te aprieta la garganta
como si nunca más fueras a ser amado.
Apollinaire

¿Pero cómo se hará de noche si la sombra
no sabe qué hacer contra el pulido
azul de la bahía?
Los cascos de los barcos ya están negros
y el cielo rayado de mástiles negros
y el agua todavía resplandece.
En el bar, siluetas
que la tarde cortó de su papel plateado
toman whisky y murmuran
en media docena de lenguas. Y mi botella
se va poniendo igual a todas las botellas;
ya no es posible leer las etiquetas.
¿Pero cómo se hará de noche
si la noche vacila
ante el escudo azul de la bahía?
Alguien tal vez venga nadando
de los barcos, y por la estela negra
que dejen sus brazadas invisibles
entre la noche al mar. Entonces sí,
antes que llegue el nadador
será de noche y se habrá abierto
la mano que en un puño mi corazón tenía.

Daniel Samoilovich *(Argentina)*

Porto Dos Ossos

Love's anguish grabs your throat
as though you were never to be loved again.
Apollinaire

But how will night fall if the shadow
does not know how to oppose the polished
blue of the bay?
The hulls of boats are already black
and the sky streaked with black masts
and the water still shimmers.
In the bar, silhouettes
that the evening cut from its silver paper
drink whisky and murmur
in half a dozen languages. And my bottle
becomes the same as all bottles;
it is no longer possible to read their labels.
But how will night fall
if it hesitates
before the blue shield of the bay?
Perhaps someone might come swimming
from the boats, and through the black wake
left by his invisible strokes
night may enter the sea. Then, yes,
before the swimmer arrives
it will be night, and the hand that held
my heart in its grip will have opened.

Daniel Samoilovich *(Argentina)*

Mi corazón era un hotel

mi corazón era un hotel
vestido de fiesta
los huéspedes se iban sin pagar
a los portazos

es cierto
a veces
una mujer lloró en sus ventanas
hasta cansarse

es cierto
yo era el que lustraba los zapatos

es cierto
hubo temporadas malas
problemas de humedad
palmeras muertas

todo eso es cierto
también la luna
y el loco que cantaba

mi corazón era un hotel
ahora parece una casa

una casita blanca.

Alejandro Schmidt (Argentina)

My heart was a hotel

My heart was a hotel
dressed up for a party
the guests would leave without paying
and slam the door

it's true
at times
a woman tired herself out
crying at the window

it's true
I was the one who polished the shoes

it's true
there were bad spells
problems of humidity
dead palm trees

all of this is true
also the moon
and the singing madman

my heart was a hotel
now it resembles a house

a little white house

Alejandro Schmidt (Argentina)

Razón de todas las cosas

(Los amantes antes y después)

De tal manera imaginaria, las cosas sucedían
para que todo fuera deshora en lo desusado:
la racha entrometida del dedo en el deshabillé,
las alabanzas a la blusa azul al soltarla hasta el
desacato de desabotonar de las polainas a las
bragas en remedo de ilusiones todo lo demás,
y así, la castidad a su holocausto, él y el final.
Aposento de cuanto es cuando a la vida huía
y a los labios venía a darse por vencido, pero
igual, no. Nadie en el hado más de la cuenta.
El cuerpo importa a partir del arte por detrás.
Una idea se da, puede ser donde menos nace.
Todo nombra, la piel a solas cede al resultado.
Está la realidad para decir adiós hace un rato.
En la ducha los afeites hermosean el enredo
y regresa el agua a la noche donde se bañan.
El amor, es la única imposibilidad necesaria.

Eduardo Espina *(Uruguay)*

Reason for All Things

(the lovers before and after)

In just such an imaginary way, things were happening
so that everything would be untimely in the unusual:
the meddler streak of the finger in the *déshabillé*,
praises for the blue blouse as it is being undone even the
disrespect in unbuttoning from spats to
knickers in imitation of illusions all the rest,
and so, chastity to its holocaust, he and the ending.
Lodging of all that is when he fled life
and searched the lips to surrender, but
no. No one in destiny for longer than necessary.
The body matters, with the backing of art.
An idea offers itself, it could be where it is least born.
Everything denominates, the skin alone gives in to the outcome.
Reality is there to say goodbye a while ago.
In the shower care gives beauty to the tangle
and the water returns to the night where they bathe.
Love, it's the only necessary impossibility.

Eduardo Espina *(Uruguay)*

Poema de la última vez

No hay más preguntas.
El deseo es más bien
el recuerdo del deseo
rodando en cámara lenta.
El sudor es el llanto indiscreto
de la despedida.
La lengua murmura voces de aliento,
suaves caricias para limar
las últimas asperezas.
Los amantes se abrazan
como hermanos siameses
antes de la separación de los cuerpos,
antes de arduos días de convalecencia
en que se intentará establecer
el número preciso de ausencias.
No tiene que ser la última vez.
Pero es como si lo fuera.

John Galán Casanova (Colombia)

Poem of the Last Time

There are no more questions.
Desire has now become
the memory of desire
tumbling in slow motion.
Sweat is the indiscreet weeping
of farewell.
The tongue murmurs words of encouragement,
soft caresses to smooth over
the final bitterness.
The lovers embrace
like Siamese twins
before their bodies' separation,
before the difficult days of convalescence
in which attempts will be made
to establish the precise number of absences.
It doesn't have to be the last time.
But it's as if it were.

John Galán Casanova (Colombia)

Introduction to Part 6: 'What becomes of us?'

The area addressed in this final selection made for difficult reading during the preparation of the anthology. The resulting poems are often hard to bear, and might suggest an intentional singling out of the worst elements in the human condition. This was not the case, nor was the question 'What becomes of us?' intended to suggest that 'conflict, sickness, violence and death' constitute (apart from the last of these) an unavoidable ending to existence. However, many of the strongest poems did reflect the proposition that, if the history of the twenty-first century thus far is anything to go by, the world still contains much that is nasty and brutish, and many lives remain short.

It is not by chance, therefore, that this section is dominated by Mexican poets. Violent death has become a terrifyingly familiar feature of everyday life for countless Mexicans since the government's declaration of war on the cartels by President Felipe Calderón in 2006. But, as readers of Roberto Bolaño's novel *2666* will know, Mexico was already famous during the 1990s for its so-called 'femicides'; the rape, murder and disappearance of hundreds of female factory workers in and around the northern city of Juárez. That murder and misogyny are inseparably associated in Mexico is of concern to at least two of the poets here: Maria Rivera, whose long eulogy for her country's dead opens Part 6, 1 and Claudia Hernández de Valle-Arizpe, whose 'I kill out of rage' – the penultimate poem – adopts the voice of an assassin, reciting a list of random, barbaric 'reasons' for random, barbaric murder.

A *Tzompantli* is a wall of skulls, constructed on a scaffold of poles, through which human heads are placed after holes have been made in them. These extraordinary objects are associated with the cultures of Mesoamerica from around 600 AD up until the time of the Spanish conquest. Perhaps the most famous example is in the museum of the Templo Mayor, built upon the ruins of the old Aztec capital's principal religious centre, sacked by Cortés in 1521. The *Tzompantli* has currency in today's Mexico also: victims of narco-violence are frequently decapitated, their heads exposed in public places. In Luis Felipe Fabre's poem 'Xochicuicatl' (p321), the poet mimics the physical structure of the *Tzompantli* both through sonic repetition and by contriving to build a small 'wall of skulls' in the second stanza: 'one skull next to another skull next to another skull / on top of / another skull next to another skull . . .' and so on. Fabre's other poem in Part 6, 'Infomercial' (p345) ironises the marketing of cleaning materials to an imaginary consumer whose blood-spattered home has her 'scrubbing night and day'.

Staying in Mexico, the speaker in Julián Herbert's poem 'Dark' (p331) sleeps anxiously, with his arm in the crack between two beds, to avoid his infant son from slipping and hurting his head on the floor, in acknowledgment of the poet Javier Sicilia, who lost his own son through a crack into the terrible chasm of corruption and violence.[3]

The Argentinian Beatriz Vignoli's poems are like sharp stabs to the conscience. And the many drafts it took to arrive at this version of 'The War of the Idiots' (p321) were a perfect illustration of Susan Bassnett's comment (see Preface) that apparently simple poems are often the hardest to translate. In the poem, the collective 'we' is responsible for the act of dynamiting the bridge that gave access to collective memory (the 'bridge over the river of forgetting'). No wonder, then, that history repeats itself.

Illness – physical and mental – and the suffering it causes, is also the topic of poems in Part 6. The Bolivian Mónica Velásquez, with 'Seven ways of talking about pain' (p324) offers a type of 'curse poem', addressed to a recipient of the same name as the poet, and promising that: 'Today, Mónica, I'd like to make you ill for a long time, mortally ill'; while the Costa Rican poet Luis Chaves, in his 'Free translation of an unpublished piece by Chan Marshall' (p335) uses the image of pulling up ivy by the root as a backcloth or or 'shadow story' to the pained and painstaking account of his sixteen year old subject's mortal illness.

Two different responses to the dictatorships in Chile and Argentina during the 1970s-80s are offered by Leonardo Sanhueza and Irene Gruss.[4] The title of Sanhueza's poem, 'Fist' (pxxx), refers to the iron fist emblem used by the Chilean secret police, the DINA, under Pinochet's dictatorship. The protagonist, we can reasonably propose (although the poem is far too subtle to do so) is a retired DINA agent, for whom, unlike his victims, 'the evenings / stretch out pleasantly . . . with a rosy sun over the mountains.' This meditation on a peaceful retirement strikes a particularly malignant note with the line 'a hand fallen to one side, as motionless / as a sack of wet sand'. Speculation over whether justice will ever be done is sustained by the image of '(t)he bug climbing the rose', which 'has not yet reached the thorns.' Meanwhile Irene Gruss's speaker in 'And in the meantime' (pxxx) confesses that 'I was washing clothes / while many people / disappeared'. Her retrospective discomfort and guilt – an 'unawareness' of what was going on, such as many middle class Argentinians would later admit to – is poignantly evoked in the imagery: 'I was rocking the cradle, / singing, / and the shutters dark.'

Like much of his work, the quartet of poems by Raúl Zurita is haunted by the Chilean dictatorship (p351-355). Here, in the 'middle of the desert', a ship lies stranded on the rocks. This powerful image of abandonment is compounded by the repetition of certain motifs: the 'screaming' rocks; plastic flowers placed before the ship as a memorial to the disappeared; the 'rising breakers' of stones that surround the ship's rusting hull; and the figure of Mireya, who 'says she is the Mother of Chile', the mother of this ship that was once a ship of the living, 'but now ploughs through the sea of rocks / with her dead children.'

Responses to the process of dying, and to death itself are offered in poems by Jacqueline Goldberg (p335) and Jorge Fondebrider (p349), while the afterlife of the dead is explored variously by Osvaldo Hernandez (p323) and Ramón Cote (p329), the last with a poignant reminder 'that it takes only a minor carelessness for time / to disperse everything that solitude and love have brought together.'

The anthology closes with 'Sobbing', by the Mexican Fabio Morábito (p359), the poem's narrator arriving late at a funeral, in order to incite a great weeping – 'the weeping of a returning tide' – so that the mourners 'forget about their dead / or remember them with greater clarity'. Only when he has achieved his goal does he reveal that 'it is my misfortune / they are weeping for, / that they are weeping for my dead / and bestow their weeping on me'.

1. A video of the poet reading this poem is available at https://m.youtube.com/watch?v=gYtLFMwQZhQ
2. Tamaulipas murders. This refers to the San Fernando massacre of immigrants by cartel gangs in 2010: https://en.wikipedia.org/wiki/2010_San_Fernando_massacre. There was another massacre of migrants in the same place the following year, when 177 were killed.
3. Javier Sicilia: A reference to the founder of the *Movimiento por la paz con justicia y dignidad* (Movement for peace with justice and dignity), whose motto is *estamos a la madre* meaning, approximately, 'we've had enough'. This group was set up by the poet, writer and activist Javier Sicilia, following the torture and murder of his teenage son Juan Francisco, along with six others, by drug gang assassins in March 2011. Since then, Sicilia – at huge personal risk to himself – has developed a formidable organisation that calls for an end to the drug wars, withdrawal of the military presence from the streets, the legalisation of drugs, and a crackdown on political corruption.
4. General Augusto Pinochet (1915-2003) violently ousted the elected socialist government of Salvador Allende in Chile in September 1973, and remained in power until 1988, when he was voted out in a national plebiscite. The dictatorship in Argentina (known also as the National Reorganization Process) was in place between 1976-83, power being shared between four senior army officers in turn, Videla, Viola, Galtieri and Bignone. The dictatorship fell after the country's defeat by the United Kingdom in the Falklands/Malvinas conflict. Both regimes were marked by sustained brutality against all opposition.

Los Muertos

Allá vienen
los descabezados,
los mancos,
los descuartizados,
a las que les partieron el coxis,
a los que les aplastaron la cabeza,
los pequeñitos llorando
entre paredes oscuras
de minerales y arena.
Allá vienen
los que duermen en edificios
de tumbas clandestinas:
vienen con los ojos vendados,
atadas las manos,
baleados entre las sienes.
Allí vienen los que se perdieron por Tamaulipas,
cuñados, yernos, vecinos,
la mujer que violaron entre todos antes de matarla,
el hombre que intentó evitarlo y recibió un balazo,
la que también violaron, escapó y lo contó viene
caminando por Broadway,
se consuela con el llanto de las ambulancias,
las puertas de los hospitales,
la luz brillando en el agua del Hudson.
Allá vienen
los muertos que salieron de Usulután,
de La Paz,
de La Unión,
de La Libertad,
de Sonsonate,
de San Salvador,
de San Juan Mixtepec,
de Cuscatlán,
de El Progreso,
de El Guante,
llorando,

The Dead

Here they come
the decapitated,
the amputees,
the torn into pieces,
the women with their coccyx split apart,
those with their heads smashed in,
the little ones crying
inside dark walls
of minerals and sand.
Here they come
those who sleep in buildings
that house secret tombs:
they come with their eyes blindfolded,
their hands tied,
shot between their temples.
Here come those who were lost in Tamaupilas,
in-laws, neighbours,
the woman they gang raped before killing her,
the man who tried to stop it and received a bullet,
the woman they also raped, who escaped and told the story
comes walking down Broadway,
consoled by the wail of the ambulances,
the hospital doors,
light shining on the waters of the Hudson.
Here they come
the dead who set out from Usulután,
from La Paz
from La Unión,
from La Libertad,
from Sonsonate,
from San Salvador,
from San Juan Mixtepec,
from Cuscatlán,
from El Progreso,
from El Guante,
crying,

a los que despidieron en una fiesta con karaoke,
y los encontraron baleados en Tecate.
Allí viene al que obligaron a cavar la fosa para su hermano,
al que asesinaron luego de cobrar cuatro mil dólares,
los que estuvieron secuestrados
con una mujer que violaron frente a su hijo de ocho años
tres veces.
¿De dónde vienen,
de qué gangrena,
oh linfa,
los sanguinarios,
los desalmados,
los carniceros
asesinos?
Allá vienen
los muertos tan solitos, tan mudos, tan nuestros,
engarzados bajo el cielo enorme del Anáhuac,
caminan,
se arrastran,
con su cuenco de horror entre las manos,
su espeluznante ternura.
Se llaman
los muertos que encontraron en una fosa en Taxco,
los muertos que encontraron en parajes alejados de Chihuahua,
los muertos que encontraron esparcidos en parcelas de cultivo,
los muertos que encontraron tirados en la Marquesa,
los muertos que encontraron colgando de los puentes,
los muertos que encontraron sin cabeza en terrenos ejidales,
los muertos que encontraron a la orilla de la carretera,
los muertos que encontraron en coches abandonados,
los muertos que encontraron en San Fernando,
los sin número que destazaron y aún no encuentran,
las piernas, los brazos, las cabezas, los fémures de muertos
disueltos en tambos.
Se llaman
restos, cadáveres, occisos,
se llaman
los muertos a los que madres no se cansan de esperar

those who were given the goodbye at a karaoke party,
and were found shot in Tecate.
Here comes the one they forced to dig his brother's grave,
the one they murdered after collecting a four thousand dollar ransom,
those who were kidnapped
with a woman they raped in front of her eight year old son
three times.
Where do they come from,
from what gangrene,
oh lymph,
the bloodthirsty,
the heartless,
the murdering
butchers?
Here they come,
the dead so alone, so mute, so much ours,
set beneath the enormous sky of Anáhuac,
they walk,
they drag themselves,
with their bowl of horror in their hands,
their terrifying tenderness.
They are called
the dead that they found in a ditch in Taxco,
the dead that they found in remote places of Chihuahua,
the dead that they found strewn across plots of crops,
the dead that they found shot in la Marquesa,
the dead that they found hanging from bridges,
the dead that they found without heads on common land,
the dead that they found at the side of the road,
the dead that they found in abandoned cars,
the dead that they found in San Fernando,
those without number they cut into pieces and have still not been found,
the legs, the arms, the heads, the femurs of the dead
dissolved in drums.
They are called
remains, corpses, the deceased,
they are called
the dead whose mothers do not tire of waiting,

los muertos a los que hijos no se cansan de esperar,
los muertos a los que esposas no se cansan de esperar,
imaginan entre subways y gringos.
Se llaman
chambrita tejida en el cajón del alma,
camisetita de tres meses,
la foto de la sonrisa chimuela,
se llaman mamita,
papito,
se llaman
pataditas
en el vientre
y el primer llanto,
se llaman cuatro hijos,
Petronia (2), Zacarías (3), Sabas (5), Glenda (6)
y una viuda (muchacha) que se enamoró cuando estudiaba la primaria
se llaman ganas de bailar en las fiestas,
se llaman rubor de mejillas encendidas y manos sudorosas,
se llaman muchachos,
se llaman ganas
de construir una casa,
echar tabique,
darle de comer a mis hijos,
se llaman dos dólares por limpiar frijoles,
casas, haciendas, oficinas,
se llaman
llantos de niños en pisos de tierra,
la luz volando sobre los pájaros,
el vuelo de las palomas en la iglesia,
se llaman
besos a la orilla del río,
se llaman
Gelder (17)
Daniel (22)
Filmar (24)
Ismael (15)
Agustín (20)
José (16)

the dead whose children do not tire of waiting,
the dead whose wives do not tire of waiting,
they imagine them in subways, among gringos.
They are called
baby clothes woven in the casket of the soul,
the little tee shirt of a three-month-old
the photo of a toothless smile,
they are called *mamita*,
papito,
they are called
little kicks
in the tummy
and the newborn's cry,
they are called four children,
Petronia (2), Zacarías (3), Sabas (5), Glenda (6)
and a widow (a girl) who fell in love at primary school,
they are called wanting to dance at fiestas,
they are called blushing of hot cheeks and sweaty hands,
they are called boys,
they are called wanting
to build a house,
laying bricks,
giving food to my children,
they are called two dollars for cleaning beans,
houses, estates, offices,
they are called
crying of children on earth floors,
the light flying over the birds,
the flight of pigeons in the church,
they are called
kisses at the river's edge,
they are called
Gelder (17)
Daniel (22)
Filmar (24)
Ismael (15)
Agustín (20)
José (16)

Jacinta (21)
Inés (28)
Francisco (53)
entre matorrales,
amordazados,
en jardines de ranchos
maniatados,
en jardines de casas de seguridad
desvanecidos,
en parajes olvidados,
desintegrándose muda,
calladamente,
se llaman
secretos de sicarios,
secretos de matanzas,
secretos de policías,
se llaman llanto,
se llaman neblina,
se llaman cuerpo,
se llaman piel,
se llaman tibieza,
se llaman beso,
se llaman abrazo,
se llaman risa,
se llaman personas,
se llaman súplicas,
se llamaban yo,
se llamaban tú,
se llamaban nosotros,
se llaman vergüenza,
se llaman llanto.
Allá van
María,
Juana,
Petra,
Carolina,
13,
18,

Jacinta (21)
Inés (28)
Francisco (53)
gagged
in the scrubland,
hands tied
in the gardens of ranches,
vanished
in the gardens of 'safe' houses,
in some forgotten wilderness,
disintegrating mutely
and in secret,
they are called
secrets of hitmen,
secrets of slaughter,
secrets of policemen,
they are called sobbing,
they are called mist,
they are called body,
they are called skin,
they are called warmth,
they are called kiss,
they are called hug,
they are called laughter,
they are called people,
they are called pleading,
they were called I,
they were called you,
they were called us,
they are called shame,
they are called weeping.
Here they go
María,
Juana,
Petra,
Carolina,
13,
18,

25,
16,
los pechos mordidos,
las manos atadas,
calcinados sus cuerpos,
sus huesos pulidos por la arena del desierto.
Se llaman
las muertas que nadie sabe nadie vio que mataran,
se llaman
las mujeres que salen de noche solas a los bares,
se llaman
mujeres que trabajan salen de sus casas en la madrugada,
se llaman
hermanas,
hijas,
madres,
tías,
desaparecidas,
violadas,
calcinadas,
aventadas,
se llaman carne,
se llaman carne.
Allá
sin flores,
sin losas,
sin edad,
sin nombre,
sin llanto,
duermen en su cementerio:
se llama Temixco,
se llama Santa Ana,
se llama Mazatepec,
se llama Juárez,
se llama Puente de Ixtla,
se llama San Fernando,
se llama Tlaltizapán,
se llama Samalayuca,

25,
16,
breasts bitten,
hands tied,
their bodies burned to a crisp,
their bones polished by the sand of the desert.
They are called
the dead women that no one knows no one saw being killed,
they are called
women who go out alone to bars at night,
they are called
working women who leave their homes at dawn,
they are called
sisters,
daughters,
mothers,
aunts,
disappeared,
raped,
burnt,
chucked away,
they are called meat,
they are called meat.
Here,
without flowers,
without tombstones,
without an age,
without a name,
without weeping,
they sleep in their cemetery:
its name is Temixco,
its name is Santa Ana,
its name is Mazatepec,
its name is Juárez,
its name is Puente de Ixtla,
its name is San Fernando,
its name is Tlaltizapán,
its name is Samalayuca,

se llama el Capulín,
se llama Reynosa,
se llama Nuevo Laredo,
se llama Guadalupe,
se llama Lomas de Poleo,
se llama México.

María Rivera (México)

La Guerra de los tontos

Dinamitamos antes de cruzarlo
el puente, el bello puente
que habíamos construido.

El puente sobre el río del olvido era.

Ahora, moriremos olvidados.
Muramos ya, y de esto.

Beatriz Vignoli (Argentina).

Xochicuicatl

Una flor: abierta como una boca diciendo abierta:
    un canto.

Otra flor pero la misma flor marchita: no dos,
no tres: sólo un instante, sólo un colibrí
dura el hombre aquí en la tierra.

Una calavera junto a otra calavera junto a otra calavera

its name is el Capulín,
its name is Reynosa,
its name is Nuevo Laredo,
its name is Guadalupe,
its name is Lomas de Poleo,
its name is Mexico.

María Rivera (Mexico)

The War of the Idiots

We dynamited the bridge before ever
crossing it, the lovely bridge
that we built.

The bridge over the river of forgetting, it was.

Now we will die forgotten.
Let's die then, and from this.

Beatriz Vignoli (Argentina)

Xochicuicatl

A flower: open like a mouth saying open:
  a song.

Another flower but the same but withered: not two,
not three: only an instant only a hummingbird
man lasts here on earth.

One skull next to another skull next to another skull

sobre
otra calavera junto a otra calavera junto a otra calavera
   sobre
otra calavera junto a otra: estrofa-tzompantli.

Una pregunta a los muertos:
¿Al canto le sigue el silencio o le sigue otro canto?

Otro canto: el silencio de los muertos: otra flor
pero la misma flor pero otra
calavera, etcétera.

Luis Felipe Fabre (México)

Vinieron los muertos

Vinieron los muertos.
Y mi padre dijo: "—Vinieron los muertos".
Había un aire podrido tras la puerta,
un aire parecido al aire de los muertos.

Había también una puerta reclinada en su marco
del modo en que lo hacen los padres cuando esperan
a alguien que ya ha tardado tanto,
y es de noche, oscuro, tan de noche,
que el aire es, de tan frío, una advertencia.

Pero no era un padre,
era solo una puerta que de vieja
parecía una cortina que se cree puerta
y que mece y golpea el viento de los muertos
a su albedrío.

Y vi también unas palomas
en la última línea de la cerca. Y había viento.

   on top of
another skull next to another skull next to another skull
      on top of
another skull next to another skull: tzompantli-verse.

A question to the dead:
Is the song followed by silence or by another song?

Another song: the silence of the dead: another flower
but the same flower but another
skull, et cetera.

Luis Felipe Fabre (Mexico)

The Dead Arrived

The dead arrived.
And my father said: "The dead have arrived."
The air was foul behind the door,
air resembling the air of the dead.

There was also a door leaning on its frame
the way that fathers do when they're waiting
for someone who is already very late,
and it's night, dark, so very much night,
that the air, being so cold, is a warning.

But it was not a father,
it was only a door that, being old,
seemed like a curtain that thinks it is a door
and which swings and blows the wind of the dead
where it will.

And I also saw some pigeons
on the uppermost wire of the fence. And there was a wind.

Yo querría deciros cuán bellas eran aun a pesar del viento,
o quizás a costa del viento. Y os digo que eran bellas.
Mas no en manera tal que uno diga: "Ved, qué bellas",
sino del modo en que basta oírlas
para beber de ellas tantísima hermosura.

Osvaldo Hernández *(El Salvador)*

Siete maneras de decir el dolor

(fragmento)

Posibilidad 1

Hoy quisiera, Mónica, enfermarte larga, mortalmente,
sacarte lejos del mundo, convaleciente:
distanciar del cuerpo su llanto, su sudor solitario
de manera que todo quede, ahora sí, bien vacío
y ser un desierto rencoroso resuelto a envenenarse de sed.
Quiero hoy quebrarte un hueso imprescindible
esparcir las astillas de la estructura fundamental
que implores ayuda y extiendas anchas las manos
y no tengas pasos ni pies para darlos.
Quiero una úlcera que cuente de tu furia
músculos torpes pidiendo a gritos
abrazos que no han de venir
epilepsias que transparenten tu confusión
tu dificultad para contenerte
insomnio eterno para salvarte de los sueños
que anuncian cuando alguien va a morir.
Ningún consuelo, eso quiero darte,
para hacer visible tu necesidad de otro
para que te vean dolerte, partirte en pedazos y se sepa
y te sepulten, te lloren, te perdonen
aunque a nadie salve tu muerte,

I would like to tell you how beautiful they were in spite of the wind,
or maybe to the cost of the wind. And I tell you they were beautiful.
But not in the way that one says: "Look, how beautiful,"
but rather in the sense in which it is enough to hear them
in order to drink in so much beauty.

Osvaldo Hernández *(El Salvador)*

Seven Ways of Talking about Pain

(a fragment)

Possibility 1

Today, Monica, I'd like to make you ill for a long time, mortally ill,
take you out of the world, a convalescent:
distance from your body its weeping, its lonely sweating
so that everything is left, at last, entirely empty
to become a resentful desert, resolved on poisoning itself with thirst.
Today I want to break one of your crucial bones
scatter the splinters of your basic structure
so that you beg for help and stretch your hands out wide
but make no steps forward have no feet to take them.
I want an ulcer to account for your rage
clumsy muscles that plead out loud
for embraces that will not come
epilepsy that reveals your confusion
your difficulty in containing yourself
eternal insomnia to save you from the dreams
that announce someone's approaching death.
No solace, that's what I want to give you,
so everyone can see your neediness
so that they see the pain in you, how you are shattered into pieces,
so that they bury you, weep for you, pardon you,
although your death saves no one,

el viento aleje tu nombre, todo sea casi igual.
Hay demasiado peso en tu sombra
y yo quiero curarte, lenta, con mi saliva...
Quiero restablecerte la balanza aún sin par
murmurarte que no hace falta,
que no hace falta morir así.

Mónica Velásquez Guzmán (Bolivia)

Palimpsesto desde Rimbaud

Escribo sobre palabras escritas
En la piel de otras palabras.
Soy eco de otros ecos. Trazo de otros trazos.
Escribo tachando voces
Como si el papel fuera una pizarra fugaz.
Advierto que al fondo de esta hoja
Arrancada a su diario de prisionero,
El poeta fijó vértigos
Antes de erigirse emperador del silencio,
Y aunque resulte herejía
Escribo encima de su voz.
Tachono su A negra, su E blanca, su I roja,
Su O azul, su U verde
Y estampo mi grafía, impunemente,
Pero él insiste en tenderme una celada.
No sé por qué persiste,
Sobre mis precarias palabras
Una divisa imborrable:
"He aquí el tiempo de los asesinos".
A ver, repitan en coro:
"He aquí el tiempo de los asesinos".

Juan Manuel Roca (Colombia)

and the wind will blow your name away, and everything remain much the same.
There is too much weight in your shadow
and I want to heal you, slowly, with my saliva . . .
I want to restore your unique balance,
whisper to you that there's no need,
there's no need to die like this.

Mónica Velásquez Guzmán (Bolivia)

Palimpsest from Rimbaud

I am writing over words written
On the skin of other words.
I am an echo of other echoes. A trace of other traces.
I write crossing out voices
As if the paper were a transient slate.
I realize that at the bottom of this page
Torn away from his prison diary
The poet attached vertigo
Before proclaiming himself emperor of silence,
And despite this being heresy
I write over his voice.
I cross out his black A, his white E, his red I,
His blue O, his green U
And I stamp my symbols with impunity,
But he insists on setting a trap for me.
Over my precarious words
I don't know why
An indelible motto persists:
"This is the time of the killers."
Once again, all together now:
"This is the time of the killers."

Juan Manuel Roca (Colombia)

Ausencia

A Marie, a su lápida de humo

El olvido es sepia e inconmensurable.

Eres el nunca Marie si no te hablo
y aún así el jamás
quién puede saber . . .
Quién
cuál es el sueño que voló tu traje enfermo de pliegue
cuál la vergüenza que cargaste inhóspita
que el salvarse no fue tarea posible
y la muerte apiló zapato sobre zapato
horrores de cuero a la venta en esquinas de entonces
como si todo fuese moneda
y nada más tuviese importancia.

Hoy son otros y nada cambia.

Verónica Zondek *(Chile)*

Premonición en San Librario

Esta mañana me llamaron para avisarme
que estaban a la venta un buen número de libros
pertenecientes a la biblioteca de un joven
fallecido hace más de ocho años.

Revisando las columnas en las que estaban
dispuestos, con asombro y cierto pavor descubrí
que la mayoría de esos cientos de ejemplares
eran semejantes a tantos de los míos.

-De qué te extrañas, me dijo el librero

Absence

To Marie, to her tombstone of smoke

Oblivion is sepia and immeasurable.

You are neverness Marie if I don't speak to you
and even this way nevermore
who can say . . .
Who
which is the dream that gave flight to your suit sick with creases
which is the shame you bore unaided
that saving yourself was not possible
and death stacked up shoe upon shoe
horrors of hide for sale at the corners of those times
as if everything were coin
and nothing else had importance.

Today they are others and nothing changes.

Verónica Zondek *(Chile)*

Premonition in San Librario

This morning someone called to tell me
there was a sale of a quantity of books
belonging to the collection of a young man
dead for more than eight years.

Checking through the list of what was
up for offer, with shock and a kind of dread
I discovered that most of these five hundred titles
were the same as so many of my own.

– What's so surprising, the bookshop manager said,

como si me leyera la mente, si al fin y al cabo
ustedes pertenecieron a la misma generación-.

Pero no era comprobar la similitud de gustos
o ediciones o preferencias comunes lo que más me perturbaba
en ese momento, ni tampoco el tiempo verbal
tan involuntariamente hostil
empleado por el librero, era más bien
la inquietante sensación de saber
que basta un mínimo descuido para que el tiempo
disperse todo lo que la soledad y el amor han reunido,
era la desoladora sensación de saber
que el tiempo no perdona lo que la vida ordena,
era, también, sobre todo, la culpable sensación de saber
que mi codicia colaboraba con la extinción
de su memoria.
Salí de allí con apenas un par de libros
firmados con su nombre -Aurelio, Bogotá
1983 - llevando entre las manos el más claro anuncio
de mi muerte anticipada.

Ramón Cote Baraibar *(Colombia)*

Oscura

a Javier Sicilia

Pasé toda la noche con el brazo en una grieta.
No era un aula de santos.
Era un hotel a las afueras de Querétaro.
Dos camas individuales provisionalmente pegadas
Para caber los tres (siempre tres) juntos.
Ascesis: duermevela: Aníbal Barca, mi hijo, cayendo
        cada 15 minutos por el hueco.
Es vulgar pero no es falso: pasé toda la noche con el

as if reading my mind, – when's all said and done
you and he belonged to the same generation – .

But it wasn't to confirm our similarity of tastes
or editions or common preferences that perturbed me most
right then, nor even the involuntarily
hostile choice of tense
employed by the bookshop manager, it was rather
the disquieting sense of knowing
that it takes only a minor carelessness for time
to disperse everything that solitude and love have brought together,
it was the devastating sense of knowing
that time does not condone that which life puts in order,
it was, also, above all, the guilty sense of knowing
that my covetousness collaborated in the extinction
of his memory.
I left there with just a couple of books
signed with his name – Aurelio, Bogotá
1983 – carrying between my hands the clearest announcement
of my own eventual death.

Ramón Cote Baraibar *(Colombia)*

Dark

For Javier Sicilia

I spent the whole night with my arm in a crack.
It was not a hall of saints.
It was a hotel on the outskirts of Querétaro.
Two single beds provisionally pulled together
to hold the three of us (always three) together.
Ascesis: a light sleep: Hannibal Barca, my son, falling
       every 15 minutes into the gap.
It's trite, but it's true: I spent the whole night with

        brazo en una grieta.
Me inculcaba el demonio de una negra rabia acústica:
        ¿para qué escribir poemas
si todo lo que hiere tiene el tacto vacío, usura de una
        tumba?
Encandilado, muy orondo y sin luz (sin otra luz y guía
        Sino etcétera etcétera),
Escribí de memoria estos versos:

"Al menos toca lo que matas.
Siéntelo babosa lumbre negro caracol con la que marcas
        – meas –
plásticos: Identidad.
Recuerda, cuando vayas al cine a ver películas de nazis,
        que tú no eres judío.
Pero si eres judío no recuerdes nada: al menos toca lo
        que matas.
No te metas en dios. No vueles coches. No hagas citas
        sagradas. No discutas conmigo.
No me vendas muñones. No me traigas cabezas. No me
        pidas que aprenda a respetar.
Toca.
Al menos toca lo que matas."

Son pésimos. Lo supe de inmediato.
Hace un par de años que no logro hacer poemas.
Lo extraño pero no lo lamento.
Todos sabemos que la poesía no es más (ni menos) que
        una destreza pasajera.
Una destreza que, perdida, se hace tú y alumbra oscura.

Igual que un padre pasará toda la noche con el brazo en
        una grieta
procurando que la cabeza de su hijo no toque nunca el
        suelo.

Julián Herbert *(México)*

my arm in a crack.
The devil instilled in me a black acoustic fury:
    why write poems
if everything that wounds has an empty touch, a tomb's
    usury?
Dazzled, very smug and without light (without another light and guide
    without etc., etc.),
I wrote these verses from memory:

"At least touch what you kill.
Feel it slug fuel black snail with which you mark
    – you piss –
plastics: Identity.
Remember, when you go to the cinema to watch films about Nazis,
    that you are not a Jew.
But if you are a Jew, don't remember anything: at least touch what
    you kill.
Don't try to act god. Don't blow up cars. Don't quote
    the scriptures. Don't argue with me.
Don't sell me the stumps of limbs. Don't bring me heads. Don't ask me
    to learn respect.
Touch.
At least touch what you kill."

They are appalling. I knew it at once.
For a couple of years I haven't been able to make a poem.
I miss it, but don't regret it.
We all know that poetry is nothing more (or less) than
    a temporary skill.
A skill which, once lost, becomes you and shines dark.

The same as a father will spend the whole night with his arm in
    a crack
making sure his son's head never touches the floor.

Julián Herbert (Mexico)

El moribundo nos convoca

el moribundo nos convoca
para recapitular su vida

forzado como está
a respirarse a sí mismo hasta el fin
su confesión es de segunda mano
carece de voluntad
para ocultar ciertas lealtades

en la vastedad del adiós
la verdad es siempre un escándalo

Jacqueline Goldberg (Venezuela)

Traducción Libre de un tema inédito de Chan Marshall

I

Arrancaron la hiedra.
De raíz. No les fue fácil, sin embargo.
Emplearon podadoras,
palas y guantes para no lastimarse.
Esa hiedra que tardó años en cubrir
la pared al fondo del patio.
Aferrada al concreto, parecía resistirse.
Era su territorio.
Si hubiera podido hablar
no lo hubiera hecho,
habría gritado,
no hubiera perdido el tiempo
en hacerlos entrar en razón

The dying man

the dying man calls us together
to review his life

forced as he is
to breathe his own breath until the end
his confession comes second hand
lacks the will
to conceal certain loyalties

in the vastness of farewell
the truth is always a scandal

Jacqueline Goldberg (Venezuela)

Free translation of an unpublished piece by Chan Marshall

I

They pulled up the ivy.
By the root. It wasn't easy for them, however.
They used secateurs,
shovels and gloves, so as not to hurt themselves.
That ivy which took years to cover
the wall at the end of the patio.
Anchored in the concrete, it seemed to fight back.
It was its territory.
If it could have spoken
it wouldn't have,
it would have yelled,
it wouldn't have wasted its time
in making them see reason

porque el objetivo de esta mañana
era cortarla, ver la pared lisa, perpendicular.
La hiedra dejó marcas
como huellas de ave pequeña,
similares a las que dejan en la arena
los pájaros marinos.

Tenías dieciséis en esa foto,
atrás la hiedra crecía como un cáncer.
Sin simetría, con determinación.
Dieciséis y ya sabías
lo que las manos no alcanzaban,
lo que era tu nombre escrito en tinta china,
lo que era una canción repetida hasta dormir,
despertar con ella.
Sabías de esta ciudad de tullidos,
obesos y descompensados,
condenada a la pequeñez.
La hiedra nada sabía de eso
pero crecía detrás tuyo
en la misma foto
donde aún tenés dieciséis
y la pared está totalmente verde,
cubierta por la hiedra que no sabe
lo que nosotros sí.
Por eso pueden cortarla de raíz,
con esfuerzo pero con éxito.
Al sol le da lo mismo,
igual cae directo sobre la pared
donde no está tu sombra.
Ni la hiedra.

II

La lluvia sobre tu nombre
escrito con tinta china, ¿recuerdas?
Empezó a correr sobre el papel,
sin simetría con la voluntad propia.

because the objective of this morning
was to cut it down, to see the wall smooth, perpendicular.
The ivy left marks
like the tracks of a small bird,
similar to those that sea birds
leave in the sand.

You were sixteen in that photo,
behind you the ivy was growing like a cancer.
Without symmetry, with determination.
Sixteen and already you knew
what the hands were not able to reach,
what your name written in china ink was,
what a song repeated till you fell asleep was,
to wake up with it.
You knew about this city of cripples,
the obese and the unhinged,
condemned to pettiness.
The ivy knew nothing of that
but grew behind you
in the same photo
where you are still sixteen
and already the wall is completely green,
covered by the ivy which doesn't know
what we know.
That's why they can cut it from the root,
with effort, but with success.
To the sun it's all the same,
it still falls on the wall
and your shadow isn't there.
Nor the ivy.

II

The rain on your name
written with china ink: do you remember?
It began to run over the paper,
without symmetry, of its own will.

Como lo haría una hiedra en la pared
donde alguien hubiera podido tomar una foto
a la niña de dieciséis,
que ya no era niña,
obsesionada con la palabra deformidad,
dormida escuchando la misma canción
que ya es difícil precisar de dónde proviene
si de adentro o de afuera
yellow hair / you are such a funny bear
y las cosas que crecían sin saber nada de esto.
Durmiera o no la niña, crecían, como el cáncer.
La hiedra también.
Entonces el nombre se convertía en otra cosa:
una mancha negra sobre papel,
como una enfermedad
o la idea que tenemos de la enfermedad.

La hiedra en cambio
no tiene ideas.
Si se enferma, muere.
La niña tiene ideas,
se enferma, muere.
Pero la hiedra estaba sana,
seguía creciendo,
empezaba a invadir la casa del vecino.
El vecino tullido que vive con su madre,
la madre obesa,
la familia descompensada
que tenemos de vecinos.
De todas formas, la cortaron de raíz
aunque estaba sana,
de un verde temperamental.
No porque tuviera ideas la planta
sino por cosas que explicaría mejor
un biólogo o un botánico
o tal vez la gorda de al lado
que vive hablando de su jardín,
del jardín y de la voluntad de un dios

Just like ivy on the wall
where someone would have been able to take a photo
of a girl of sixteen,
who was not a girl anymore,
obsessed by the word deformity,
sleeping while listening to the same song
now difficult to determine where it came from
whether from within or without
yellow hair / you're such a funny bear
And the things which grew without knowing anything of this.
Whether the girl slept or not, they grew, like cancer.
The ivy also.
Then the name changed into something else:
a black stain on the paper,
like an illness
or the idea we have of illness.

Ivy, by contrast,
does not have ideas.
If it gets sick, it dies.
The girl has ideas,
she gets sick, she dies.
But the ivy was healthy,
it continued growing,
it began to invade the neighbour's house.
The crippled neighbour who lives with his mother,
the obese mother,
the unhinged family
we have as neighbours.
In any case, they cut the root,
even though it was healthy,
of a temperamental green.
Not because the plant had ideas
but for reasons that would be better explained
by a biologist or botanist
or maybe the fat woman next door
who passes her time talking of her garden,
of the garden and the will of a god

que le envió un hijo tullido
como castigo tal vez,
por obesa,
por gorda,
por solterona ,
por vecina,
porque sí.

Porque no hay razón para nada,
un día algo está sano,
la mañana siguiente lo arrancan de raíz.
Un día se tiene dieciséis
y la vida es una extensa playa en la tarde,
la arena tatuada con huellas de pájaros marinos.
Y ese momento dura lo que dura
una canción que se repite
hasta entrar en el sueño
mientras lo demás sigue creciendo,
dentro y fuera,
en silencio,
lejos de la simetría,
con determinación.

Luis Chaves *(Costa Rica)*

Cuerpos de todos los tamaños por donde corre la misma sangre

Mil novecientos ochenta y nueve agujeros
que hacen del rancho un colador
para que el clima de las cuatro estaciones
se suceda en concierto por el único ambiente
sin necesidad de ventanas. Recién despierto,
acodado en las mantas Lescano barre con la vista
los cuerpos tendidos de la madre, la esposa,

who sent her a crippled son
as a punishment, perhaps,
for being obese,
for being fat,
for being unmarried,
for being a neighbour,
or just because.

Because there's no reason for anything,
one day something's healthy,
the next morning they pull it out by the root.
One day you are sixteen
and life is a long beach in the afternoon,
the sand tattooed with the tracks of sea birds.
And that moment lasts as long
as a song on repeat lasts
until entering sleep
while the rest keeps on growing,
inside and out,
in silence,
far from symmetry,
with determination.

Luis Chaves (Costa Rica)

Bodies of all sizes where the same blood runs

One thousand nine hundred and eighty nine holes
that turn the farmhouse into a colander
so that the climate of the four seasons
pass in concert through the same atmosphere
without any need for windows. Recently woken,
resting on blankets, Lescano's gaze sweeps over
the laid-out bodies of mother, wife,

un cuñado, las hijas que son tres
más los dos perros que, sin contar el loro,
ascienden al número de ocho como víctimas
de una masacre de la cual, en estado de ebriedad,
él pudo haber sido el agente; pero no se acuerda
de nada y el flequillo sobre los ojos
le da un aspecto de pony tardíamente alfabetizado.

D.G. Helder *(Argentina)*

Puño

Aun así tuvo tiempo para ver crecer a sus hijos
y hacerse perdonar. Las tardes
se estiran apacibles en su casa
como siempre las imaginó:
con un sol rosado sobre las montañas.
A veces saca una silla de playa al jardín
y se pone a leer libros sobre el big-bang
o la vida de Napoleón. Su mujer lo observa:
el libro desparramado sobre el vientre,
pequeños espasmos en las mejillas
y a un lado la mano caída, inmóvil,
como una bolsa de arena mojada.
El piojo que trepa hacia la rosa
aún no llega a las espinas. Ya llegará.

Leonardo Sanhueza *(Chile)*

brother-in-law, three daughters
plus two dogs, which, not including the parrot,
bring to eight the number of victims
of the massacre in which, in a drunken state,
he could have been the perpetrator; but he remembers
nothing and the fringe over his eyes
gives him the look of a pony who has learned to read too late.

D.G. Helder *(Argentina)*

Fist

In spite of everything he had time to see his children grow
and to be forgiven. The evenings
stretch out pleasantly in his house
as he always imagined they would,
with a rosy sun over the mountains.
Sometimes he takes a deck chair out to the garden
and settles into a book about the Big Bang
or the life of Napoleon. His wife watches him,
the book unfolded on his stomach,
his cheeks twitching slightly
and a hand fallen to one side, as motionless
as a sack of wet sand.
The bug climbing the rose has not yet reached
the thorns. It'll get there soon enough.

Leonardo Sanhueza *(Chile)*

Mientras tanto

Yo estuve lavando ropa
mientras mucha gente
desapareció
no porque sí
se escondió
sufrió
hubo golpes
y
ahora no están
no porque sí
y mientras pasaban
sirenas y disparos, ruido seco
yo estuve lavando ropa,
acunando,
cantaba,
y la persiana a oscuras.

Irene Gruss *(Argentina)*

Infomercial

(para los tiempos que corren)

Señora ama de casa: ¿está harta
de tallar día y noche

coágulos de sangre imposibles de limpiar
en la ropa de toda su familia?

¿Las vísceras embarradas en las paredes de su casa
no le permiten dormir?

¿Se ha descubierto a sí misma

And in the meantime

I was washing clothes
while many people
disappeared
not just because
but they hid
they suffered
were beaten
and
they are no more
not just because
and while there were
sirens and shots, harsh sounds
I was washing clothes,
rocking the cradle,
singing,
and the shutters dark.

Irene Gruss *(Argentina)*

Infomercial

(for the times we live in)

Señora Housewife: are you sick and tired
of scrubbing night and day

clots of impossible-to-remove blood
from the clothes of all your family?

Do the entrails spattered on the walls of your house
prevent you from sleeping?

Have you found yourself exclaiming like a sleepwalker:

exclamando sonámbula: "¡Fuera, fuera mancha maldita!"?

Compre ahora
el Limpiador Quitamanchas Lady Macbeth
y póngales fin a esa viscosas pesadillas.

El Limpiador Quitamanchas Lady Macbeth

está compuesto a base de microorganismos carroñeros
que harán por usted el trabajo sucio
eliminando

los restos cadavéricos
sin dañar la superficie en la que se encuentran adheridos:
¡científicamente comprobado!

Señora, usted lo sabe: matar
es fácil, lo difícil viene después.

Pero ahora
el Limpiador Quitamanchas Lady Macbeth le ofrece
una increíble solución que revolucionará la higiene doméstica:

¡Diga adiós al rastro de sesos en su sillón favorito! ¡Diga adiós
a esas alfombras ensangrentadas!

Marque ahora el número que aparece en su pantalla
o llame al 01800 666
y obtenga junto con su compra

el aplicador multifuncional y un paquete de bolsas para cadáveres
¡totalmente gratis!

Con el Limpiador Quitamanchas Lady Macbeth
usted volverá a dormir

como una verdadera reina.

Luis Felipe Fabre (México)

"Out, damned spot, out I say!"?

Now you can buy
Lady Macbeth Stain Remover
and put an end to those viscous nightmares!

Lady Macbeth Stain Remover

is made up from a base of scavenger micro-organisms
that will do your dirty work for you
eliminating

cadaverous remains
without damaging the surfaces to which they are stuck:
scientifically proven!

Señora, you know it: killing
is easy. The difficult part comes later.

But now
Lady Macbeth Stain Remover offers you
an incredible solution that will revolutionize domestic hygiene:

Say goodbye to the trace of brains from your favourite armchair!
Say goodbye to those bloodied rugs!

Take a note now of the number that appears on your screen
or call 01800 666
and receive along with your purchase

a multifunctional applicator and a packet of body bags
absolutely free!

With the Lady Macbeth Stain Remover
you will be able to sleep

like a true queen.

Luis Felipe Fabre (Mexico)

Plaza St. Exupéry

a E.A.F., i.m.

– Prométeme que nunca
vas a morir – dije.

Por la puerta entreabierta del Unión
vimos bajar la noche.

Ascuas recuerdo:
flotaban en lo azul.

Beatriz Vignoli *(Argentina)*

Desmantelar la casa

Más allá de la ausencia y del enorme despropósito que sigue
–costumbres que cuesta desterrar,
como llamar todos los días, por ejemplo–
no estoy seguro de que haya algo así
como la verdadera medida de la muerte
hasta que la casa se vacía, porque entonces
lo que tenía un sentido y por supuesto historia
apenas se resume en inventarios:
dos cuadros, un sillón, el samovar,
la cama y el bargueño.
La porcelana inglesa ya no cuenta,
ni el baccarat, la plata,
primeras ediciones de nada que ahora importe.
Son cosas viejas,
objetos que boyan en los cuartos sin razón.

Jorge Fondebrider *(Argentina)*

Plaza St. Exupéry

to E.A.F., i.m.

– Promise me
you'll never die – I said.

By the door of the Union
we watched night fall.

Embers I remember:
they were floating in the blue.

Beatríz Vignoli *(Argentina)*

Closing up the House

Beyond the absence and the tremendous absurdity of what follows
– habits, such as calling every day,
for example, are hard to banish –
I am not sure that there is any such thing
as the true measure of death
until the house is empty, because
what once had a meaning and, of course, history
can barely be summarized in an inventory:
two paintings, an armchair, the stove,
the bed and the sideboard.
The English china already doesn't count,
nor the cut glass, the silver,
first editions of nothing that now matters.
They are old things,
objects that float about the rooms with no purpose.

Jorge Fondebrider *(Argentina)*

La muerte está en casa

La muerte está en casa.
Nos movemos como pedazos descosidos
y ya nadie pregunta qué ha pasado,
qué nos hace mirarnos sin queja.
El cuerpo vacío de la muerte
entró y se desvistió en casa,
a pesar del sol,
a pesar de los nacimientos,
a pesar de los llamados alegres.
Y nadie de nosotros le
pregunta hasta cuándo,
nadie de nosotros la golpea,
nadie vuelve a vestir a la muerte.

Irene Gruss (Argentina)

de 'El desierto'

Abajo las infinitas piedras del desierto, montañas
de piedras, laderas, infinitas piedras sobre el
desierto como un mar. Arriba el cielo, el cielo
azul que cae. Las piedras gritan al estrellarse con
al aire, con el cielo que cae.

El desierto grita. Hay un muro de cal con
nombres. Hay un muro blanco y pequeñas
botellas con flores de plástico que gritan al
doblarse bajo el viento.

Un poco más lejos hay un barco. Nadie diría que
puede haber un barco en el medio del desierto. Es
un barco grande, herrumbroso, recostado encima
de las piedras. Nadie lo diría, pero está allí. El

Death is At Home

Death is at home.
We move like unstitched patches
and no one now is asking what has happened,
what makes us look at each other without complaint.
The empty body of death
came in and undressed at home,
despite the sun,
despite the births,
despite the happy calls.
And not one of us
asks how long he's staying,
not one of us beats him up,
no one puts death's clothes back on.

Irene Gruss (Argentina)

from 'The Desert'

Below: the infinite rocks of the desert, mountains
of rocks, hillsides, an infinity of rocks upon the
desert like a sea. Above: the sky, the blue sky
that is falling. The rocks scream when they smash themselves
against the air, against the falling sky.

The desert screams. There is a limestone wall
with names. There is a white wall and small
bottles with plastic flowers that scream as they
bend beneath the wind.

A little further on there's a ship. No one would
think there could be a ship in the middle of the
desert. It's a big rusty ship, lying on top of the
rocks. No one would think it, but there it is.

mismo cielo que cae sobre las piedras cae sobre él.
Todas las piedra gritan.

Gritan, el desierto de Chile grita. Nadie diría que
esto puede ser, pero gritan.

★

Hay un barco en medio del desierto. Un barco
reclinado sobre las piedras del desierto y arriba la
losa a pique del cielo. El océano invertido del
cielo cae sobre las piedras y éstas gritan. Nadie,
salvo las piedras son capaces de gritar así. Mireya
se tapa los oídos para no oír el chillido del
desierto. Chile grita, el desierto del Chile grita.
Mireya acumula pequeñas flores de plástico frente
a un barco arrumbado en el pedrerío.

Están las costas, las tercas costas sin mar trepando
para atrás sobre las olas muertas de los cerros.
Mireya dice que es la madre de Chile. Que es la
madre de un barco reclinado en medio del desierto.

★

De lejos parece una mancha negra, pero es un
barco. Debajo las piedras amontadas contra su
casco asemejan olas. Pero no son olas, son sólo
piedras y gritan. Las rompientes encaramadas
gritan. Está también el sol cayendo a pique y
flores de plástico coloreadas como soles
minúsculos. Está el mar del desierto, está el mar
de piedras del desierto hirviendo frente a Chile.

Están las diminutas flores y las costas gangrenadas
del mar reseco.

Mireya les pone nombre a cada una de esas flores.

The same sky that falls on the rocks falls on it.
All the rocks scream.

They scream, the desert of Chile screams. No one
would think that could be, but they scream.

⋆

There is a ship in the middle of the desert. A ship
reclining on rocks in the desert and above it the
wrecked slab of the sky. The inverted ocean of the
sky falls on the rocks and they scream. No one
except the rocks is capable of screaming like this.
Mireya covers her ears so as not to hear the shrieking
of the desert. Chile screams, the desert of Chile screams.
Mireya gathers little plastic flowers in front of a ship
discarded on a pile of rocks.

There are shores, stubborn sea-less shores climbing
from behind over the dead waves of the rock-hills.
Mireya says she is the mother of Chile. That she is the
mother of a ship lying in the middle of the desert.

⋆

From a distance it seems like a black stain, but it's
a ship. Below it, the rocks piled up against its
hull resemble waves. But they're not waves, they're
only rocks, and they scream. The rising breakers
scream. There is also the sun falling sharply and
coloured plastic flowers like tiny suns. There is
the sea of the desert, there is the sea of rocks
in the boiling desert facing Chile.

There are little flowers and the gangrenous shores
of the parched sea.

Mireya gives a name to every one of those flowers.

Ante el barco parecen minúsculos soles
despidiéndolo.

★

El desierto grita, el puerto reseco grita, el mar de
piedras grita azotado por el viento. Mireya le pone
flores a la tripulación de un barco herrumbroso y
negro. Cada flor tiene un nombre y se doblan
juntas como pañuelos despidiéndolo. Mireya dice
que es madre de un barco de desaparecidos
arrumbado en el desierto. Dice que el barco es
Chile, que una vez fue un barco de vivos, pero
que ahora surca el mar de piedras con sus hijos
muertos.

Las flores se doblan. Oleadas y oleadas de piedras
chocan contra los bordes de un casco
herrumbroso.

Hay un puerto reseco y un barco con una
tripulación de muertos encallado en la mitad del
desierto. Mireya dice que son sus hijos. El mar de
piedras grita.

Chile encalla y naufraga en el pedrerío reseco de
las olas.

Raúl Zurita (Chile)

Mato por rabia

Mato por rabia, por odio, por despecho; mato por celos,
por venganza; mato para hacer(me), hacer(te) justicia.
Para que entiendas de una vez y para siempre, para descansar
de ti; mato por miedo, para robar, para huir, para defenderme;
mato por hábito, para divertirme; mato por reacción,

Before the ship they seem like tiny suns
bidding it farewell.

*

The desert screams, the parched harbour screams, the sea
of rocks scream, lashed by the wind. Mireya lays down
flowers for the crew of a rusty black ship.
Every flower has a name and they bend together
like handkerchiefs waving it goodbye. Mireya says
she is the mother of a shipload of the disappeared
forgotten in the desert. She says that the ship is
Chile, that once it was a ship of the living, but
now it ploughs through the sea of rocks with her dead
children.

The flowers bend over. Wave after wave of rocks
crash against the sides of
a rusty hull.

There is a parched harbour and a ship with
a crew of the dead run aground in the middle of the desert.
Mireya says they are her children. The sea
of rocks screams.

Chile runs aground and is wrecked on the parched rock-heap
of the waves.

Raúl Zurita (Chile)

I Kill out of Rage

I kill out of rage, out of hatred, out of spite; I kill from jealousy,
for revenge; I kill to bring justice (for me or for you).
So that you understand for once and for all, to get a rest
from you; I kill out of fear, to rob, to flee, to defend myself;
I kill out of habit, for fun; I kill as a reaction;

para que no me mates, para que no me violes. Mato porque
ya no aguanto, porque quiero morirme pero no me atrevo,
porque hasta los niños matan, porque estoy enfermo, porque
estoy loco, porque estoy triste, porque ya nadie me quiere.
Mato en nombre de mi religión, en nombre de mi pueblo,
de la libertad, de la democracia. Mato en nombre de Dios.
Y también mato porque se me da la gana aquí, en la chabola,
en el barrio, en el antro, en la carretera, en tu casa, en la mía.
Mato por droga, porque me excita, porque me ejercito, porque
un día a mí me van a matar. Mato perros, gatos, puercos, gente.
Mato al que va en la calle, al que duerme, al que se divierte.
Mato con armas para que haya sangre, para que corra la sangre
como mi rabia, mi hartazgo, mi injusticia, mi fealdad, mi sexo,
mi gordura, mi diabetes, mi cirrosis, mi cáncer, mi retraso mental,
mi estupidez, mis pesadillas, mi vida sin remedio.

Te mato a ti pero puedo matar a tu hermana, a tu padre, a tu mujer,
a tus hijos, a tu amante, a tu abuela, a tu perro. Te mato hoy pero
no confíes porque puedo matarte mañana, cualquier día,
con las balas que van a perforar tu pulmón y tu estomago
y que se alojarán, muy calientes, en tu cuello, en tus ingles,
en tu cabeza. Y lo tuyo no será de nadie, ya ves, lo que pregonaste,
lo que hiciste, lo que sabías, lo que tanto te gustaba: tus mañanas,
tus noches acompañado, tus recuerdos, tus planes, todo se lo comerá
el acero. Bullets, hermano, bullets; qué tragedia, que dolor,
van a gritar los que te conocieron, y tú ya en cenizas, hombre,
mujer, niño, feo, bonito, bruto, genial, pobre, rico, qué importa.
¿Mataste alguna vez? ¿Lo has intentado?
Dispara, le dice el asesino al muchacho,
¿o es que no te atreves?
Nunca ha habido un arma en mi casa, nunca la hubo,
nunca he disparado.

Claudia Hernández de Valle-Arizpe *(México)*

so that you don't kill me, so that you don't rape me. I kill because
I can't bear it anymore, because I want to die but don't dare,
because even children kill, because I'm sick, because
I'm crazy, because I'm sad, because nobody loves me anymore.
I kill in the name of my religion, in the name of my people,
of freedom, of democracy. I kill in the name of God.
And also I kill because here I feel like it, in the shack,
in the neighbourhood, in the nightclub, on the road, in your house, in mine.
I kill for drugs, because it excites me, because it's exercise, because
one day it's me they're going to kill. I kill dogs, cats, pigs, people.
I kill who's going past in the street, or sleeping, or having fun.
I kill with weapons so that there's blood, so that the blood runs
like my rage, my weariness, my injustice, my ugliness, my sex,
my obesity, my diabetes, my cirrhosis, my cancer, my mental retardation,
my stupidity, my nightmares, my hopeless life.

I kill you but could kill your sister, your father, your wife,
your children, your lover, your grandmother, your dog. I kill you today but
don't trust me, because I can kill you tomorrow, any day,
with bullets that will pierce your lung and your stomach
and will lodge, very hot, in your neck, in your groin, in your head.
And what is yours will be no one's, you see; what you proclaimed,
what you did, what you knew, what you liked so much; your mornings,
your nights in company, your memories, your plans, all of this will bite
the dust. Bullets, brother, bullets; what a tragedy, what sorrow,
those who knew you will cry, and you now in ashes, man,
woman, child, ugly, pretty, ignorant, brilliant, poor, rich, whatever.
Have you ever killed? Have you tried to?
Shoot, says the killer to the boy,
or don't you dare?
There has never been a weapon in my house, there never was,
I have never fired a shot.

Claudia Hernández de Valle-Arizpe (Mexico)

Sollozos

Yo siempre llego tarde
a los entierros,
cuando los ojos
de los concurrentes
se han secado
y algunos ya olvidaron
la cara del difunto,
qué edad tenía,
de qué murió.
Entonces llego yo
con mi llanto anacrónico,
con el negro de mi luto
en todo su candor aún,
reparto abrazos
como incendios,
retengo entre mis manos
las manos de la viuda
y de los huérfanos,
todo el cortejo asiste
a mi dolor,
nadie se atreve a contrariarlo,
la gente se avergüenza
y vuelve a apretujarse
alrededor del muerto,
la viuda no resiste
y rompe a sollozar,
los huérfanos también
y el llanto crece nuevamente,
alcanza a todos,
a los que no habían llorado aún,
a los que andan por ahí,
que advierten que es un llanto de reflujo,
de envergadura,
y entran en él,
se olvidan de sus muertos
o los recuerdan con más claridad,

Sobbing

I always arrive late
at funerals,
when the eyes
of those attending
have dried
and some have already forgotten
the face of the deceased,
how old he was,
the cause of his death.
Then I arrive
with my anachronistic weeping,
in my mourner's black
with its sincerity intact,
and like a conflagration
I offer out hugs,
clasp the hands of the widow
and of the orphans
between my hands,
the whole cortège witnesses
my pain,
no one dares refute it,
people are embarrassed
and crowd together again
around the dead man,
the widow caves in
and breaks into sobs,
the orphans also
and the sound of weeping grows once more,
reaching everyone,
those who have not yet wept,
those who are there
who observe that it is the weeping of a returning tide
of considerable magnitude,
and they enter into it,
they forget about their dead
or remember them with greater clarity,

y el llanto se hace caudaloso,
arrastra llantos de otras épocas,
se advierte su bramido de gran llanto
que se expande
y se desliga de los muertos,
por eso llego tarde
al llanto de los otros,
vengo con otro llanto
en la garganta
que suelto entre los cuerpos húmedos
y veo cómo se prende en cada lágrima,
se enrosca,
crepita en cada uno,
y soy el único que sabe
que es mi desdicha
la que están llorando,
que están llorando por mis muertos
y me regalan sus sollozos.

Fabio Morábito (México)

and the weeping flows faster,
dragging with it the weeping of other occasions,
its roar warns of a great weeping
which broadens out
and detaches itself from the dead,
for this I arrive late
at the weeping of others,
I come with another weeping
in my throat
which I let loose among the damp bodies
and I see how it clings to every tear
coils around,
crackles in each of them,
and I am the only one who knows
it is my misfortune
they are weeping for,
that they are weeping for my dead
and bestow their weeping on me.

Fabio Morábito (Mexico)

General Acknowledgements

In researching and making the selection for this anthology, I have drawn on the help of many friends. In the first instance, I would like to thank the poets themselves for allowing me to translate and publish their poems. While many were happy to accept my translations without comment, others offered useful contextual information, or provided help with the translation of particular words or phrases.

So I'd like to start by acknowledging my thanks to the poets with whom I discussed their own or other poems face-to-face or by email, namely: Héctor Abad Faciolince, Jorge Aulicino, Piedad Bonnett, Rómulo Bustos Aguirre, Damaris Calderón, Gabriel Chávez Casazola, Carlos Decap, Jorge Fondebrider, Irene Gruss, Darío Jaramillo Agudelo, Carlos López Beltrán, Tedi López Mills, Andrés Neuman, Sergio Raimondi, María Rivera, Juan Manuel Roca, Daniel Samoilovich, Leonardo Sanhueza, Pedro Serrano, Enrique Winter and Verónica Zondek. I asked many questions of some of these people, fewer of others, but they all demonstrated patience and understanding in providing me with answers.

I would like to express my extraordinary gratitude to Tom Pow for insisting that I meet Alastair Reid, and for putting me up so generously at his home in Dumfries in July 2014. Like Tom, several of the contributors to the anthology offered me hospitality when I visited their countries, inviting me to stay in their houses for indeterminate periods and at very short notice. In this last category I am especially grateful to the northernmost and southernmost of my hosts: Julián Herbert in Saltillo, Mexico, and Verónica Zondek in Valdivia, Chile, and to their respective partners, Mónica and Menashe. To Paulo Slachevsky and Silvia Aguilera I owe thanks for the use of their home in Santiago de Chile, and similarly to Enrique Winter, on two visits to Valparaíso. I also wish to thank Pedro Serrano, Ana Franco and Lucrecia Orensanz for their kindness to me during my time in Mexico City, and Pura López Colomé, for showing me Cuernavaca, under the volcano.

I owe a debt of gratitude to all those who invited me to the literary festivals I attended while researching the book: Francisco de Asis and Gloria Gabuardi (Granada, Nicaragua, 2011 and 2012); Pablo

Braun and Pablo Makovsky (Buenos Aires and Rosario, Argentina, respectively, 2011); Fernando Rendón (Medellín, Colombia 2012); Federico Díaz-Granados (Bogotá, Colombia, 2014); Paulo Slachevsky and Silvia Aguilera (Santiago, Chile, 2014); Graciela Aráoz (Buenos Aires, Argentina, 2015), and Nubia Macias Navarro and Laura Niembro (Guadalajara, México, 2011 and 2016).

Many thanks to Jorge Fondebrider, with whom the whole journey started, for our many conversations regarding Latin American poetry and its diverse trends and movements, as well as for his advice on just about everything. Thanks too for the warm welcome I have received from Jorge and his family on several trips to Buenos Aires.

I am indebted to Patrick McGuinness, George Szirtes, David Greenslade, Tom Pow, Bill Herbert, Daniel Hahn and Edith Grossman for reading and commenting on the manuscript. All of you contributed to the final stages of the book's making.

The support of Rose, my wife, and of our daughters, Sioned and Rhiannon, has been inestimable. Rose, an astute reader of both Spanish and English, was willing to discuss obscure points of translation with me at all hours of night and day. Special thanks also to Rhiannon, herself a translator, for copy-editing the drafts and helping with preparation of the final manuscript.

The biggest thanks of all is reserved for my dear friend Inés Garland, a fine writer and skilled translator, who read every poem in this book, and commented in detail on my translations, displaying exemplary patience and helping me avoid several potential pitfalls or embarrassments. Without her, the task would have been far more difficult, and infinitely less enjoyable. If any errors remain, the fault is entirely mine.

I am grateful to the Arts Council of Wales for appointing me Creative Wales Ambassador for the year 2014, which enabled me to travel in Latin America – an award that would not have been possible without the untiring support of Sioned Puw Rowlands at Wales Literature Exchange. I am grateful too for the award of research leave by Cardiff University that enabled me to complete this work. Finally, many thanks to Mick Felton at Seren for offering to do the book in the first place. It's been an interesting journey already, and it's not over yet.

Source Acknowledgements

The translator and publishers would like to thank the authors and publishers of the poems included in this anthology, which originally appeared as follows:

Héctor Abad Faciolince: 'Memento' was first published in *Testamento involuntario* (Bogotá: Alfaguara, 2011); **Humberto Ak'Abal**: the poem 'Chinumutux' was first published in *El animalero* (Guatemala: Editorial Cultura 1990) and 'Camino al revés' in *Guardián de la caída de agua* (Guatemala: Editorial Serviprensa Centroamericana, 1993); **Roberto Appratto**: 'Es la voz' was first published in *Levemente ondulado* (Montevideo: Librería Linardi y Risso, 2005) and 'Todos los poetas' first appeared in *Lugar* perfecto (Montevideo: Yaugurú, Montevideo, 2011); **Teresa Arijón**: 'La vida nueva' first appeared in her book *Os* (Málaga: Puerta del Mar, 2008). **Jorge Aulicino**: 'La ciudad y los bárbaros' is from *Paisaje con autor* (Buenos Aires: Último reino, 1988), La ley de la calle comes from *Hombres en un restaurante* (Buenos Aires: Libros de Tierra Firme, 1994), and 'Cierta dureza en la sintaxis' is from the collection of the same name (Buenos Aires: Selecciones de Amadeo Mandarino, 2008); **Frank Baéz**: 'Maullido' and 'Los beach poets' both first appeared in *Postales* (Santo Domingo: Ediciones De a Poco, 2009); **Gustavo Barrera Calderón**: 'El espacio vacío' was published in *Adornos en el espacio vacio* (Santiago de Chile: El Mercurio-Aguilar, 2002). **Igor Barreto**: 'Ladrón de gallos' was published in *Soul of Apure* (San Fernando de Apure: Ediciones Sociedad de Amigos del Santo Sepulcro, 2006); **Diana Bellessi**: 'Crucero ecuatorial' first appeared in *Crucero ecuatarial* (Paraná: Sirirí, 1981) and 'Detrás de los fragmentos' in *Danzante doble máscara* (Buenos Aires: Ediciones Ultimo Reino, 1985). **Gioconda Belli**: 'Dios dijo' was first published in *Línea de fuego* (La Habana: Casa de las Américas, 1978); **Javier Bello**: 'La jaula de sentencia' is from the collection *Las jaulas* (Madrid: Visor, 1998) and 'XI' is taken from *El fulgor del vacío* (Santiago de Chile: Editorial Cuarto Propio, 2002); **Piedad Bonnett**: 'Biografía de un hombre con miedo' was first published in *El hilo de los días* (Bogotá: Colcultura, 1995) and 'Lección de supervivencia' in *Explicaciones no pedidas* (Madrid: Visor, 2011); **Osvaldo Bossi**: poems are from the collection *Tres* (Buenos Aires: Bajo la luna, 1997); **Coral Bracho**: the poem 'Cabras' first appeared in *Si ríe el emperador* (México DF: Era, 2010); **Camilo Brodsky**: 'Las naturalezas muertas: mirlos, tordos y otras aves' was first published in *Whitechapel* (Santiago de Chile: Das Kapital, 2009); **Rómulo Bustos Aguirre**: 'Balada de la Casa' was published in *En el traspatio del cielo* (Bogotá: Colcultura, 1993), 'Escena de Marbella' in *La estación de la sed* (Bogotá: Editorial magisterio, 1998) and 'Del cangrejo ermitaño' and 'Cuento' in *Muerte y levitación de la ballena*. (Cali: Universidad del Valle, 2011); **Damaris Calderón**: 'Está será la única mentira en la que siempre creeremos' was first published in *Con el terror del equilibrista* (La Habana: Matanzas, 1987) and 'Instantanéa' in *Guijarros* (La Habana: UNEAC,

1994); **Fabián Casas**: 'Despertarte' was published in *El salmón*, (Buenos Aires: Ediciones Deldiego, 1996) and 'Tratando de sepultar' was published in *Pogo* (Buenos Aires: Ediciones Deldiego, 1999); **Luis Chaves**: the poem 'Traducción libre de un tema inédito de Chan Marshall' was published in *Chan Marshall* (Madrid: Visor, 2005); **Gabriel Chávez Casazola**: both 'He nacido en los confines' and 'La canción de la sopa' were published in *El pie de Eurídice*, (Bogotá: Gamar, 2014); **Micaela Chirif**: 'Un amigo' was first published, untitled, in *Sobre me almohada una cabeza* (Valencia: Pre-Textos, 2012); **Eduardo Chirinos**: The poems 'Un perro mojado de rocío' and 'La herida' both form part of the book *No tengo ruiseñores en el dedo* (Valencia: Pre-Textos, 2006). **Alejandro Cortés González**: The poem 'Jurar en vano' was first published in *Pero la sangre sigue fría* (Bogotá: Editorial Kimpres, 2012); **Ramón Cote Baraibar**: 'Premonición en San Librario' was first published in the book *Como quien dice adios a lo perdido* (Granada, Spain: Valparaíso ediciones, 2014); **Rafael Courtoisie**: . 'Those who are not here' was first published in *Umbría* (Caracas: Colección Vitrales de Alejandria, 1999); **Alejandro Crotto**: The poems 'En el Haras Vadarkablar' and 'Las Palomas' were both published in *Abejas* (Buenos Aires: Bajolaluna, 2009). **Carolina Dávila**: 'Postal de Buenos Aires' was published in *Como los catedrales* (Bogotá: U. Nacional de Colombia, 2011); **Carlos Decap**: 'American Bar' and 'Batalla del Ebro' are both taken from *Asunto de Ojos* (Viña del Mar: Ediciones Altazor, 2014); **Antonio Deltoro**: The poem 'Primavera' was published in *Los árboles que poblarán en el Ártico* (México DF: Era, 2012); **Edgardo Dobry**: The poem 'Mandado' was first published in *El lago de los botes* (Barcelona: Lumen, 2005); **Paula Einöder**: 'La escritura de arcilla' was first published in the collection also titled *La esctiura de arcilla* (Montevideo: Ediciones imaginarias, 2002); **Siomara España**: 'La Casa Vacía' first appeared in *Concupiscencia*, (Quito: Editorial El Ángel, 2007) and 'El Regreso de Lolita' appeared in the book of that title (Guayaquil: El Quirófano, 2014). **Eduardo Espina**: 'Razón de todas las cosas' first appeared in *La caza nupcial* (Buenos Aires: Último Reino, 1992); **Fabricio Estrada**: 'El espejo' was first published in *Poemas contra el miedo* (Tegucigalpa: Editorial Pez Dulce, 2001); **Luis Felipe Fabre**: 'Xochicuicatl' first appeared in *Cabaret Provenza* (México DF: Fondo de Cultura Económica, 2007). 'Imagen de la desconocida' and 'Infommercial' were both published in *Poemas de terror y de misterio* (México DF: Almadía, 2013); **Jorge Fernández Granados**: 'Las cosas' was originally published in the book *Los hábitos de la ceniza* (México DF: Joaquín Mortiz, 2000); **Damsi Figueroa**: 'Execración de la luz' was first published in *Cartografia del éter* (Santiago de Chile: Ediciones del Temple, 2003); **Jorge Fondebrider**: 'De cómo el amor se vuelve recuerdo del amor' was first published in *Imperio de la luna* (Buenos Aires: Libros de Tierra Firme, 1987); 'All The Things You Are' was first published in *Standards* (Buenos Aires: Terra Firme, 1993); 'Regent's Canal (A La Altura De Danbury Street)' first appeared in *Los últimos tres años* (Buenos Aires: Terra Firme, 2006), and 'Desmantelar la casa' appears in his collected poems, *La extraña trayectoria de la luz* (Buenos Aires: Bajolaluna, 2016); **Ana Franco**: 'Peligro de extinción' was first published in a bilingual (Spanish-Mixteco) plaquette (Barcelona, 2012); **Jessica Freudenthal Ovando**: The fragment 'Arbol' is from *Demo* (La Paz: Plural Ediciones, 2011); 'La casa del loco' is available online at: http://www.puntoenlinea.unam.mx/images/stories/pdf/cartografias-54-jessica-freuedentahl.pdf; **John Galán Casanova**: 'Poema de la primera vez' and 'Poema de la última vez' were both published in *Al pie de la letra* (Bogotá: Universidad Externado de Colombia, 2008); **Alicia García Bergua**: 'Metafísica zoológica' was first published in *Ser y seguir siendo* (México DF: Textofilia, 2013); **Jacqueline Goldberg**: the poem 'El moribundo nos convoca' was first published in *La salud* (Caracas: Editorial La nave va, 2002); **Catalina González Restrepo**: both 'Alimento' and 'Viaje' were published in *La última batalla* (Valencia: Pre-Textos, 2010); **Irene Gruss**: 'Mientras tanto' is from *Sobre el asma* (Buenos Aires: Ed. de la autora, 1995), 'Tea' is from *Solo de contralto*, (Buenos Aires: Editorial Galerna, 1997) and 'La muerte está en casa' appeared in *De Humo: Antología personal* (Madrid: La Palma y Eme, 2015); **Marcelo Guajardo Thomas**: 'Cochrane' was first published in *Un momento propicio para el exilio* (Santiago de Chile: Das Kapital Ediciones, 2011); **Wendy Guerra**: 'El viaje inverso', 'Un rostro en la muchedumbre' and 'Palabra de esquimal' all appeared in *Ropa interior* (Barcelona: Bruguera, 2008); **Otoniel Guevara**: 'Nunca tuve una casa' was first published in the cultural supplement *Tres Mil, Diario Colatino, El Salvador 2010*; **Tomás Harris**: 'Argel' is taken from the collection *Diario de navegación* (Concepción: Editorial Sur, 1986); **D.G. Helder**: 'Intrascedencia' first appeared in *El faro de Guereño* (Buenos Aires: Libros de Tierra Firme, 1990), while 'No clarea y ya se oyen cacareos' and 'Cuerpos de todos los tamaños...' were both first published in *El Guadal* (Buenos Aires: Libros de Terra Firme, 1994); **Carlos Henrickson**: 'Pequeña canción realista' was first published in the book *Despoblados* (Santiago de Chile: Ed. Fuga, 2011); **Julián Herbert**: 'Los Mezquites' first appeared in *Kubla Khan* (México DF: Era, 2005) and 'Oscura' first appeared in *Álbum Iscariote* (México DF: Era, 2013); **Osvaldo Hernández Alas**: both 'Canción para Manuel' and 'Vinieron los muertos' first appeared in *Parábola de los ríos*, (San José, Costa Rica: Casa de Poesía, 2015); **Claudia Hernández de Valle-Arizpe**: 'Mato por rabia' was first published in *Perros muy azules* (México DF: Era, 2012); **Ricardo Herrera Alarcón**: the poem 'Un hombre solo en una casa sola' first appeared in *El cielo ideal* (Santiago de Chile: LOM ediciones, 2013); **Jaime Luis Huenún**: 'En la casa de Zulema Hualquipán' was first published in *Reducciones* (Santiago de Chile: LOM ediciones, 2013); **Miguel Ildefonso Huanca**: 'Odiseo' was first published in *Canciones de un bar en la frontera* (Lima: El Santo oficio ediciones, 2001); **Darío Jaramillo Agudelo**: 'Razones del ausente' was first published in *Tratado de retórica – o de la necesitad de poesía* (Cúcuta: Instituto de Cultura y Bellas Artes: 1978); 'Testimonio acerca del hermano' was originally published in *Poemas de Amor* (Bogotá: Fundación Simón y Lola Guberek, 1986) and the sequence 'Gatos' is from the book *Gatos* (Valencia: Pre-Textos, 2003); **Carlos López Beltrán**: 'Desabrigo' was published in the *Anuario de poesía mexicana*, edited by Julián Herbert (México DF: Fondo de Cultura Económica, 2007); **Pura López**

Colomé: 'Y el anturio, impávido' was first published in *Santo y seña* (México DF: Fondo de Cultura Económica, 2007); **Tedi López Mills**: 'La guerra sutil' was first published in *Segunda persona* (México DF: UAM, 1994); 'Fiestas' is as yet uncollected; **Edwin Madrid**: 'Delicias de la noche' first appeared in *Tambor secreto y otros poemas* (Quito: Sistema nacional de bibliotecas, 1995); 'Muchacho de corazón amarillo' was published in *Mordiendo el frío* (Madrid: Visor, 2004); **Diego Maquieira**: 'La Tirana' (Me sacaron por la cara) is the title poem from the collection *La Tirana* (Santiago de Chile: Edición Tempus Tacendi, 1983); **Eduardo Milán**: 'decir ahí es una flor difícil' first appeared in *Nervadura* (Barcelona: Llibres del Mall, 1985) and 'El salto del tigre, metáfora' appeared in *Por momentos la palabra entera* (México: Ediciones Idea, 2006); **Alessandra Molina**: 'Ronda infantil' was published first in *As de triunfo* (La Habana: Ediciones Unión, 2001); **Mauricio Molina**: 'El Viejo licántropo' appeared in *Abominable libro de la nieve* (México DF: Conaculta, 1999); **Tania Montengro**: 'El ñatazo' was first published in *La Revolvición* (Managua: Fondo centroamericano de mujeres, 2014); **Fabio Morábito**: 'Despedida' and 'Ajusco' are from *Lotes baldíos* (México DF: FCE, 1985); 'Time of Crisis' and 'Weeping' are from *De lunes todo el año*, (México DF: Joaquín Mortiz, 1992); **Andrés Neuman**: the poem 'Buenos Aires al vuelo' was first published in *El tobogán* (Madrid: Hiperión, 2002); **Carmen Ollé Nava**: the poem 'Bares' was first published in the book *Todo Orgullo humea la noche* (Lima: Lluvia, 1988); **Miguel Ángel Petrecca**: 'Novelista' first appeared in the collection *La voluntad* (Buenos Aires: Bajo la Luna, 2013). **Paula Piedra**: 'Sí hay sueño Americano' was first published in the book *Ejercicios Mentales* (Costa Rica: Perro Azul, 2003); **Jaime Pinos**: 'Vista general' was first published in the collection *80 días* (Santiago de Chile: Alquima Ediciones/Siega, 2014); **Nadia Prado**: 'Siempre escribía' was first published in the collection *Job* (Santiago de Chile: LOM Ediciones, 2005); **Aleyda Quevedo Rojas**: 'Por fortuna' appeared in *La otra, la misma de Dios* (Quito: Editorial Conejo, 2011); **Sergio Raimondi**: 'Qué es el mar' and 'El verbo inglés ante la acción del fuego' were both published in *Poesía civil* (Bahía Blanca: VOX, 2001); **Clemente Reidemann**: 'El hombre de Leipzig' was first published in *Karra Maw'n* (Valdivia: Alborada, 1984); **María Rivera**: the poem 'Los Muertos' was published in the collection *Los Muertos* (México DF: Mantarraya Ediciones, 2010); **Juan Manuel Roca**: 'Lo que ocurre en el poema', Paisaje con mendigos', 'Mester de servidumbre' and 'Palimpsesto desde Rimbaud' were all originally published in *Biblia de pobres* (Madrid: Visor, 2009); **Mirta Rosenberg**: 'Una carta convertida en cosa' was published in *El arte de perder* (Buenos Aires: Bajolaluna, 1998) and 'Si alguien querría ser una tortuga' is from *El paisaje interior* (Buenos Aires: Bajolaluna, 2012); **Daniel Samoilovich**: 'La casa del Tigre' and 'Libélulas' are both from *El mago* (Buenos Aires: De la Flor, 1984); 'Porto dos Ossos' was first published in *La Ansiedad Perfecta* (Buenos Aires: De la Flor, 1991); **Leonardo Sanhueza**: 'Puño' was first published in *La ley de Snell* (Santiago de Chile: Ediciones Tácitas, 2010); **Juan Ramón Saravia**: 'De cómo algunas curaciones resultan peor que la enfermedad misma' was first published in *Paisajes bíblicos: de* *ida y vuelta* (Tegucigalpa: Guaymuras, 1985); **Osvaldo Sauma**: 'Mirándola dormir' was first published in *El libro del adiós* (Costa Rica: Perro Azul, 2006). **Alejandro Schmidt**: 'Mi corazón era un hotel' was first published in *Esquina del universe* (Córdoba, Argentina: Alcion Editora, 2001); **Marina Serrano**: 'What did we go to see, Simón . . .?' and 'You never said yes' were both first published in *La única cosa necesaria* (Córdoba, Argentina: Ediciones del Copista, 2012); **Pedro Serrano**: The three poems are uncollected in book form: 'El conejo y la chistera' first appeared in *Revista Sibila*, no. 39, April 2012; 'Berwick' in *Revista Estación Poesía*, no. 5, September 2015; 'Dark Ages' is first published here. **Alicia Torres**: 'Like Percival' is taken from *Consideración de la rosa* (Caracas: Pequeña Venecia, 2000); **Julio Trujillo**: 'Diez tequilas' was published in *Una sangre* (México DF: Trilce, 1998); **Malú Urriola**: the extract published here is from *Hija de perra* (Santiago de Chile: Cuarto propio, 1998); **Mónica Velásquez Guzmán**: 'Siete maneras de decir el dolor (Posibilidad 1)' is from *El viento de los náufragos* (La Paz: Plural, 2005); **Beatriz Vignoli**: 'La guerra de los tontos', 'La caída', 'Función de la lírica', 'Plaza St. Exupéry and 'Escrito en la mesa de luz de un hotel ****' were all published in *Viernes* (Buenos Aires: Bajolaluna, 2001); **Ariel Williams**: The extract consists of the first three poems in *Discurso del contador de gusanos* (Buenos Aires: El Suri Porfiado, 2011); **Enrique Winter**; 'El piso sucio y la luz prendida' and 'Polaca' both appeared in *Rascacielos* (México DF: Limón partido, 2008); **Laura Wittner**: 'Plastic Moon' and 'Otra ciudad' were first published in *La tomadora de café* (Bahía Blanca: Ediciones Vox, 2005); **Verónica Zondek**: 'Profundo en el mapa' first appeared in *El libro de los valles* (Santiago de Chile: LOM Ediciones, 2003); 'Progreso' and 'Ausencia' first appeared in 'Por gracia de hombre' (Santiago de Chile: LOM Ediciones, 2008); **Raúl Zurita**: the four poems included in this anthology constitute the first half of the 'Desierto' section of *Inri* (Madrid: Visor, 2003).

Contributor Biographies

Héctor Abad Faciolince is a Colombian writer, most widely known for his work as a novelist, especially for his bestselling *Angosta* (2004). Born in 1958 in Medellín, Abad has also spent extended periods in Spain, Italy and later Berlin, largely because it was dangerous for him to remain in Colombia. Abad began writing at an early age, and at 21 was awarded the 1980 Colombian National Short Story Prize for *Piedras de Silencio*, but it was while in Italy that he published his first book, *Malos Pensamientos*, a collection of short stories. His memoir, *El olvido que seremos*, published in English as *Oblivion*, recounts the murder of his father, a prominent doctor, by paramilitary thugs in 1993.

Humberto Ak'Abal was born in 1952 in Momostenango, Guatemala, of the Maya k'iche people. He writes in Maya-k'iche and Spanish, and his work has been widely translated, into French, English, German, Arabic and Italian, amongst other languages. Ak'Abal has published twenty books of poetry, including: *El Animalero, Guardián de la caída de agua, Gaviota y sueño, Ovillo de seda, Oscureciendo, Las palabras crecen, Solitud*, and *Cantares de hojarasca*. He has also written three books of short stories, and two books of essays.

Roberto Appratto was born in Mondevideo, Uruguay in 1950. A poet, novelist and literary critic, Appratto has published ten poetry collections and six novels. He has taught literature classes, literary theory and cinematographic narrative classes in high schools and Universities in Uruguay, and continues to run writing and reading workshops.

Teresa Arijón was born in Buenos Aires in 1960 and is a poet and translator. Her published poetry collections include *La escrita* (1988), *Alibí* (1995), *Poemas y animals sueltos* (2005) and *Os* (Puerta del Mar, 2008). *Óstraca* (2011) features poems from Arijón's previous collections as well as some previously unpublished poems.

Jorge Aulicino, born in Buenos Aires in 1949, is a poet, journalist and translator. He has published a number of poetry collections, a large selection of which appear in *Estación Finlandia: Poemas Reunidos* (Buenos Aires: Bajolaluna, 2012). Aulicino has translated a number of Italian poets, including Cesare Pavese and Pier Paolo Pasolini; and in 2015 published his translation of Dante's *Divine Comedy*. He worked for the Buenos Aires newspaper Clarín for 28 years and from 2005 to 2012 was the editor of the newspaper's weekly cultural magazine, Ñ. In 2015, he won the Argentine National Poetry Prize.

Frank Báez, born in Santo Domingo, Dominican Republic, in 1978, is a poet, editor and writer. He has published three books of poetry, one book of short stories and three books of chronicles. His poetry collection *Postales*

(Santo Domingo: Ediciones De a Poco, 2009) has been published in five countries and was awarded the Salome Ureña National Prize for Poetry in 2009. In 2014 a selection of his poetry was published in English, titled *Last Night I Dreamt I was a DJ* (Miami: Jai-Alai Books, 2014). His work is included in the anthology *El canon abierto: última poesía en español* (Madrid: Visor Libros, 2015), brings together many of the most relevant Spanish-language poets born after 1970. Báez also forms part of the multidisciplinary collective El Hombrecito, combining performance in music, literature and visual arts.

Gustavo Barrera Calderón, born in Santiago, Chile, in 1975, is a poet and performance artist. He has participated in a number of urban interventions integrating music, poetry and performance. Calderón obtained a degree in architecture at the Pontifica Universidad Católica, Chile. His publications include *Exquisite* (del Temple, 2001), *Adornos en el espacio vacio* (El Mercurio-Aguilar, 2002), *Creatur* (RIL, 2009), *Cuerpo perforada es una casa* (La Calabaza del Diablo, 2011), and a poetic sequence, *Carácter* (Barrera Real, 2008). Calderón has also published the book *Dinero, muerto y un rostro sin cejas* (Barrera Real, 2006), which includes a photographic record of a 'poetic intervention' in Santiago General Cemetery.

Igor Barreto was born in Venezuela in 1952. He was resident in Romania for a number of years and studied Theory of Art at the University of Bucharest (1973-1979). Barreto has published ten books of poetry, including *Crónicas llanas* (1989), *Carama* (2001), *Soul of Apure* (2006) and *El llano ciego* (2006), all published by Sociedad de Amigos, Caracas. Barreto has been translated into English, Italian and French. In 2008 he won a Guggenheim fellowship. He has also worked as Professor of Literature at both the Central and Metropolitan Universities of Venezuela. In 2014 the Spanish publisher Pre-textos published *El campo/El ascensor*, his Collected Poems.

Diana Bellessi was born in Santa Fe, Argentina, in 1946. She studied philosophy at the Universidad Nacional de Litoral. She coordinated writing workshops in Buenos Aires prisons for two years, an experience which is recorded in the book *Paloma de contraband* (Torres Aguero, 1988). In 1993 Bellessi was awarded a Guggenheim Fellowship. She has numerous publications to her name, including *Destino y propagaciones* (Casa de la cultura de Guayaquil, 1970); *Tributo del mudo* (Sirirí, 1982); *El jardín* (Bajo la Luna Nueva*, 1993); *La edad dorada* (Adriana Hidalgo, 2003) and *Tener lo que se tiene* (Adriana Hidalgo, 2009).

Gioconda Belli, born in Nicaragua in 1948 is a novelist, poet and political activist. Her publications include novels, poetry collections, a memoir, children's books, essays and political commentary, and her work has been translated into more than 14 languages. Belli's first book *Sobre la Grama* (1972) won the Universidad Nacional de Nicaragua poetry prize. *La Mujer Habitada* is a semi-autobiographical novel which received widespread attention, exploring gender narratives within the Nicaraguan revolution. Belli went on to win a number of awards including the Premio Internacional de 'Poesía Generación del 27' for her collection *Mi íntima multitud* (2002). Her memoir *El país bajo mi piel*, which chronicles her time as a Sandinista revolutionary, is published in English as *The Country Under my Skin* (Bloomsbury, 2002).

Javier Bello was born Concepción, Chile, in 1972. He studied Hispanic Language and Literature at the Universidad de Chile. It was also there that he formed the 'Grupo Códice' and collaborated in the publications of the bulletin *Cave Canem*, the magazine *Licantropía* and the anthology *Códices*, which he co-authored. In 1994 Bello won first prize in the unpublished category of the 'Juegos Literarios Gabriela Mistral' for *La rosa del mundo* (1996, Santiago). In 2006 he won the Premio Hispanoamericano de Poesía Juan Ramón Jiménez, and in 2007 the prestigious Pablo Neruda prize.

Piedad Bonnett was born in Amalfi, Colombia in 1951. She is a poet and novelist, whose awards include the Casa de América Prize (2011) for her collection *Explicaciones no pedidas* and the Poetas del Mundo Latino Prize (2012). Her memoir, *Lo que no tiene nombre* (That which has no name), recording the life and suicide of her son, received extraordinary plaudits across Latin America and Spain on its publication in 2013. She lives in Bogotá.

Osvaldo Bossi was born in Buenos Aires in 1963. He is a poet and novelist whose publications include *Tres* (Buenos Aires: Bajolaluna, 1997), *El muchacho de los helados y otros poemas* (Bajolaluna, 2006), *Ruego por el tornado* (Sigamos enamoradas, 2006), *Esto no puede seguir así* (Letras y Bibliotecas de Córdoba, 2010), *Como si yo fuera su novia* (Editorial Mágicas naranjas, 2013), as well as the novels *Adoro* (Bajolaluna, 2009) and *Yo soy aquel* (Nudista, 2014). He also features in a range of Argentinian and Latin American poetry anthologies. Since 2014 he has been editor of the poetry publishing house Viajero insomne.

Coral Bracho, born in Mexico City in 1951, is a poet and translator whose work has been published in several languages. Her publications include the poetry collections *El ser que va a morir* (J. Mortiz, 1982), *La voluntad del ámbar* (Ediciones Era, 1998), *Ese espacio, ese jardín* (Era, 2003), *Si ríe el emperador* (Era, 2010) and *Marfa, Texas*, (Era, 2015). She has been a Guggenheim fellow for poetry (N.Y.), and a SNCA fellow (México). She has received the National Poetry award (Aguascalientes, 1981), the Book of the Year award (Xavier Villaurrutia 2004) and the Jaime Sabines-Gatien Lapointe Prize (Quebec, 2011), among other awards.

Camilo Brodsky is a poet and editor, and was born in Santiago de Chile in 1974. He is one of the founders of the publisher Das Kapital, which, since 2009, has contributed to revitalising the Chilean literary scene, publishing novelists and poets such as Jaime Huenún, Ignacio Fritz and Leonardo

Hernández. In terms of his own writing, Brodsky received the 'Premio Municipal de Literatura de Santiago' in 2010 for his poetry collection *Whitechapel* (Das Kapital, Santiago, 2009), and in 2011 he won the CNCA prize for 'best unpublished work' for *La noche del zelota* (Das Kapital, 2013).

Rómulo Bustos Aguirre was born in 1954 in Santa Catalina de Alejandria, Colombia, and is the author of nine volumes of poetry, including, most recently *La pupila incesante: Obra poética* 1988-2013 (Universidad de Cartagena, Colombia, 2016). Using a language rich in metaphysical allusion and sensual imagery, Rómulo Bustos is a writer of 'slow' poetry, inspired by the landscape and themes of his native Caribbean. A professor of literature at the University of Cartagena, he has won the National Poetry Prize from the *Instituto Colombiano de Cultura*, and the Blas de Otero Prize from the Universidad Complutense de Madrid.

Damaris Calderón, born in 1967 in La Habana, Cuba is a poet, novelist and essayist. Her poetry collections include *Con el terror del equilibrista* (Ediciones Matanzas, 1987), *Duras aguas del trópico* (Ediciones Manzanas, 1992), *Duro de roer* (Ediciones Las Dos Fridas, 1999), and *Los amores del mal* (El billar de Lucrecia, 2006). Her poetry appears in anthologies of current Cuban and Latin-American poetry, and has been translated into English, Dutch, Portuguese and French.

Fabián Casas was born in 1965, in Buenos Aires, Argentina. He is the author of fiction, essays, poetry and screen plays. He is also a philosopher and journalist. Casas' literary career began in 1988 with the poetry book *Otoño, poemas de desintoxicación y tristeza* (Ediciones Filosalfia). His subsequent poetry publications include *Tuca* (1990), *El Salmón* (1996), *Pogo* (1999), *Bueno, eso es todo* (2001) and *El hombre de overol* (2007). In 2007 Casas received the German literary prize Anna Seghers.

Luis Chaves (b. 1969) is a Costa Rican poet, novelist and translator. Chaves' works have been published in Costa Rica, Mexico, Argentina, Spain, Germany, Italy and Slovenia. His publications include *Los animales que imaginamos* (1997, awarded the Isor Juana Inés de la Cruz Poetry Prize, Mexico); *Chan Marshall* (2005, awarded the III Fray Luis de Leon Poetry Prize, Spain), and *La máquina de hacer niebla*, which won the Costa Rican National Poetry Prize in 2012.

Gabriel Chávez Casazola is a Bolivian poet and journalist. Born in 1972, he published his first poetry collection, *Lugar Común* in 1999. Following this came *Escalera de Mano* (2003), *El agua iluminada* (2010) and *La mañana se llenará de jardineros* (2013). His work has been translated into Portuguese, Italian, English and Romanian. He is a columnist for Bolivian newspapers and a contributor to several international poetry magazines. His awards include the Medalla al Mérito Cultural del Estado Boliviano and in 2013 he was finalist for the Premio Mundial de Poesía Mística Fernando Rielo.

Micaela Chirif is a Peruvian poet and children's short story author. Born in Lima in 1973, Chirif's first poetry collection, *De vuelta* was published by Colmillo Blanco in 2001. Following this came *Cualquier cielo* (Mundo Ajeno, 2008), and *Sobre mi almohada una cabeza* (Pre-Textos, 2012). In 2015, Galería Estampa published an illustrated selection of her poetry as part of the Biblioteca Americana. Her work in children's literature has won her the Münich White Ravens de la Internationale Jugendbibliothek twice, for *Buenas noches, Martina* (2010), and *Desayuno* (2014).

Eduardo Chirinos, born in Lima, Peru in 1960, is a poet, essayist, translator and children's short story writer. His most recent poetry collections include *Breve historia de la música* (2001), which won the 2001 Premio Casa de América de Poesía, and *Mientras el lobo está* (2010), which won the 2010 XII Premio de Poesía Generación del 27. Chirinos has published translations from Mark Strand, Louise Glück and by the Filipino poet José Garcia Villa. He currently lives in Missoula, where he works as a Professor of Hispanoamerican and Spanish literature at Montana University.

Alejandro Cortés González was born in Bogotá, Colombia, in 1977. He has published the novel, *Notas de inframundo* (2005) and the poetry collections *Pero la sangre sigue fría* (2012) and *Sustancias que nos sobreviven* (2015). He won the 6th National Poetry Contest UIS (2014) for *Sustancias que nos sobreviven*. Cortés has participated in literary events in South America, Mexico and France. He is a member of the Trilce Foundation and director of cultural programming at the Trilce bookshop, Bogotá.

Ramón Cote Baraibar, born in Colombia in 1963, is a poet, novelist, and essayist. Baraibar's publications include *Poemas para una fosa común*, *Botella papel*, *Colección privada* (winner of Casa de América Prize, 2003), *Los fuegos obligados* (winner of the Unicaja de poesía prize, 2009), *Como quien dice adiós a lo perdido* (2014) and *Hábito del tiempo* (2015). His poems have been translated into English, French, German and Greek. He lives in Bogotá.

Rafael Courtoisie, a poet, novelist and essayist, was born in Montevideo, Uruguay, in 1958. Courtoisie is the author of seven novels, five books of short stories, and twenty books of poetry. His work has been translated into more than fifteen languages and he has been awarded a number of prestigious international awards including the Plural Prize, Jaime Sabines Prize (Mexico), Loewe Prize, Blas de Otero Prize (Spain), and was a finalist of the Romulo Gallegos prize in 1995. He has been an invited professor in universities across Latin America, the United States and Europe.

Alejandro Crotto was born in 1978 in Buenos Aires, Argentina. Crotto has a degree in literature and has published the poetry collections *Abejas* (2009), *Chesterton* (2013) and *Once personas* (2015), all with the Buenos Aires publishing house Bajolaluna. Crotto has published poems in the literary magazines *Diario de Poesía*, *Letras libres* and *Hablar de Poesía*, and has featured in a number of anthologies. He runs the blog losporquesdelarosa.blogspot.com, which is dedicated to poetry and the translation of poetry.

Carolina Dávila was born in Bogotá, Colombia in 1982. As well being as a poet, she is a lawyer specializing in women's and human rights. Dávila's first book of poems, *Como las catedrales* (Universidad Nacional de Colombia, Bogotá), won the 2010 national poetry prize, awarded by the Colombian Ministry of Culture. She has collaborated in a number of publications in Colombia and Latin America, including magazine publications in Colombia and Chile and poetry anthologies in Colombia and Venezuela.

Carlos Decap was born in Chile in 1958. He studied in Madrid at the Universidad de Concepción y Complutense and currently lives in Valaparaíso. His poetry publications include *Asunto de ojo* (1991), *Golpes de vista* (2005) and *Asunto de ojos* (2014). He works at the *El mundo* publishing house.

Antonio Deltoro was born in Mexico City in 1947. He has published, amongst others, the following collections of poetry: *Algarabía inorgánica* (1979), *¿Hacia dónde es aquí?* (1984), *Los días descalzos* (1992), *Balanza de sombras* (1996), *El quieto* (2008) and *Los árboles que poblarán el Ártico* (2012). In 2012, Deltoro published the book of essays *Favores recibidos*. He won the 1996 Premio Nacional de Poesía Aguascalientes for *Balanza de sombras* and the Premio Iberoamericano de Poesía Carlos Pellicer for *Los árboles que poblarán el Ártico*. In 2014 he won the Serbian Novi Sad International Festival of Literature prize and in 2015 the *Poetas del Mundo* Latino prize.

Edgardo Dobry, writer and translator, was born in Rosario, Argentina in 1962 and currently lives in Barcelona, where he is a professor in Hispano-American literature and theory of literature at Barcelona University. Dobry is the author of the poetry collections *Contratiempo* (Buenos Aires: Adriana Hidalgo, 2013) – which was written following the award of a Guggenheim fellowship in 2010; *Pizza Margarita* (México DF: Mangos de Hacha, 2011); *Cosas* (Barcelona: Lumen, 2008) and *El lago de los botes* (Lumen, 2005), amongst others. He has also published the collections of essay *Orfeo en el quiosco de diarios; ensayos sobre poesía* (Buenos Aires: Adriana Hidalgo, 2007) and *Una profecía del pasado; Lugones y la invención del "linaje de Hércules"* (Buenos Aires: FCE, 2010).

Paula Einöder was born in September 1974 in Montevideo, Uruguay, to a family of German origin. She holds a degree from the Universidad de la República de Uruguay, and works as an English teacher. Her first book *La escritura de arcilla* (Montevideo, 2002) was granted two Honourable Mentions in the annual literary awards of the Uruguayan Ministry of Culture and Education, and her poetry has appeared in national and international anthologies, as well as being translated into English and Italian. Her most recent project, *266 días* is published online. She currently lives in Munich, Germany.

Siomara España was born in Manabí, Ecuador, in 1976. She is a poet and lecturer at Guayaquil University, cultural editor of the newspaper *El Emigrante* and departmental editor of the Casa de la Cultura, Guayaquil. Her publications include: *Concupiscencia, Alivio demente, De cara al fuego, Contraluz, El regreso de lolita, Jardines en el aire,* and *Construcción de los sombreros encarnados, música para una muerte inversa*. She has won a number of awards and has been included in several international anthologies, including *Tapestry of the Sun: an anthology of Ecuadorian poetry* (San Francisco: Coimbra, 2010).

Eduardo Espina was born in Uruguay in 1954. He is the author of numerous books of essays, literary criticism and poetry. His publications also include more than 40 academic articles and 100 book introductions, notes and reviews. In 1980, Espina was the first Uruguayan participant in the prestigious International Writing Program at the University of Iowa. He has won the Uruguayan Premio Nacional de Ensayo twice, for *Las ruinas de lo imaginario*, (1996) and *Un plan de indicios* (2000). In 1998 he received the Premio Municipal de Poesía. In 2011 he was awarded a Guggenheim fellowship in poetry.

Fabricio Estrada is a poet and leading literary figure in Honduras, where he was born in 1974. He has published a large number of poetry collections since the first, *Sextos de lluvia* in 1998. His poetry has also been widely anthologised.

Luis Felipe Fabre was born in 1974 in Mexico City, where he still lives and teaches. His stark and striking poetry has a large following among a younger generation of Mexican writers. He was awarded grants from the National Fund for Culture and the Arts in the category for Young Artists both in 2004-5 and 2007-8. In 2014 He curated *Todos los originales serán destruidos (All the originals will be destroyed)*, an exhibition of contemporary art by Mexican poets.

Jorge Fernández Granados is a poet and essayist. Born in Mexico in 1965, he has received prestigious literary awards in his country, including the Premio Internacional Jaime Sabines, the Premio Nacional Aguascalientes and the Premio Iberoamericano Carlos Pellicer. He belongs to the Sistema Nacional de Creadores de Arte in Mexico.

Damsi Figueroa was born in Talcahuano, Chile in 1976. Her first poetry collection, *Judith y Eleofante* (Concepción: Editorial Letra Nueva, 1995) brought her to the attention of the reading public, and she was invited to participate in a number of anthologies, as well as in the first and second editions of the *Encuentro de Poetas Universitarios*, organized by the *Federación* *de Estudiantes* of the Universidad de Concepción. Her output also includes installations and works of conceptual art.

Jorge Fondebrider (born 1956 in Buenos Aires) is an Argentinian poet, critic and translator. Alongside his own collections, and several anthologies and studies of Argentinian poetry, he has published widely on such diverse topics as a history of Lycanthropy, a study of Argentinians in Paris, and books on Patagonia and Buenos Aires. Fondebrider is also a well-known music journalist, and a translator from both French and English, notably of recent Irish writing. A bilingual Selected Poems, *The Spaces Between*, translated by Richard Gwyn, is available from Cinnamon, Blaenau Ffestiniog (2013). His Collected Poems were published in 2016 as *La extraña trayectoria de la luz* (Buenos Aires: Bajolaluna).

Ana Franco Ortuño was born in Mexico City in 1969. She has a Master's in Hispanic literature from UNAM. As a poet, her publications include *De la lejanía* (Tinta nueva, 2005), *Sólo 8 poetas* (Arlequín, 2007) and *Parques o El imán de la tierra* (H. Vera, 2009). Her work has also been published in several anthologies including *Animales distintos: muestra de poetas argentinos, españoles y mexicanos nacidos en los sesenta* (Arlequín-Fonca-Conaculta, 2008). She is assistant editor for *Periódico de poesía* at UNAM, Mexico City.

Jessica Freudenthal Ovando, born in Madrid in 1978, is a Bolivian writer who lives in La Paz. She promotes children's reading with the Colectivo Lee and teaches Spanish on the International Baccalaureate Programme. She received an honorary mention in the *Premio nacional de poesía Yolanda Bedregal* for her book *Hardware* (2004 and 2009) and since then her work has appeared in various anthologies throughout America and Europe. Her second collection *Demo*, was published in 2010, and her third, *El filo de las hojas*, in 2015. A new collection, titled *Tree*, is forthcoming.

John Galán Casanova, born in Bogotá, Colombia, in 1970, is a poet and essayist. His first book *ALMAC N AC STA* (Bogotá, 1993), won the Premio Nacional de Poesía Joven de Colcultura, to which he added the International Poetry Prize *Villa de Cox* in 2009. Between 1998 and 2002 he worked as coordinator and editor for the network of literary workshops *Raíz de cinco*. His most recent publications are *LI poemas para Li* and a major translation of Brazilian poets into Spanish: *Once poetas brasileros* (both 2013).

Alicia García Bergua was born in Mexico City in September, 1954. She is a poet, essayist and translator. Bergua is editor of texts on popular science for the magazine *¿Cómo ves?* She has published numerous poetry collections and a book of essays. She is a member of Mexico's Sistema Nacional de Creadores.

Jacqueline Goldberg was born in Venezuela in 1966. She is a poet and novelist. Her novel *Las horas claras* won the XII Premio Transgenérico de la Sociedad de Amigos de la Cultura Urbana in 2012 and the *Premio Libro del*

Año de los Libreros Venezolanos in 2014. She has also won a number of awards for her poetry, including the *Premio de Poesía Bienal Mariano Picón* in 2001. Goldberg's poetry has appeared in a number of anthologies published in Spain, Peru, Venezuela and Argentina.

Catalina González Restrepo was born in Medellín, Colombia, in 1976. She obtained her undergraduate degree in Spanish and Literature from the Universidad de Antioquia and a Master's from the Pontificia Universidad Javeriana in Bogotá, the city in which she began her career as an editor, which she still pursues. Her two most recent poetry collections are *La última batalla* (Pre-Textos, 2010) and *Una palabra brilla en mitad de la noche* (Universidad Externado de Colombia, 2012). Her work has also appeared in national and international anthologies and magazines and has been translated into French, Portuguese, Italian and English.

Irene Gruss was born in Buenos Aires, Argentina, in 1950. She forms part of the group of poets who founded the workshop 'Mario Jorge De Lellis 'at the beginning of the 1970s. A prominent figure on the Argentine poetry circuit of the 1980s and 90s, she is a minimalist, writing in an intimate and sometimes brutal register about everyday and prosaic subject matter. A Collected Poems, *La mitad de la verdad*, was published by Bajolaluna (Buenos Aires) in 2008.

Marcelo Guajardo Thomas is a Chilean writer. He was born in Santiago in 1977. His most recent books are *Un momento propicio para el exilio* (2011), which unites all of the texts written between 2002 and 2010, and *Puerta azul en muro de adobe* (2014). In addition to the high praise he has received for his poetry, his novel *La bicicleta mágica de Sergio Krumm* won the Premio Barco de Vapor in 2013.

Wendy Guerra was born in 1970 in Cienfuegos, Cuba. She is part of a generation of Cuban writers and artists who express themselves in a mix of genres and across media. She came to fame with the publication of an autobiographical novel based on her diaries, *Todo se van* in 2006, which won the *Premio Bruguera de Novela* and gained critical acclaim across Spain and Latin America, and was published in English as *Everyone leaves* (2012). *A Cage Within* is a collection of translations of Guerra's poetry published by Harbor Mountain Press (2013).

Otoniel Guevara was born in El Salvador in 1967. He studied journalism at the El Salvador University, and since then has worked as a publicist, cultural journalist, and editor. His poems have been translated into eight languages, and in addition to his 30 published titles, he has numerous publications in magazines, newspapers and anthologies. He has been a cultural ambassador for El Salvador in 17 countries and has received more than 20 literary prizes. He is executive director of the *Fundación Metáfora* and the director of a new publishing house, *La Chifurnia*.

Tomás Harris was born in Serena, Chile, in 1956, one of the so-called 'generation of the 80s'. He studied to be a Spanish teacher, and in 1979 published his first collection, *La vida a veces toma la forma de los muros*. With *Crónicas maravillas*, he was awarded the *Casa de Américas* prize in 1996. He has edited, among others, one of the most important anthologies of Chilean poetry in recent years: *Veinticinco años de poesía chilena: 1970-1995*. His work has appeared in English and Swedish translation. He has been employed as a senior researcher in the National Library of Chile since 1995.

Daniel García (D.G.) Helder was born in Argentina in 1961. He is a poet and critic, and one of the most authoritative commentators on contemporary and twentieth century Argentine literature. He has been co-editor of the website *Poesía.com* (1996-2006), director of the *Casa de Poesía* in Buenos Aires (2001-2008) and was the curator of the XVII Festival Internacional de Poesía de Rosario (2009). In addition to his own publications, his poetry has been included in numerous national and international anthologies.

Carlos Henrickson was born in Santiago in 1974. He is a writer, translator and critic. In addition to several poetry collections, he has also published literary criticism, translations and has organised a number of poetry conferences. He lives in Valparaíso.

Julián Herbert was born in Acapulco, Mexico in 1971 and now lives in Saltillo. His difficult childhood is described, in part, in his award-winning 2011 memoir, *Canción de Tumba*. He is a leading figure in Mexico's contemporary poetry scene and has been the vocalist for the rock groups *Los Tigres de Borges* and *Madrastras*. He is coordinator for the interdisciplinary art collective, *Taller de la Caballeriza*. He has won a number of prizes including the Premio Nacional de Literatura Gilberto Owen in 2003 and the Premio Nacional de Cuento Juan José Arreola in 2006.

Osvaldo Hernández Alas is a poet and editor. He was born in Chalatenango, El Salvador, in 1976. He has taught creative writing at the Escuela de Jóvenes Talento en Letras in El Salvador. His books include *Parqueo para sombrillas* (2004) *y Parábola de los ríos* (2015). In addition, he has been included in a number of anthologies and magazines in El Salvador and internationally. He directs the *Laberinto Editorial* project.

Claudia Hernández de Valle-Arizpe was born in Mexico City in 1963. She has been editor, workshop leader and teacher at several universities. Author of nine collections of poetry and two volumes of essays, in 1997 she won the *Efraín Huerta* National Poetry Prize for *Deshielo*. Her poems appear in anthologies from Mexico and other countries, and have been translated into English, Dutch, French and Mandarin Chinese, among other languages. Other awards include the Jaime Sabines Ibero-American Poetry Prize in 2010 for *Perros muy azules* and the Sor Juana Inés de la Cruz poetry prize for *A salvo de la destrucción*.

Ricardo Herrera Alarcón was born in Temuco, Chile, in 1969. He is a teacher and poet and lives in the city of Carahue. He has twice been awarded literary research grants from the Chilean Ministry of Culture, in 2007 and 2011. His poetry collection, *Sendas perdidas y encontradas*, won the Premio Mejores Obras in 2008. He co-edited, with Cristian Cruz, the *Antología Poética Chilena* (2005). His most recent book is *El cielo ideal* (Santiago de Chile: LOM ediciones, 2013).

Jaime Luis Huenún was born in Valdivia, Chile in 1975. He is a writer and editor and has worked on the magazines *Pewma, literatura y arte* and *Ulampu: literatura y arte indígena latinoamerica*. He is organiser of the poetry festival Los Cantos Ocultos, and has himself been an invited writer at numerous literary festivals. His work has been translated into a number of languages. He won the Pablo Neruda young poetry award in 1999, the Municipalidad de Santiago literary prize in 2000, and the Premio Nacional de Poesía Pablo Neruda in 2003, amongst others. He lives in Santiago de Chile.

Miguel Ildefonso, poet and novelist, was born in Lima, Peru in 1970. He studied literature at the Universidad Católica of Peru and completed a Masters in Creative Writing at University of Texas at El Paso. His books include *Vesitigios* (1999), *Los Ciudades Fantasmas* (2002) and *Dantes* (2010). In 2005 he published the book of short stories *El Paso*, which won the Premio Nacional de Cuento in Peru. Other awards include the Juegos Florales de Poesía from The University of Texas (El Paso) and the Peruvian national poetry prize *Copé de Oro*.

Darío Jaramillo Agudelo (born 1947, Santa Rosa de Osos, Colombia) is an internationally acclaimed poet, novelist and essayist. He graduated in law and economics from the Universidad Javeriana of Bogotá, and worked for many years in various roles with state cultural and arts organisations. He has been shortlisted or winner of several awards for his work, including the Colombian National Eduardo Cote Lamus prize for poetry (1978), and the José María de Pereda Prize for the short novel (2010). The most recent edition of his Selected Poems is his personal anthology *Basta cerrar los ojos* (México DF: Era, 2014).

Carlos López Beltran was born in 1957 in Minatitlán, in the Gulf of Mexico. He has a PhD from King's College, London. Since 1992 he has worked as a historian and philosopher of bioanthropological sciences at UNAM, Mexico City. Previously, he worked as science writer, magazine editor and translator. He has published several collections of poetry, of which the most recent is *Hembras desarboladas y otros hombres fuera de lugar* (2014). He has published two collections of essays: *El material de los años* (2014) and *La Ciencia como Cultura* (2005). With Pedro Serrano he co-edited *La Generación del Cordero* (2000, an anthology of contemporary British poetry) and *359 Delicados* (2012, an anthology of contemporary Mexican poetry).

Pura López Colomé is a Mexican writer and translator. She was born in Mexcio City in 1952 and completed her BA and MBA in Mexican Literature at UNAM. She is the author of 11 books of poems, and a Collected: *Poemas reunidos 1985-2012* (México DF: Conaculta, 2013). Her work has been translated and published in a number of countries. In 2011 she recorded a bilingual anthology of poetry on CD with Alastair Reid: *Resonancia/Resonance: Poetry in Two Languages* (Fondo de Cultura Económica). She has received many awards for her writing and translation, including the Premio Xavier Villaurrutia, the Premio Nacional de Traducción Literaria and the Premio Nacional Alfonso Reyes. She is a member of Sistema Nacional de Creadores de Arte, and lives in Cuernavaca.

Tedi López Mills was born in Mexico City in 1959. She studied at UNAM, Mexico City, and at the Sorbonne, Paris. She was the first recipient of the Fundación Octavio Paz poetry grant in 1998, and was awarded the Jóvenes Creadores grant in 1994. She forms part of the Sistema Nacional de Creadores de Arte, and has won numerous prizes, including the Premio Nacional de Literatura José Fuentes Mares in 2006; the Premio Xavier Villaurrutia de Escritores para Escritores in 2009; and the Premio de Narrativa Antonin Artaud in 2013.

Edwin Madrid was born in Quito, Ecuador in November 1961. He studied literature at the Universidad Andina Simón Bolívar. In 1990 he was awarded the Premio Nacional de Poesía Joven Djenana. He has worked as a journalist, specialising in cultural affairs for a number of publications, and has edited a bilingual (Spanish-English) edition of the complete poems of the Ecuatorian poet Jorge Carrera Andrade (2003). His poetry collections include *Celebriedad* (1992), for which he won the Concurso Nacional Cuento y Poesía and more recently a Selected Poems, *Mordiendo el frío* (La Habana: Casa de las Américas, 2010). His work appeared in the bi-lingual publication, *Tapestry of the Sun: an anthology of Ecuadorian poetry* (San Franciso: Coimbra, 2010).

Diego Maquiera (born Santiago de Chile, 1951), grew up in a diplomatic family with periods living in New York and various Latin American capitals. He achieved considerable success as a poet during the 1980s, notably with the collections *La Tirana* (1983) and *Los Sea Harrier* (1986). He was awarded the Pablo Neruda Prize for poetry in 1989. Maquiera has also been active in the visual arts, his 2012 collection *El Annapuma* appearing as an audiovisual work. He has published an anthology of the Chilean poet Vicente Huidobro, and claims to have been influenced strongly by the 'musical poetics' of Igor Stravinsky.

Eduardo Milán was born in Rivera, Uruguay in 1952. He is a poet and essayist, and has written over twenty books of poetry, collections of criticism and two anthologies of Spanish-language poetry. He chose exile in Mexico in 1979 for political reasons and has lived there ever since. He has published a number of books of poetry, including a recent major collection with critical essays: *Disenso* (México DF: Fondo de Cultura Económica, 2010). His *Selected Poems* has also appeared in a bilingual English edition with translations by Patrick Madden and Steven J. Stewart (Bristol: Shearsman, 2012).

Alessandra Molina was born in Havana, Cuba in 1968, and currently lives in the United States. She graduated from Havana University in 1991 and has published the collections *Anfiteatro entro los pinos* (1996), *Usuras del lenguaje* (1999), *As de trinufo* (2001) and *Otras maneras de lo sin hueso*, a bilingual German-Spanish edition (Graz: Leykam, 2008). She has won the Premio de Poesía Luis Rogelio Nogueras, and the Premio de Poesía de la Gaceta de Cuba, amongst others awards.

Mauricio Molina was born in Costa Rica in 1967. While living in Colorado, USA, he wrote his first book; *Abominable libro de la nieve* (México DF: Conaculta, 1999) for which he received the 1998 *Sor Juana Inés de la Cruz* Poetry Prize from the Mexican Cultural Centre. Between 2002 and 2007 he lived in Greece, where he wrote *Cuadernos de Salónica* (San José: Espiral, 2012). He is currently a professor at the University of Costa Rica.

Tania Montenegro, a poet and journalist, was born in Estelí, Nicaragua, in 1969, and studied journalism at the Universidad Centroamericana. She worked as an editor on several publications for 14 years and is currently a freelance consultant in communication, and editor of the 'Bolsillo' and 'El Oriental' sections of the newspaper *Hoy (Today)*. She has contributed to the Spanish newspaper *El País*, and has worked on producing educational materials about domestic violence and sexual abuse. She has published two collections of poetry, *Revolvición* and *Lakursi*.

Fabio Morábito was born in Alexandria in 1955 and has lived in Mexico City since the age of fifteen. His award-winning poetry and short stories have established him as one of Mexico's best-known writers over the past 25 years. Despite Italian being his first language, all of his writings are in Spanish: poetry, short stories, essays and novels. He is also a translator from Italian, and his own books have been made available into German, English, French, Portuguese and Italian.

Andrés Neuman is a poet, novelist, short story writer and translator. He was born in Buenos Aires in 1977, and has lived in Granada, Spain for many years. At the age of 22 he published his first novel, *Bariloche*, which has been followed by five others. His novel *Traveller of the Century* won both of Spain's most prestigious awards for fiction and was shortlisted for *The Independent* foreign fiction prize. He is a prolific poet, with several collections, including a collected poems, *Década* (2008). His most recent poetry collection is *Vendaval de bolsillo* (Almadía, 2014).

Carmen Ollé Nava was born in Lima, Peru, in 1947. She has participated in literary festivals and conferences across Latin America, the United States and Europe. She has published a number of books across genres, the most recent being a collection of short stories, *Monólogos de Lima* (2005). She edited the anthology of Peruvian poetry: *Antología de poesía peruana* for LOM ediciones (Santiago, 2008), and has won a number of awards, including the Homenaje de La Cámara Peruana del Libro for the FIL (2014), and Premio Casa de La Literatura (2015).

Miguel Petrecca was born in Buenos Aires in 1979. He is a poet, journalist, editor and translator. The poetry books he has published include *El gran furcio* (2004), *El Maldonado* (2007) and *Un país mental* (2013). He is the founder of *Gog y Magog*, a Buenos Aires based publishing house which has produced some of the most exciting new poetry collections of recent years. He has lived in Shanghai and translates from Chinese. He currently lives in Paris, where he manages a Latin American bookshop, and is a contributor to various cultural journals and magazines including *Ñ, Perfil, Periódico de poesía* and *Brando*.

Paula Piedra was born in Costa Rica in 1976. She studied interior design, and published her first book of poetry, *Ejercicios Mentales*, in 2003. In addition to her own poetry collections she has been included in a number of anthologies published in Costa Rica, Ecuador, Mexico, Argentina and Guatemala. She has written articles and columns for magazines in Costa Rica. She currently works as a curator of contemporary art projects.

Jaime Pinos was born in Chile in 1970: he is a poet, editor and cultural entrepreneur. He is creator and editor of the independent publisher *La Calabaza del Diablo* and the magazine *Homónima*. He is a member of the collective *Lanzallamas*. His poems have been included in anthologies both in Chile and elsewhere in Latin America, and have been translated into a number of languages. He is one of the organisers of *A Cielo Abierto*, the Valparaíso poetry festival. He is currently director of the Casa-Museo La Sebastiana, Pablo Neruda's home.

Nadio Prado was born in Santiago de Chile, 1966. She has a degree in philosophy from ARCIS and a PhD in literature from the Universidad de Chile. She has won a number of awards for her writing, including the Premio Mejores Obras Literarias in the unpublished work category, in 2004; a grant from the Fundación Andes in 2005, and the Consejo Nacional del Libro y la Lectura award in 2003. Her work has appeared in various anthologies: *Poesía latinoamericana del siglo XXI: El turno y la transición* (1997); and *Cuerpo plural: Antología de la poesía hispanoamericana contemporánea* (2010).

Aleyda Quevedo Rojas was born in Quito, Ecuador in 1972. She is a poet and journalist. In 2006 she won the Premio Nacional de Poesía Jorge Carrera Andrade with her book *Algunas rosas verdes*. She has represented Ecuador at international poetry festivals and conferences in Colombia, Peru, Chile, Argentina, Spain, Mexico, Brazil and Venezuela. Her poetry has been included in magazines in Ecuador, Colombia, Venezuela, Brazil and the USA. Various of her poems have been translated into Hebrew, Portuguese, German and English. Her most recent poetry collection, *La otra, la misma de Dios* (2011) was described by one critic as 'eroticism as a path to self-knowledge.'

Sergio Raimondo was born in 1968, in Bahía Blanca, Argentina. He is a poet, academic, cultural entrepreneur and professor of Contemporary Literature at the Universidad Nacional del Sur. Until June 2011 he was the director of the Museo del Puerto, de Ingeniero White. In 2007 he was awarded a Guggenheim Fellowship for the Creative Arts (Latin America and the Caribbean). He has a particular interest in Latin poetry, and has previously translated Catullus into Spanish, as well as versions of William Carlos Williams. *Poesía Civil* (ediciones Vox, 2001) is to date his only collection of poetry.

Born in Valdivia, Chile in 1953, **Clemente Riedmann** was trained as an anthropologist, a background which has coloured his poetic enterprise, focussing as he does on the use of colloquial, hybrid and universal language. He conceives poetry as a kind of communication that exceeds the artistic sphere, where irony and parody are in the service of both ancient and recent memory. Author of nine books of poetry, his work has been translated into English, German and Italian. He has been awarded the Pablo Neruda Prize (1990), and the Premio Casa de las Américas (Cuba, 2006).

María Rivera was born in Mexico City in June 1971. She is a poet and peace activist. She was awarded the Premio Nacional de Poesía Joven Elías Nandino in 2000 with her first book, *Translación de dominio*. In 2005 she received the Premio Nacional de Poesía Aguascalientes with the poetry collection *Hay batallas* (2005). She has been awarded a grant from the Centro Mexicano de Escritores grant and is an active member of the Sistema Nacional de Creadores de Artes in Mexico.

Born in Medellín in 1946, **Juan Manuel Roca** is one of the most respected figures in contemporary Colombian poetry and fiction. Also a well-known journalist and social commentator, he has a long association with the world-famous poetry festival in the city of his birth, set up in defiance of many years of war and civil strife in his country. He has received numerous awards; was a finalist for the Rómulo Gallegos Prize for the Novel (2004), winner of the Cuban Casa de América Prize in 2008 for his *Antología personal*, and of the Spanish prize, Casa de América de Poesía Americana in 2009, for his collection *Biblia de Pobres*.

Mirta Rosenberg was born in Rosario, Argentina in 1951, but has lived in Buenos Aires for many years. Rosenberg's debut collection, *Paisajes*, was published in 1984. In 1990 she took over the publishing house Bajolaluna, renaming it Bajo la nueva luna (Under the new moon). She works as a translator from English and French and as a journalist has written for the Argentinian newspaper *La Nación*. Rosenberg's poetry has been included in numerous anthologies, and has been translated into French, English, and German.

Daniel Samoilovich was born in Buenos Aires in 1949. He has published a dozen collections of poetry since his first, *Párpado*, in 1973. A bilingual collection of his poetry has appeared in English, translated by Andrew Graham Yooll (Nottingham: Shoestring Press, 2007) and his Collected Poems, *Rusia es el tema* were published by Bajolaluna in 2014. He is a translator from Latin, Italian, English and French. He has translated, amongst others, the Latin poet Horace and Shakespeare's *Henry IV*. Between 1986 and 2012 he directed the Buenos Aires cultural newspaper *Diario de Poesía*.

Leonardo Sanhueza was born in Temuco, Chile, in 1974. He studied geology at university, along with classics. He began writing early, winning his first literary prize at the age of twenty. He has authored four collections of poetry of which the most recent is *Tres bóvedas* (Santiago: Bastante, 2014). His work has gained critical acclaim and won several more awards, including the Premio Academia Chilena de la Lengua in 2011 and the Premio Pablo Neruda in 2012. In addition to his own poetry, he is the author of an anthology: *El bacalao* (Ediciones B, Santiago, 2004), and two volumes of chronicles. His book *Leseras* (Santiago: Tácitas, 2010) offers translations of Catullus into Chilean Spanish

Born in Honduras in 1951, **Juan Ramón Saravia** is a poet, columnist, publisher and translator. In 1993 he was awarded an International Writing Program grant from the University of Iowa, and in 1994 was writer in residence at Hamline University, Minnesota. He has received a number of prizes for his work including the Premio de Poesía, Casa de las Américas in 1988, and the Premio de Estudios Históricos 'Rey Juan Carlos I' in 2005. As well as eight poetry books, Saravia has published a collection of essays, a collection of short stories and a novel, *Ciguanaba con migrañas*.

Osvaldo Sauma was born in Costa Rica in 1949. He worked as Professor of Literature at the Conservatorio Castella, San Jose, Costa Rica from 1981 to 2010. He has participated in numerous international poetry festivals across Latin America, the USA, Europe and India. He worked as Literature Branch Coordinator at the International Festival of Arts of Costa Rica. He has also been juror in several international poetry awards. In 2013 he won the Costa Rican National Poetry Award 'Achilles J. Echeverria' with the collection *La Canción del Oficio*. His work has been translated into English, Italian, French, Portuguese, Arabic and Hindi.

Alejandro Schmidt was born in Villa María, in the province of Córdoba, Argentina, in 1955. He has published many books of poetry, beginning with

Tajo en la piedra (1984), and most recently *La dificultad y otros libros* (2015). His awards include the Premio Municipal de Villa María, 1992. His poetry has been translated into English, German, Italian, French and Romanian. Two of his books are available in Braille, and his work has been adapted for the theatre.

Marina Serrano was born in 1973 in Quequén, in the Province of Buenos Aires, Argentina. Her poetry was published in the Argentinian anthology *Hotel Quequén* (Sigamos enamoradas, 2006). In November 2006, her first collection, *Formación Hospitalaria* (Sigamos enamoradas, 2006) was published, for which she won a commendation in the 2nd Premio Internacional de Poesía from the cultural review *Promoteo*. Amongst other awards, she was also commended for the 'Luis Tejada' Prize in 2010 for the book *Divulgación científica*. He most recent collection is *Segunda Fundación* (Cabiria, 2015).

Pedro Serrano, born in Montreal in 1957, is a poet and teaches at UNAM in México DF. He is Director of the Banff International Literary Translation Centre in Canada. His translations include the anthology *La generación del cordero* (containing many of the most prominent British poets of the 1980s), Shakespeare's *King John* and the poetry of Edward Hirsch. He recently published *DefenβaS*, a book on poetry and other wanderings. *La construcción del poeta moderno*, an essay on T.S. Eliot and Octavio Paz, was published 1n 2012. He is the editor of the online poetry monthly *Periódico de Poesía*. He was granted the Guggenheim fellowship in 2007.

Alicia Torres was born in Caracas, Venezuela, in 1960. She is a poet and psychotherapist. She currently lives in Caracas where she has a private practice. She has previously lived in London, San Francisco and India. Torres has published two poetry collections; *Fatal* in 1989 and *Consideración de la Rosa* in 2000.

Julio Trujillo was born in Mexico City in September 1969. He studied Hispanic language and literature at UNAM. He has been editor of the *Revista Universidad de México* and *Lectura*, director of the *Revista Mexicana de Cultura* and *El Nacional*, editorial coordinator of *El Huevo*, and chief editor of *Letras Libres*. He was awarded an INBA grant in 1993 and a FONCA grant in 1994 and 1996. He has been a member of the SNCA since 2004. He won the Premio de Poesía Punto de Partida in 1991 and the Premio Nacional de Poesía Joven Elías Nandino in 1994 for *Una sangre*.

María de la Luz Urriola González, known as **Malú Urriola**, is a Chilean dramatist and poet. She was born in Santiago in 1967. Her work has been included in numerous anthologies, including *16 poetas chilenos* (Santiago: Ediciones Cámara Chile, 1987). She participated with other Latin American writers in the *Guía del Nuevo siglo*, edited by Julio Ortega (Editorial de la Universidad de Puerto Rico, 1998). In 2004 she received the Premio

Mejores Obras Editadas del Consejo Nacional del libro and the Premio Municpal de Poesía for the book *Nada* (Santiagó: LOM, 2003). In 2006 she won the Premio Pablo Neruda. In 2009 she was awarded a Guggenheim fellowship.

Mónica Velászuez Guzmán was born in La Paz, Bolivia in 1972. She has a PhD in Hispano-American literature from El Colegio de México, and has published five poetry collections. She was awarded an International Writing Program of Iowa grant in 1997. In 2008 she won the Premio Nacional de Poesía Yolanda Bedregal for *Hija de Medea* (2008). She was editor of the major contemporary anthology of her country's poetry: *Antología de la poesía boliviana: Ordenar la danza* (Santiago de Chile: LOM, 2004). She currently teaches Literature at the Universidad Mayor de San Andrés and the Universidad Católica Boliviana.

Born in Rosario, Argentina in 1965, **Beatriz Vignoli** is a novelist, poet, journalist, translator and art critic: to date she has published four novels and seven collections of poetry. In the eighties she contributed to magazines in Rosario and Buenos Aires; between 1992 and 1997 she initiated a series of lectures on poetry and narrative with a group of young writers in Rosario. Between 1993 and 1995 she was art critic for the newspaper *Buenos Aires Herald*. Since 2000 she has written for the *Rosario/12* supplement of the national newspaper *Página/12*.

Ariel Williams was born in Trelew, Patagonia in 1967. He was a founding member of the magazine *El perseguidor*, and co-directed the online magazine *Verbo Copihue: Letras Patagónicas*. In 2008, his book *Los fronterantes* received an honourable mention in the Concurso de Poesía Olga Orozco. To date he has published two novels and six collections of poetry and prose poetry, of which the latest is *Notas de una sombra* (Espacio Hudson, 2014).

Enrique Winter was born in Santiago, Chile in 1982. His first work, *Atas las naves*, won the poetry award at the Víctor Jara Arts Festival. Following this, *Guía de despacho* won the Chilean National Young Poet Competition. *Lengua de señas* won the Pablo de Rokha Poetry Prize, and has been translated into English as *Sign Tongue*. *Rascacielos* translated and published in English as *Skyscrapers* in 2009, won the 'Goodmorning Menagerie Chapbook-in-Translation Prize'. He has translated books by Charles Bernstein and Philip Larkin. Winter holds an MFA in Creative Writing from NYU and directs the Creative Writing diploma at PUCV. He was previously a lawyer.

Laura Wittner was born in Buenos Aires, Argentina, in 1967. She has published a number of poetry books and has written books for children. Her work has been published in France, Spain and Uruguay. She has a literature degree and works as a translator. In addition, she coordinates poetry and translation workshops and runs a blog.

Verónica Zondek was born in Santiago de Chile in 1953. She is a poet, translator and editor. She has a History of Art degree from The Hebrew University of Jerusalem, and to date has published ten poetry books and an anthology of Chilean poetry, *Cartas al azar* (1989). She is a writer of diverse interests, having compiled a major study of the Chilean poet, Gabriela Mistral, and also written a children's story: *La mission de Katalia* (2002). She is a member of the editorial committee for the independent publishing house LOM Ediciones in Santiago, and has translated poetry by Derek Walcott, and most recently, by Anne Carson.

Raúl Zurita was born in Santiago in 1950. His first poetry was published while still a student at the Universidad de Chile in Santiago, where Zurita met writers and intellectuals, including Nicanor Parra, who would have a profound influence on his work. With friends he founded the artists' action group *Colectivo de Acción de Arte* (CADA) in protest against the Pinochet government. His first collection, *Purgatorio* was published in 1979, and formed part of a trilogy. He has been granted a Guggenheim and a DAAD fellowship and has won numerous awards, including the Chilean National Prize for Literature (2000), the Pablo Neruda Prize (1988), the José Lezama Lima Prize (2006), and an honorary doctorate from the University of Alicante, Spain (2015).

Bibliography of Anthologies

In addition to the numerous individual collections and online magazines consulted for the selection process, a stock of anthologies formed essential preliminary reading matter. Below are the main anthologies used in this process:

Calderón, Teresa, Lila Calderón & Tomás Harris (eds.) *Veinticinco Años de Poesía Chilena (1970 - 1995)*. México DF: Tierra Firme.

Contreras, Gonzalez (ed.) *Poesía Chilena Desclasificada (1973 - 1990)*. Santiago: Editorial Etnika (2006).

Díaz-Granados, Frederico (ed.) *México y Colombia: Antología de Poesía Contemporánea*. Bogotá: Cangrejo Editores: Embajada de México (2011).

Fabre, Luis Felipe (ed.) *La Edad de Oro: Antología de poesía mexicana actual*. México DF: UNAM (2012).

Fondebrider, Jorge (ed.) *Una antología de la poesía argentina* (1970-2008). Santiago de Chile: LOM (2008).

Fondebrider, Jorge (ed.) *Otro Río Que Pasa: un siglo de poesía argentina contemporánea*. Buenos Aires: Bajo La Luna (2010).

Ghigliotto, Galo & Allegrezza, William (eds.) *The Alteration of Silence: Recent Chilean Poetry*. New Orleans: Diágolos Books (2013).

Guerrero, Gustavo (ed.) *Cuerpo plural: Antología de la poesía hispanoamericana contemporánea*. Valencia: Editorial Pre-Textos (2010).

Levitin, Alexis & Iturburu, Fernando (eds.) *Tapestry of the Sun: an Anthology of Ecuadorian Poetry*. San Francisco, California: Coimbra Editions (2009).

Ollé, Carmen (ed.) *Antología de la poesía peruana*. Santiago: LOM Ediciones (2008).

Ramírez, Sergio (ed.) *Puertas abiertas: Antología de poesía centroamericana*. Mexico: FCE (2011).

Rodríguez Moya, Daniel (ed.) *Antología: La poesía del siglo XX en Nicaragua*. Madrid: Visor Libros (2010).

Saldaña Paris, Daniel (ed.) *Doce en punto: poesía chilena reciente (1971-82)*. México DF: UNAM (2012).

Samoilovich, Daniel (ed.) *Antologiá de la poesía argentina*. Ciudad Autónoma de Buenos Aires: Ministerio de Relaciones Exteriores y Culto (2014).

Serrano, Pedro & López Beltrán, Carlos (eds.) *359 Delicados (con filtro): Antologiá de la poesía actual en México*. Santiago: LOM Ediciones (2012).

Tono Martínez, José (ed.) *Antología de la Joven Poesía Argentina*. Buenos Aires: Instituto de Cooperación Iberoamericana (2001).

Vásquez, Samuel & Mutis, Santiago (eds.) *Poetas Colombianos*. Monterrey: Universidad Autónoma de Nuevo León (2012).

Velásquez Guzmán, Mónica (ed.) *Antología de la poesía boliviana: Ordenar la danza*. Santiago: LOM Ediciones (2004).

Weiss, Mark (ed.) *The Whole Island: Six Decades of Cuban Poetry: A Bilingual Anthology*. Berkeley: University of California Press (2009).

Winter, Enrique (ed.) *Poesía chilena reciente, Revista Viento en Vela* Nº 13 - Ciudad de México (2008).

Zaidenwerg, Ezequiel (ed.) *Penúltimos: 33 poetas de Argentina (1965-1985)*. México DF: UNAM (2014).

Zurita, Raúl (ed.) *Cantares: Nuevas voces de la poesía chilena*. Santiago: LOM Ediciones (2004).

Index of Authors

Abad Faciolince, Héctor,	136
Ak'Abal, Humberto,	84, 240
Appratto, Roberto,	234, 248
Arijón, Teresa,	206
Aulicino, Jorge,	66, 172, 242
Báez, Frank,	200, 222
Barrera, Gustavo,	56
Barreto, Igor,	160
Bellessi, Diana,	120, 282
Belli, Gioconda,	98
Bello, Javier,	186, 254
Bonnett, Piedad,	100, 182
Bossi, Osvaldo,	274
Bracho, Coral,	174
Brodsky, Camilo,	176
Bustos Aguirre, Rómulo,	44, 160, 164, 186
Calderón, Damaris,	130, 224
Casas, Fabián,	122, 280
Chaves, Luis,	334
Chávez Casazola, Gabriel,	66, 112
Chirif, Micaela,	108
Chirinos, Eduardo,	158, 286
Cortés González, Alejandro,	124
Cote Baraibar, Ramón,	328
Courtoisie, Rafael,	70
Crotto, Alejandro,	148, 166
Dávila, Carolina,	78
Decap, Carlos,	132, 244
Deltoro, Antonio,	168
Dobry, Edgar,	120
España, Siomara,	46, 264
Espina, Eduardo,	302
Estrada, Fabricio,	240
Fernández Granados, Jorge,	212
Figueroa, Damsi,	52
Felipe Fabre, Luis,	276, 320, 344
Fondebrider, Jorge,	76, 280, 282, 348
Franco, Ana,	290
Freudenthal Ovando, Jessica,	94, 124

Galán Casanova, John,	262, 304
Garcia Bergua, Alicia,	70
Goldberg, Jacqueline,	334
Gonzáles Restrepo, Catalina,	246, 294
Gruss, Irene,	106, 344, 350
Guajardo Thomas, Marcelo,	232
Guerra, Wendy,	100, 240, 264
Guevara, Otoniel,	88
Harris, Tomás,	204
Helder, D. G.,	72, 188, 340
Henrickson, Carlos,	272
Herbert, Julián,	68, 330
Hernández de Valle-Arizpe, Claudia,	354
Hernández, Osvaldo,	132, 322
Herrera Alarcón, Ricardo,	54
Ildefonso, Miguel,	290
Jaramillo Agudelo, Darío,	102, 152, 196
López Beltrán, Carlos,	134
López Colomé, Pura,	162
López Mills, Tedi,	210, 250
Luis Huenún, Jaime,	52
Manuel Roca, Juan,	198, 226, 232, 326
Madrid, Edwin,	270, 296
Maquiera, Diego,	268
Milán, Eduardo,	178, 190
Molina, Alessandra,	128
Molina, Mauricio,	184
Montenegro, Tania,	284
Morábito, Fabio,	48, 150, 358
Neuman, Andrés,	80
Ollé, Carmen,	278
Petrecca, Miguel,	216
Piedra, Paula,	220
Pinos, Jaime,	86
Prado, Nadia,	98
Quevedo Rojas, Aleyda,	286
Raimondi, Sergio,	174, 214

Ramón Saravia, Juan, 250
Riedemann, Clemente, 106
Rivera, Maria, 310
Rosenberg, Mirta, 110, 156

Samoilovich, Daniel, 44, 154, 298
Sanhueza, Leonardo, 342
Sauma, Osvaldo, 288
Schmidt, Alejandro, 300
Serrano, Marina, 218
Serrano, Pedro, 74, 146, 170

Torres, Alicia, 292
Trujillo, Julio, 226

Urriola, Malú, 268

Velásquez Guzmán, Mónica, 324
Vignoli, Beatriz, 130, 134, 230, 320, 348

Williams, Ariel, 200
Winter, Enrique, 118, 248
Wittner, Laura, 60, 74

Zondek, Verónica, 62, 244, 328
Zurita, Raúl, 350